THE UNITED STATES OF AMERICA
PASSPORT

DEPARTMENT OF STATE

To all to whom these presents shall come Greeting:

I, the undersigned Secretary of State of the United States of America, hereby request all whom it may concern to permit

Morris G. Hindus

a citizen of the United States, safely and freely to pass, and in case of need to give him all lawful Aid and Protection.

This passport is valid for use only in the following countries and for objects specified, unless amended.

All Countries
NAME OF COUNTRY

Journalistic work and travel
OBJECT OF VISIT

The bearer is accompanied by _____

Given under my hand and the seal of the Department of State at the City of Washington, the 14th day of May in the year 923 and of the Independence of the United States the one hundred and forty seventh.

Charles E. Hughes

PERSONAL DESCRIPTION

Age 32 years
Height 5 ft 9 in
Forehead high
Eyes gray
Nose straight

Mouth medium
Chin medium
Hair black
Complexion ruddy
Face square

Distinguishing marks _____

Place of birth Russia
Date of birth Feb. 27, 1891
Occupation writer – lecturer

Morris G. Hindus
SIGNATURE OF BEARER

PHOTOGRAPH OF BEARER

No 286325

By Maurice Hindus

A TRAVELER IN TWO WORLDS

THE KREMLIN'S HUMAN DILEMMA

HOUSE WITHOUT A ROOF

CRISIS IN THE KREMLIN

MAGDA

IN SEARCH OF A FUTURE

THE BRIGHT PASSAGE

THE COSSACKS: The Story of a Warrior People

MOTHER RUSSIA

RUSSIA AND JAPAN

HITLER CANNOT CONQUER RUSSIA

TO SING WITH THE ANGELS

SONS AND FATHERS

WE SHALL LIVE AGAIN

GREEN WORLDS

MOSCOW SKIES

THE GREAT OFFENSIVE

RED BREAD

HUMANITY UPROOTED

BROKEN EARTH

THE RUSSIAN PEASANT AND THE REVOLUTION

A Traveler in Two Worlds

MAURICE HINDUS

A Traveler in Two Worlds

◆

Introduction by Milton Hindus

1971

DOUBLEDAY & COMPANY, INC.

Garden City, New York

Library of Congress Catalog Card Number 70–139033
Copyright © 1971 by Frances McClernan Hindus
Introduction Copyright © 1971 by Doubleday & Company, Inc.
All Rights Reserved
Printed in the United States of America
First Edition

Contents

Contents

A Traveler in Two Worlds

Portrait of an Uncle

"If you want to write," my uncle Maurice Hindus used to say to me, "why don't you leave the city and go to work on a farm?"

I discovered later on that I was not the only one of his nephews to whom he had given similar advice to leave home and explore the real America that was to be found outside New York City, according to him, and especially among those people who worked on the land. I didn't know, until I had read his memoirs, how much little places like North Brookfield in upstate New York had meant to him. He had gone to work there as an immigrant boy of seventeen, hardly three years in this country, for a farmer named Jim Moore, who had advertised for hired help through an employment agency on the Lower East Side. Moore had eventually become almost a second father to him, and the autobiographical *Green Worlds* is dedicated to his memory: "the most irascible friend, the most sensible teacher, the most humane Americanizer I have ever known."

Like much well-meant advice from older people to younger ones, his to me, I'm afraid, fell on deaf ears. It didn't seem very pertinent to me. It was too simple for my taste and reflected, I thought, the somewhat smug attitude of a self-made man who was inclined to make a fetish out of the particular experience that had brought him success and to believe that the road which had led him to a certain goal was the only road there was to it. To connect working on a farm with the art of writing seemed a ridiculous *non sequitur* to me, for I realized even then, from a careful reading of Proust, that the material which a writer used counted for much less than the treatment which he was able to give it. Writing was "creative" precisely in the degree that it was able to perform the seemingly impossible feat of making a silk purse out of a sow's ear. Flaubert had even proposed to rival the Deity by writing a great book about *nothing at all.*

The surroundings in which my uncle's advice was given added to its incongruity. My conversations with him usually took place in the living-working room of his duplex apartment in the solid old Hotel des Artistes west of Central Park. The ceiling of this room, two stories high, with a huge wrought iron chandelier, the windows twenty feet or more in height, the bareness of much of the wall space above the low-slung bookcases lining the room on all sides with volumes in Russian, English, and other languages— all the space and filtered light gave to the studio the air of a chapel in a cathedral. There was a mixture there of elegance and asceticism, and the presence in one corner of a small desk with a typewriter on it, manuscript pages scattered about, and the portion of the heavy carpet near the desk most worn out plainly hinted that the room was more used by a working writer than it was for entertaining. The boy who had once astonished his high school principal by telling him that his ambition was to become a farmer and had subsequently actually become one before he had become an educated man and a writer had obviously gone very far, in my view, from the pastoral life to which he seemed to be seeking, as if by proxy, to return through me. I did not know, then, that no matter how far-flung his travels, he continued to return to the country around North Brookfield, where he had so many friends and memories, very nearly to the last day of his life.

How little we know and understand each other, or manage, across the vast distances and abysses that separate even members of the same family from each other, to communicate, and that little, more often than not, by chance or indirection. On one of the walls of my uncle's apartment there was a symbolic juxtaposition or balancing of two beautiful, framed photographs that may or may not have been symbolic. They were both studies of bearded old men's heads. One was of George Bernard Shaw, inscribed by him to my uncle, in gratitude as I later learned for his having acted, soon after having become famous as an interpreter of Russia to the West, as Shaw's "guide, philosopher and friend" during a trip to Russia in the 1930s. Shaw's brow in this picture is massively intellectual and his aged face of a man in his middle seventies is unmistakably individualistic and brightly observant in expression. Yet the other picture is no less impressive. The head is positively Tolstoyan in its weight and dignity, but it is a picture of an anonymous peasant, perhaps illiterate, taken by Margaret Bourke-White during a visit to some remote Russian village.

I wondered if Maurice was trying to say something by balancing off the world-famous celebrity against the nameless Russian peasant. It seemed to me that if any single idea informed the score of books he wrote during his life, it was that the common man, especially if he were one who worked on the land, was filled with spiritual and intellectual riches equaling if not exceeding those possessed by the more prominent and well-to-do who were so often empty—what Whitman liked to call "damned stimulacra," stuffed shirts devoid of real inner worth and substance. This Wordsworthian or romantic notion transpires through his most touching and tender pages, which, though they are written in prose, are transfigured by a poetic quality in the descriptions of landscape and the simpler joys of rustic life. The pictures were emblematic of the two sides of his life. He had consorted with people like Shaw, Lady Astor, Lord Lothian, Wendell Willkie, Jan Masaryk, F. Scott Fitzgerald, Clarence Darrow, William Jennings Bryan, and Helen Keller without being spoiled for the enjoyment of the company of the humble dirt farmers who had been his friends and employers in upstate New York or the unlettered muzhiks of the Russian countryside in which he had been born. If a choice had had to be made, he might even have felt more at home with the latter than in the exciting and colorful intellectual and social world that his talents had opened to him.

Maurice was born in the small Byelorussian village of Bolshoye Bykovo in 1891, a member of one of the four Jewish families in the village. It was located in the Pale of Settlement to which most Russian Jews were confined by the Czar. The law prevented people of Jewish faith from owning land, but his grandfather, who was something of a favorite of the well-known Polish Count Radziwill, the largest landowner of the vicinity, was able to rent a large acreage from the nobleman. Maurice used to recall that his own father, in the days of his greatest prosperity, owned ten horses, twenty cows, many calves, geese, and hens, as well as the only horse-drawn threshing machine, "the sole mark of the machine age in the community." Unfortunately, his father, though very kind, proved quite improvident, produced too many offspring even for his ample resources (no less than seventeen, by two wives), was a poor businessman, showed a quite uncharacteristic love of vodka in his later years, and, at his death, left an impoverished family—a widow and numerous children.

My father, who was the oldest of the eleven children of my grandfather's second marriage, came to the United States around the turn of the century. He entered the women's clothing industry, like Abraham Cahan's character David Levinsky, but unlike that tycoon he prospered only very indifferently. By 1905, however, he was sufficiently established to help his mother and some of his younger brothers and sisters, among them Maurice, to emigrate. The need to do so was dire. Nineteen-five was the year of the first of three major Russian revolutions in this century. It was an unforgettable year for anyone who managed to survive it. Unexpected defeat at the hands of tiny Japan rocked the Czar's empire to its foundations. The first Soviet, with the twenty-eight-year-old revolutionary Leon Trotsky conspicuous among its leaders, spontaneously sprang into existence. Backlash and reaction against the revolutionaries took the form of peasant pogroms against the Jews.

The village of Bolshoye Bykovo itself was spared the horrors and atrocities that occurred elsewhere in Russia, perhaps because the number of Jews was so small and their relations with the Orthodox priest of the village very amicable. There were no tales of terror among my father's people to match those of my mother's family which had come over to this country in the same fateful year. News of the social explosions in St. Petersburg and the repercussions they had provoked spread widely, of course, and all Jews were happy to find refuge in the United States, but there was no feeling, as my uncle told the story, of the kind recorded by Mary Antin in her *Promised Land* of being liberated and going from darkness into light. On the contrary, he never forgot his experience of what he called "the desolation of the uprooted." With all its faults, he had formed deep attachments to the country in which he had been born and to its people, and leaving them was "like tearing something out" of his very soul.

His memories of the fields, forests, and streams among which he had spent his childhood and boyhood became all the more tormenting when they were contrasted with the realities of the East

Side ghetto to which he came—its overcrowded tenements, sweat-shops, pushcarts, peddlers, mountainous piles of garbage, vermin, and the other signs and stigmata of urban poverty. Cooped up in a small airless bedroom with two older brothers, he soon began to dream of leaving the hellish city behind him and making his way into the interior of the country in search of a counterpart of the village he remembered. He grew literally sick of Manhattan, developed a heart murmur, a touch of tuberculosis, and began making endless dreary pilgrimages to clinics in search of the elusive state of health that neither medicines nor pills produced. Only the atmosphere that he found on Jim Moore's farm restored him, and to the end of his days, when "the world was too much with him," he claimed that, more effective than a visit to the doctor or psychiatrist, was going up to the country where he had spent his youth and helping one of his farmer friends with his chores. The prescription seemed to work for him, too. No wonder he came to think it a cure-all for everything that ever troubled anyone.

In making a name for himself eventually as a writer on Russia, war correspondent, and lecturer on public platforms throughout the country and over nationwide radio, he also gave a feeling of identity, of belonging to America, and even of pride to those of us who were related to him. It was only reflected glory, to be sure, but that may be better than nothing at all. It impressed me, for example, when I first entered college to find that my family name was recognized by more than one of my professors, who asked if I were related to him and seemed to expect something more of me because I was. Mary McCarthy observes in *The Company She Keeps* that "if you scratch a Socialist, you find a snob." The truth seems to be that if you scratch almost anyone at random you find a streak of snobbishness underneath. All of us are in need of support for our desire to be slightly special and superior in some respect, and the accomplishments of my uncle Maurice were, for a long time, the source which fed this conviction in our family.

Because this was so, it's easy to understand the feelings of excitement he inspired when he appeared at a family gathering, such as a wedding or bar mitzvah. Whispers would quickly run around the room, especially among the more impressionable youngsters: "Maurice Hindus is here!"

In family photographs on such occasions, he was always given a central place even if his relation to the event was very peripheral, but in any case, the distinction of his features, the unruliness of his hair, and the unusual brightness of his eyes (which occasionally gave him a surprised and even startled look) would have been sufficient to make his face stand out among the others in any picture. He was pleased by such attentions, less because of vanity, I think, than because, like many childless men (though married), he was intensely family-minded and had something that can only be called an avuncular vocation, which made him take an interest in his many nephews and nieces and eventually even in their children. A large number of people in the family can remember receiving from him, at one time or another, completely unexpected gifts or missives evincing his kindness and concern for them.

After he had become markedly successful, everyone in the family treated him as an "elder statesman" whose advice was sought on all sorts of subjects. Even those who were chronologically older deferred to him with "the deep almost worshiping respect enjoined by an inferior order of endowment toward a higher." But it had not always been so. There were family legends, later confirmed by himself, that his brothers had regarded his passion for reading with scant sympathy when he kept the light on late at night and interfered with the sleep they sorely needed in order to go out in the morning to work a twelve-hour day. In his memoirs he recalls having to prepare his lessons for school in the bathroom because of this. An older sister, who had married a quite affluent man, had refused at one point to lend him a mere fifty dollars which he desperately needed to pay for his tuition at Colgate University. Even after he had finished college, attended the Harvard Graduate School, and published his first book, *The Russian Peasant and the Revolution*, in 1920, but before there was any large public recognition of his talents, he was still known among the family in Brownsville as *der meshugenneh philosophe* (Yiddish, roughly meaning "the zany philosopher").

My own memories of him go back to my childhood, but his visits to our apartment I remember less directly than indirectly through the recollection of the complaints of my poor mother, who was meticulously neat and orderly as a housewife, concerning the watery mess he had made of her whole bathroom while taking a shower. Also, I seem to recollect his sleeping out on the fire escape of the apartment house in which we lived, which caused some comment. He may have acquired this habit while living on the East Side where sleeping on the fire escape or the roof was a recognized way of escaping the stifling heat of the tenements during the summer. Or else it may have been due to the health and fresh-air fads he had imbibed from the writings of Bernarr MacFadden. He had also spent some time, as I later learned, among the pacifist and vegetarian sects of Russian Doukhobor peasants who had settled in Western Canada and would occasionally annoy the government authorities by marching in the nude upon Ottawa to express their indignation about some measure. He had written his earliest articles about these schismatics for Glenn Frank's old *Century Magazine*, and he had obviously been imbued with the utmost sympathy for the naïveté of their ideas and the eccentricities of their behavior. These unlettered peasants had somehow arrived at conclusions strangely similar to those of Tolstoy whom they had never read, or perhaps it was the other way about and he had reached conclusions similar to theirs. Both their way of life and way of thought were fascinating to Maurice, and he made his magazine reports of them so interesting that the editor was inspired to commission him to go back to his native Russian village in 1923 and to do a series of articles reporting on the changes which the Revolution had made in peasant life as he remembered it. It was out of this assignment that his book *Broken Earth* came in 1926.

But at the outset, the family regarded Maurice himself as an eccentric. He was the only one who had left the city to go back to work on the land, though eventually he managed to get for himself a formal education that was unique in its extent and thoroughness among the immigrant generation of the Hinduses. His choice of the risky vocations of writer and lecturer also made his family suspect his soundness until there was hard evidence that it had worked out successfully despite the odds against him. As happens so often, public recognition preceded private recognition by those closest to him.

My own more certain memories of him begin about the time I
entered college as a freshman and promptly fell, as if through a
trap door, into one of the extreme student movements, which
were as popular among us in the 1930s as, after a long period in
the shadows, they are once more coming to be. My father, a
reader of Cahan's Yiddish paper, the *Jewish Daily Forward*, was a
mild Socialist in theory and a voting Democrat in practice, and he
was alarmed at my turn toward radicalism and revolution. He
took me, therefore, to see my uncle Maurice, hoping that the latter
might help to moderate my views somewhat. And that is what he
did in the end, not by any direct onslaught against my theories
but by counteracting my utopian view of Russia with a dose of
realism. He could appreciate the fact that my ideological development had not been entirely gratuitous. There were real grievances,
like the Depression, which had struck serious blows against my
family and me, and I was attempting to respond to these grievances. He was not one of those who forget the enthusiasms of
their youth completely. He, too, had felt the sting of social in-
justice and had been thrilled by his discovery as an immigrant of
the various peddlers of panaceas designed to perfect the world.
In his autobiography he tells how on East Broadway were to be
found "Anarchists, Social Revolutionaries, Social Democrats, Pop-
ulists, Zionists, Zangwillites, Assimilationists, Internationalists,
Single Taxers, Republicans, Democrats, each group with its own
gods, dead and alive, its own demons too . . ." The trouble was
that, as he listened to them, he discovered that "the prophets of
the various causes and their disciples were not wise or strong
enough so to fortify their ideological positions that opponents
couldn't demolish them." And so, after much reflection, he had
"decided that [he] was neither clever enough nor old and experienced enough to be a crusader for any abstract ideal."

There was no way to transmit this conclusion to me directly,
yet he must have made me feel that there was a quality of *déjà vu*,
so far as he was concerned, about theories that seemed to me then
novel and exciting. We also talked of Russia, of course, and he
brought to my attention the fact that while capitalist America was
in the grip of a great economic depression, which was the immediate source of my own unhappiness and desire for sweeping
change in the system, "Communist" Russia, to which we all looked

then as an example of what a well-planned, orderly, and idealistic society should be, was in the grip of a famine that was destroying millions of peasants and that this famine was not really necessary, but had been produced by the stubborn, pigheaded, doctrinaire policies of the Soviet government. Now it must be realized that at the time, a strenuous effort was being made by Communists and their fellow-travelers to deny the very existence of this famine. It seemed to us that only political reactionaries and the Hearst yellow tabloid press would spread such slanderous stories. I was dumfounded to hear them from the lips of my uncle, who was a liberal and progressive and recognized many positive achievements of the Revolution. Such was my impassioned intolerance and fanaticism at that moment in my youth that, for a flickering instant, I lumped my uncle together in my mind with Hearst and the right-wing reactionaries. Yet it was impossible for me to maintain this attitude for very long. Our family ties and his patent honesty of purpose prevented me from dismissing what he told me with the same ease with which I dismissed other facts that accorded uncomfortably with my radical theories.

Nor could I readily refute or discount the cogent analysis by which he sought to demonstrate to me that, in defiance of Marxist analysis, the Russian Revolution was a phenomenon that grew out of the specifics of Russian history and more particularly out of the age-old peasant hunger for land, which had caused revolts of a magnitude that had shaken the Czar's throne long before Marxism was even known in Russia. He pooh-poohed the idea that the Russian Revolution was a harbinger of world revolution. It was hardly an accident, he said, that, despite all of the fantasies and wish-fulfillments and activity of Lenin and Trotsky, the Russian Revolution had died on the Russian frontier. It was most improbable that a violent overturn along similar lines would ever occur in any of the industrialized nations of the western world, and the possibility was especially remote in such a society as that of the United States. In countries that had a land problem analogous to Russia's, such as China and those in southeast Asia, however, it was not impossible that the Russian example might prove powerful, but that was certainly not because of Marxist theory. Such observations seemed very farfetched to me, then, because they ran counter to all of my romantic notions, but, in retrospect, it appears to me that he did much in a quiet and unostentatious way to restore me to a more balanced and sounder outlook on the world than was fashionable among those of my contemporaries who shared my views. It was only much later that I learned from him what good company I had unwittingly been in at that time. Just about the period when my father had brought me to him in order to have him dampen some of my illusions about the Soviets, F. Scott Fitzgerald had sought him out in order to have him allay his fears that a violent Communist revolution might well be imminent in the United States. The substance of what he said to both of us, for those who are curious, may be found in the last chapter, entitled "The Collapse of World Revolution," of a book he published in 1933 called *The Great Offensive.*

He influenced me because he was never heavy-handed in his approach. More quickly than my parents he grasped the fact that I insisted more stubbornly than most upon finding or making my own path in life and that all attempts to force an issue with me were more likely than not to prove, as the jargon nowadays has it, "counterproductive." When he found that I did not resemble him in his attachment to the land or his romantic idealization of a rural life but that I still insisted on becoming a writer on my own terms, he did what he could for me. He helped me financially, he let me use his apartment for long periods of time while he was traveling abroad, he read everything I wrote, and gave me promptly his impressions of it. He did not flatter and he tried to be objective. In my younger days, he was more critical of what I did than later on, without ever being discouraging. Eventually he came to view my work with the kindness of a kinsman and not at all with the envy of a rival or competitor engaged in the same line of work. Such an attitude is not too usual, in my experience, even among writers who are very friendly or related to each other. It sprang in his case from a generosity that was fundamental to his character.

It may be best perhaps to conclude with an assessment of him by a man of his own generation, whose vision is unclouded by the partiality of a relation and who is inclined to express himself with restraint rather than overstatement. Here is what Louis Fischer says in his book *Men and Politics:* "Maurice Hindus came frequently to Moscow and wrote some excellent books. He could never bear Moscow for more than a week or so, and soon he would sling his shoes over his shoulder like the Russian peasant —the peasant did it to save his shoes but Maurice to save his feet—and tour the countryside. He is simple and loves simple people. He is a farmer and loves the soil. Hindus has a tremendous capacity for warmth and affection. He participates in the suffering and joys of others; and he frequently empties his purse to friends. He was born in a Russian village and appreciated what the Bolsheviks were doing to lift the villages out of the Czarist mire. Doubts frequently tormented him, as they did all of us, but when they tormented him he was disconsolate and grim and yearned either for frivolity or, more frequently, for a soul-interview with a kindred spirit . . . He understands emotions and ignores economics. He despised Communist terminology and Marxist logic and admired the Soviets only for what they did to uproot and give new life to humanity. Hindus is humble, and honestly avows his limitations, accepting assistance when he needs it. He is an American lecture audience's ideal: dramatic, passionate, personal, romantic-looking, and not too high-brow."

But I would add that there are some things in this description that I myself should change. If Maurice was something of a muzhik, he was also a muzhik with a difference; if he was simple, he was, like that peasant who posed for the photograph by Margaret Bourke-White that now hangs on my own living-room wall, also profound. But the general outlines of Fischer's sketch are certainly recognizable to me and to all who knew him. While I was driving down to New York in July 1969 to attend his funeral and reflected on the obituaries that had come not only from various parts of this country but from Europe, I suddenly recalled something that Emerson had said to Whitman on Boston Common in 1860 to buoy up his self-confidence: "You have put the world in your debt, and such obligations are always acknowledged and met." It may be that these words are applicable, in a measure, to all those who, like my uncle Maurice, are blessed with the capacity to give to others more than they have ever received from others themselves.

Milton Hindus

Chapter 1

A Village Where Time Stopped

◀▶

I grew up in wild country of forests and marshes, of streams and lowlands for which my native Byelorussia has always been famed.

Wandering among the silver birches, the somber pine, the splendid oak with whose leaves our mothers pasted the huge loaves of dark rye bread before putting them into the heated brick oven, was always an exhilarating adventure. Not only birds and beasts inhabited the wilderness, but all manner of spirits, some as innocent and playful as kittens, others as cunning and cruel as hungry she-wolves. Though I never saw any spirits, I believed in them, for other boys and their elders had told of encountering them, of talking to them, of outwitting their sly machinations to inveigle mortal souls into bondage and damnation.

I especially feared yet was fascinated by the *rusalka*, the spirit of a drowned girl who enticed boys and girls into her embrace and tickled them under the arms until they died from laughter, then dragged them down to the bottom of the river where she lived. Once I thought I heard a *rusalka* laugh, the sweet melodious laugh that enchants the hearer. My heart throbbed violently and I stood still hoping for a glimpse of the dazzling nymph —a girl with deep bosom, big sparkling eyes, and long black hair flowing loose over her shoulders. Then I remembered that if I saw her she would bewitch me and I should be helpless to resist the fatal tickling. Panic-stricken, I ran crying out of the forest, not daring to look back until I was safe by the blacksmith shop in the clearing, where the presence of people, so ran the legend, would keep the *rusalka* from showing herself.

Yet the forest lured me as it did my muzhik playmates, boys and girls. In summer the wall of swampy wood sheltering one side of our village—a village of some 150 families—was our favorite

playground. There we went swimming in the stream that meandered through bushes and trees. There we gathered berries and
mushrooms, firewood and oak leaves, for our mothers. There we
built bonfires and baked the potatoes we stole from neighboring
gardens and fields. There we climbed trees and, stick in hand,
battered down the nests of the ever-swarming black crows, the
cursed birds that picked rye seed out of the ground—the rye that
was our bread—and that snatched up newly hatched chicks.

Our muzhiks were overwhelmingly illiterate—at most, some
three per cent of them could read and write. They never read
newspapers, magazines, any agricultural journals. They knew only
the damage but none of the benefits that crows brought to their
fields. That was why they were perpetually seeking to extermi-
nate the black birds and incited us children into helping them any
way we could, which we did with alacrity and joy. But it was a
futile crusade—nature was on the side of the crows and they prospered.

Woods and more woods, thick and thin, stretched in all di-
rections from our desolate village. We were within easy driving
distance by horse and wagon from Polyesye, the vast wilderness
—some ten million acres—of forest and swamp, of streams and
lakes, of meadows and pastures, where some of our muzhiks had
purchased strips of grassland. In summer they cut and stacked the
grass and always came home loaded with mushrooms and berries.
In winter they hauled the hay home in sleighs and brought with
them endless strings of dried and frozen fish. Polyesye was the
great wonderland and those who went there, whether to work as
lumberjacks as did my two older brothers, or to cut grass on their
own strips of land, told exciting tales of its age-old and mighty
forests, its wild game, its rich fisheries, its fabulous crops of berries and mushrooms—and of course its evil spirits.

But the largest forest near our village was the Polish landlord's
berezak (birch wood). Always alive with the twitter and song of
many-colored birds, it was also famed for the variety and pleni-
tude of its edible mushrooms. During the mushroom season, we
swooped down on it in parties and loaded our willow-plaited
baskets with them, for our mothers to marinate or dry in the sun
for soup during the long winter months. To this day going mush-
rooming in some near-by wood is a favorite Russian pastime, as

much for city as for village folk, as much for professor and academician as for peasant and factory worker.

We loved the birch more than any other tree and of no other tree have Russians through the ages sung so joyfully or so sorrowfully. Summer and winter it dominates the somber Russian landscape. In spring, muzhiks who owned (as they no longer do) strips of birch in the forests adjacent to our village tapped them for sap. They did not boil the sap into sugar as American farmers do with maple sap. Instead, they stored it in barrels in a barn or cellar; and when fermented it made a refreshing beverage, especially on hot summer days. I recall many an appetizing meal I made of dark rye bread, boiled potatoes, and a glass or bowl of fermented birch sap.

Out of leafy birch twigs we fashioned brooms with which to sweep house, courtyard, street, and with which to lash ourselves in the steam bath. The white bark was precious. Out of it muzhik craftsmen constructed all manner of containers for berries and mushrooms, for *smetana* (sour cream) and honey, for *kvas* and soup to be carried to field workers, and from the wood itself they carved pretty snuff boxes and purses that fetched a handsome price in the city bazaar.

Birch made the best firewood of any tree we knew and was especially suited for splitting into *luchiny* (long faggots) with which muzhiks who could afford neither lamps nor kerosene lighted their homes—the single room that was kitchen, dining room, bedroom and hen coop, in which pigs were always fed and which in winter was shared with piglings and sometimes with a sick lamb or calf. The *sentsui*—the other room in a muzhik's dwelling—was usually without windows and without oven and remained freezingly cold all winter long. In summer people might sleep in it, but principally it served as a store room for tools, sacks of grain, or the trunks in which muzhiks kept their Sunday clothes or in which unmarried girls were gathering their bridal linen.

Thinking back to my childhood in a Byelorussian village, it seems incredible that though they lived in forested country, and close to Polyesye, the greatest forests of all, our muzhiks were so poor they could not afford to buy the necessary timber from either landlord or the state to build more commodious dwellings. They lived without "modern improvements," without even outhouses; pigpens or open fields served man's natural needs.

Because of overcrowding, the living space in muzhik homes was infested with roaches, bedbugs, fleas, and lice, which, in the absence of insecticides other than kerosene, throve and multiplied. No wonder also that in the absence of all knowledge of hygiene, with no medical service at hand, with only one elderly *feldsher* (healer) called Sklerovich serving about half a dozen or more villages, one epidemic after another, now smallpox, now scarlet fever, now diphtheria, now typhoid, swept over one village after another. In spring or autumn when an epidemic broke out, our kindly parish priest, Adam Sharantovich, was kept busy officiating at funerals. Those funeral processions, especially when all the village followed a child's small coffin, are among the saddest memories of my old life. I can never forget how torn and shaken I would be by the despairing *plach* of the women, the traditional lamentation for the dead.

My mother's best friend was Darya, the wife of a hard-working muzhik who lived across the street from us. Darya gave birth to one child after another, about a dozen children, and excepting one—a boy called Sergey, one of my closest playmates—they all died in infancy. For days after the burial of a child, Darya would come to our house, sob her heart out to my mother, accompanying her tears with the customary *plach* which ran something like this: "Why, did you leave me, my precious love . . . didn't you know that your mother loved you more than herself, more than anything in the world . . . Ay, how terrible it is to be without you . . . O, Lord, my God, why are you punishing me so cruelly? . . . What have I done to deserve such punishment . . . Gone, gone, one after another, my own loved ones and why, why?"

In the utter absence of medical facilities in our countryside, many children died in infancy. Our muzhiks knew nothing of maternity homes—the very expression—*rodilny dom*—was no part of their vocabulary. The term *akusherka* (midwife) was not unknown, but there was no midwife in our whole township, only the one *feldsher,* and obstetrics was no part of his practice. My mother gave birth to eleven children, every one of them on straw on the floor, with only an illiterate *babka* (old woman) in attendance. The *babka* was experienced in the delivery of babies, but the only disinfectant she knew was soap and hot water, and the umbilical cord she cut with an ordinary kitchen knife.

Let it be remembered that despite the good work of the *zemstvos,* the self-governing welfare organizations founded in 1864, the mortality rate of children up to the age of four was one of the highest in Europe, 273 per thousand in 1913.

Yet in our part of the immense Russian land, people were spared the periodic famines that devastated other territories. The climate of Byelorussia, especially of the region that embraced our village, protected us against the crop-killing droughts that again and again scorched the Volga and other regions. In consequence we never knew complete crop failure. If the spring harvest was poor, the autumn harvest was good, and vice versa. I do not remember a single family in our village suffering from a lack of dark rye bread, potatoes, cabbage, or sour milk, the principal items in our diet. Sugar was a luxury, so was white bread, so was pastry, except on such holidays as Easter, when *kalachi*—specially baked wheat cakes—and dyed eggs enlivened our neighbors' festivities. Butter and meat were rare, but sunflower oil was cheap as it is even today and served an endless variety of purposes in cooking and baking, and spread on bread was a favorite food for children and grownups.

In retrospect it is astonishing how primitively self-sufficient our muzhiks were, not only in the food they ate but in the clothes they wore. Out of home-grown flax, women spun and wove the linens which they sometimes dyed and out of which they sewed shirts and trousers for boys and men, blouses and skirts for girls and women. Out of their own sheep's wool they spun and wove cloth for *svitky* (cloaks) for winter use; and migrant artisans from the city visited our village in winter, and processed dried sheepskins into heavy overcoats and wool into *valenki* (felt boots). Underwear and handkerchiefs were completely unknown, and men and women who had leather shoes wore them on Sundays and holidays or when they went to the parish church a little more than a mile away. In summer week-days old and young went barefooted or wore *lapti*—home-plaited bast sandals, which to me have always symbolized the backwardness of the Russian village.

Actually, our muzhiks were still living in the age of wood. With rare exceptions their plows were wood-framed. Steel pitchforks for loading and unloading hay and straw or sheaves of grain were unknown; with their own hands they fashioned pitchforks out of appropriate limbs of trees. Grain drills too were unknown, and muzhiks seeded their fields by hand, throwing handful after handful of the seed from a wooden basket slung from the neck over the breast. Grain was threshed with handmade flails and winnowed with handmade wooden scoops. Even spoons were made of wood and so were water and milk pails. Knives and forks were unknown and muzhiks ate meat and spread butter with their fingers.

Of course they had steel axes and steel saws for cutting logs and splitting firewood. They also had steel scythes for mowing hay. But only landlords in the neighborhood had begun to use mowing machines, grain drills, threshing machines, and other implements, imported principally from Germany. Muzhiks had to content themselves with the hand tools they could afford to buy or make themselves. Even axles of their carts and wagons were usually made of wood, and except for a few nails here and there, no metals were used in the construction of houses and barns.

Ours was the only house with a shingled roof, part of an inheritance from my grandfather who for some reason had once been favored by Count Radziwill, a Polish landlord who had held vast acreages in various parts of Byelorussia. But my improvident and vodka-loving father had drunk up most of the inheritance, so we got down to one cow and one horse and the big house with the shingled roof. All other houses and barns in the village were thatched. Now and then sparks from a chimney set the thatch afire and in the absence of fire-fighting machinery, even of water barrels, the house burned to ashes. If there was a strong wind, other houses and barns caught fire, leaving the muzhiks destitute and homeless. Then these *pogoreltsui* (burned-out folk) would take to begging, wandering from one village to another, going from house to house, explaining that they were *pogoreltsui* and receiving alms, rarely in money, usually in eggs, bread, measures of rye or potatoes, bundles of flax, cuts of pork or sausages, or any other home-processed commodity that they could sell and start life anew. Muzhiks never refused alms to *pogoreltsui* or beggars.

Being "burned out" was one of the direst calamities for the muzhik in the old days.

Bolshoye Bykovo was the name of our village. Across the river that meandered through the woods and behind a dense birch lot lay the village of Maloye Bykovo. Other villages stretched around us within a mile or two: Brantchitsi, Iserno, Igrayevo, Pratsavitshy. Our own village, like all the others, had a single street lined on each side with log-built thatch-roofed cottages. There were no sidewalks or pavements; though ditches at the sides drained off flood water, water holes and mud puddles rarely dried up. The highways that connected us with the outside world were not always passable after a siege of autumn rains or spring floods. There were times when we were completely cut off from the outside world. But then—our village like the others, was largely self-sufficient and self-governing.

Ages of struggle with inhospitable nature under an autocratic Czarist state had cultivated in the muzhik—even where there was no *mir* (communal land ownership) but where the land was individually owned as was the case in our part of Russia—a superb spirit of co-operativeness. This spirit was most dramatically expressed in the *skhod* (mass meeting), where any and all communal problems were solved: mending roads and bridges, hand-clearing the communal pastures of shoots of bush and shrub, the election of local officials—an elder who was the link with the state, a watchman for the communal *magazin* (storage barn for grain), shepherds for the communal pastures, one for horses, one for cattle, one for sheep and pigs that were always pastured together. The *skhod* knew no parliamentary rules; people just talked and argued as loudly and passionately as they chose until they all agreed, so no vote-taking was necessary.

The *skhod* did not concern itself with problems of state or with any political questions, which was why it was permitted freedom of expression. The local prerogatives of the state were the concern of the *pisar* (record-keeping clerk) and the *uryadnik* (constable), both of whom maintained their offices and homes in the small town of Pohost, seat of the township, some four miles away from our village.

The *zemsky nachalinik* (rural chief) and the *stanovoy* (district police officer) rarely visited our region. Nor did the *pisar* travel around. His was an office job, and people in the township who had business of one kind or another with the government were obliged to go to his office. Not so with the *uryadnik*. He was always on the go, from one village to another. Muzhiks hated him only a little more than the *pisar* because both extracted bribes under any pretext.

Vividly I remember how my widowed mother used to shiver whenever the uniformed *uryadnik*, sheathed sword at his side, drove into the village. The moment he strutted into our house we children hid under the table or the bed. We looked on him as on a man of evil omen, and Mother, knowing well the purpose of his visit, would hasten to present him with a pot of butter, a dried cheese, foods that she needed for her own family. But this was the only way she and others like her in the village could keep out of trouble with the law, which the *uryadnik* interpreted to suit his own purposes. Nobody would dare complain against him to the *zemsky nachalinik* for fear of incurring his vengeance. But since he, more than any officer the muzhik knew, personified the power of state and law, the muzhik had an abiding hatred of both, a hatred with which all political parties had to reckon after the abdication of the Czar in March 1917. Even Lenin as early as January 1919, some fifteen months after the Bolshevik seizure of power, was obliged to complain that "millions of inhabitants grew accustomed to regard the Central Power of the nation as an organization of landlords, exploiters, murderers." This was manifestly true of the muzhik. Despite his century-old adulation of the Czar as the "Little Father," he had been persuaded that the powers that ruled him, of whom he might never encounter anybody higher than the *uryadnik*, were as much his natural enemies as fires and floods. It was this age-old hatred of "the millions" for the "Central Power" that Lenin turned to his advantage during the months of his fight for the dictatorship.

At the time (1905) that our family migrated to America there was no schoolhouse in our village nor in any of those near by. In 1923, when I returned to Russia as an American journalist, there were classes but no schoolhouses in any of these villages except Brantchitsi, the seat of the parish church. The school had been built a few years before the Revolution, not by the state but by the Polish landlord whose fields and forests adjoined the village. Bulhak was the landlord's name, and though he was a Roman Catholic he put up the schoolhouse for muzhiks who were Greek Orthodox. A handsome man of early middle age, as I remember him, with pink cheeks and light reddish hair, he was famed for his benevolence, not only to muzhiks but also to the scatter of Jews in the surrounding villages. I know nothing about his background or his education, but obviously he belonged to the more progressive landed gentry. Often while on his way to Slutsk, the nearest city, of some 15,000 inhabitants and about fifteen miles away from his estate, he would stop at our house to give his horses a rest. He always gave us children pieces of candy wrapped in gaily colored paper, pinched our cheeks, and spoke to us with playful humor. And if late in winter one of our muzhiks ran out of fodder for his cow, he could count on Bulhak for a load of straw to keep the cow alive. Winter after winter my own father went to him for help, now for a load of straw, now for a sack of rye for bread, now for a sleighload of firewood, and Father never came back empty-handed.

Our village was lucky to have had so benevolent a landlord. Muzhiks blessed him and prayed for him. We were equally lucky to have had a kindly parish priest, an honest and sober man, who did not chase after women and who neither grumbled nor protested if a muzhik was too poor to compensate him for a rite he might perform, whether a christening, a burial, or the blessing of field crops. He loved children, and when apples and pears in his magnificent orchard ripened he would gather the windfalls and distribute them free among boys and girls who lingered hopefully outside the high picket fence that enclosed the orchard. Whenever in summer I happened to be in his village, I too benefited from the good man's generosity. I ate my fill of fruit and took some home for my mother.

When I returned to Russia after the Revolution, Bulhak was dead; he had died during the civil war, and it was shocking to hear the Bolshevik overseer of his estate, which had become a state farm, speak of the monstrosities muzhiks had perpetrated on the dead man's body and on his properties, principally on his livestock and his forests. The parish priest and his wife were still alive, and my visit to their home when, old, withered and poverty-stricken, they found themselves alone in the world, hounded by the Soviets and forsaken by the muzhiks who had once blessed and prayed for them, was one of the most heartbreaking experiences I had in those days. The Revolution had released the pent-up hatred of the muzhiks against people of privilege, even against those who had been kind to them and against whom they had never whispered a word of reproach or disrespect. It is well to emphasize here that the outward docility of the muzhik as I had known him in Czarist times was as deceptive as was the seemingly unshakable power of the Czar himself.

There were four Jewish families in our village. The head of one was a blacksmith, another was both trader and farmer, while the other two, including my father, lived off small landholdings. Jewish children, boys and girls, had to be taught Hebrew so they could read the Bible and recite their prayers. The four families therefore engaged a tutor in the city of Slutsk to teach Hebrew and Yiddish and who knew enough Russian to teach us to read and write the language. The first Russian book I ever read—a collection of fairy tales—was lent to me by the most remarkable muzhik in our village. Blind in one eye, the lids of which seemed glued together, he was called Blind Sergey. A handsome man in the early forties, with thick black hair brushed back from a lofty forehead and a thick black mustache under a thin, straight nose, he was one of the few muzhiks I ever knew who never had cultivated a beard. He was literate in Russian and Slavonic, the language of the Russian Greek Orthodox Church, and was a brilliant storyteller and a gifted singer. He especially loved religious music, and it was always affecting to hear him intone in his soft baritone voice the solemn and long-drawn-out chants of the Orthodox Church.

Like nearly all our people, Sergey believed in spirits—he had seen them, talked to them, had outsmarted them in their cunning plots to ensnare him into captivity and doom. There was no end to the stories he could tell, and during the long winter evenings when muzhiks, principally men, gathered in our house, because it was the largest in the village, Sergey would tell story after story with such consummate artistry that he made the flesh of his listeners creep, of none more than of my own spellbound, shivering self.

I looked up to Sergey as the most learned man in the village. He lent me the few paper-bound books he had bought in the city bazaar, and he talked of books as the source of all wisdom with such eloquence and ardor that he roused in me the desire to read and read, one book after another. But there was no library in our village or in any of the villages around us, not even in Pohost, seat of the township. It was not until after I had entered a Russian state school for boys in the city of Slutsk that I found myself close to a small library.

I had never before been in a city and Slutsk was a revelation —so many people, so many streets, so many styles of dress, so many varied types of humanity! A small city, still backward in its development, with no electric lights, no telegraph, no telephone, no railroad, with not a single factory, except two steam-powered flour mills, with only the long main street cobbled all the way. The population was made up of traders, principally Jews, artisans both Russian and Jewish, and officials, oh, so many, all Russians and all wearing resplendent uniforms, a few physicians and lawyers, retired landlords or those preferring to maintain homes away from their village estates. All these were overshadowed by the few nobles who were invariably addressed as "Your Highness" or "Your Illustriousness," titles that emphasized the sharp social cleavages in the community. Muzhiks in their rough homemade clothes were readily identified as the lowest of the low on the scale of feudal social values; and this applied to all villagers, Jew or non-Jew.

My father had a distant relative in the city who was a pharmacist and who therefore ranked as one of the local elite. Whenever Father took me to visit him we were received in the kitchen, and if we were invited to stay for a meal, it was not to eat it with the family in the dining room, but there in the kitchen with the maid. Never once did we sit down to dinner with our relatives.

One day the son of the house, who was about my own age and a student at the most celebrated gymnasium in the city, suggested a game of handball in the backyard. We had hardly begun to play when a servant called out that his mother wanted to see him "for a little minute." He dashed indoors, saying he'd be back right away, but though I waited and waited he never did come back.

The son of a pharmacist should not be seen by the neighbors playing ball with a child whose father grubbed in the earth for a living, like any dirty muzhik.

Though Father never seemed to resent his relatives' snobbery, I was humiliated and angered at being treated as an inferior by them. I had never known anything like it to happen in the village. But finally I dismissed the matter as just one more example of the incomprehensible ways of city folks, as much a part of the scheme of things as the bitterness of winter and the harshness of muzhik life in general.

Like all cities and towns spread across the vastness of Russia, Slutsk would have starved to death without the produce the villagers brought to the cobbled outdoor market place: cereals and dairy foods, meats and animals to be butchered, vegetables, mushrooms and fruits. Yet nobody ever addressed the muzhik, regardless of his age, by the polite *vy* (you) or by his given name and patronymic like "Ivan Ivanovich." Everybody, even children, called the muzhik, even if he was an elderly white-haired man, as *ty* (thou), a term of disrespect. There was always plenty of haggling over prices between city folk and muzhiks, and at times tempers flared and muzhiks were scorched with such epithets as "muzhik dumbbells," "muzhik idiots," "muzhik cholera," "muzhik this-and-that," the very term "muzhik" signifying a creature of a lower breed, too debased to be worthy of acceptance as a social equal.

No wonder that the muzhik cherished an abiding hostility to the city, its traders and intelligentsia, its plain folk and officials, its landlords and noblemen. In my early months in school, I too felt this hostility. But study was a broadening experience, principally because of the excellence of the teachers, who in time mitigated my village-bred animosity to the city. Still, despite its illiteracy and wretchedness, I loved the village more than the city. I felt at home there as I never did in the city, and I never failed to return there for summer vacations and winter holidays. I continued to play with muzhik boys and girls and made the rounds of homes, especially to Blind Sergey's to listen to the talk, always frank and sometimes passionate, of everyday events and of modest ambitions, chief of which was somehow to get possession of another strip of land. In winter, I especially enjoyed the nightly gatherings in our house when men from all over the village talked themselves out about their grievances against nature or neighbors, argued and quarreled over personal and community problems, and what was particularly fascinating to me, told ghost stories and of encounters with the Evil One in the woods, in the swamp, on the road, or in the barn. Now and then Blind Sergey, tiring of conversation, would start a song and everybody would join in. Then Sergey would stand in the middle of the room like a choirmaster on a stage and lead the gathering in one song after another. And how fervently we all sang!

I had never known of any anti-Semitism among our muzhiks. The four Jewish families in the village carried the common burden of backwardness and poverty as stoically as did their non-Jewish neighbors. Nor did I ever acquire the anti-Christian bias of so many Jews in towns and cities. Adam Sharankovich, our priest, was a remarkable man and he would no more call Jews "Christ-killers" than Jews, even in the privacy of their homes, would call him "pogrom-maker," an epithet that fitted many priests in the Pale of Settlement where Jews were confined under the Czars. Mother always addressed the priest as *batyushka* (little father) and whenever he stopped at our house she fired the samovar for him. She never took money from him but he always brought her a gift of one kind or another—fresh fruit from his orchard, honey from his hives, or eggs that some parishioner had offered as payment in kind for some clerical ministration.

Living in the village, I grew up a peasant myself, steeped in peasant lore, peasant music, peasant ways, and peasant psychology. I could not know then what a unique treasure I was storing up in my memory against a distant future when as a traveler between two worlds I would devote myself to interpreting my old world to my new.

Chapter 2

The Uprooted

◆►

Three of us, my two closest friends and I, recent graduates from the Czarist elementary school, went for a long walk in a wood outside the school town. This was our last walk together. The following morning I was to leave by diligence for the nearest railroad station, some forty miles away, on the long journey to America. Though we had read Mark Twain, Fenimore Cooper, Jack London, Harriet Beecher Stowe, of life in real America we knew nothing, and as we walked along we entertained ourselves with speculation of the mechanical wonders I should see in the new and far away country.

Twilight came and we fell silent. There was nothing to say that had not already been said. So we started singing, the melancholy songs of Pushkin, Lermontov, Nekrasov, and the lively folk ditties we had learned in school. Singing was as important a subject in our curriculum as history and geography, grammar and literature. We loved singing so much that mornings before class and during recess we sang more than we played. Russia was always a singing nation. She still is. Wars, plagues, famines, revolutions, dictatorships come and go, but song never dies. "Song became our life," wrote Nikolay Tikhonov, the Soviet poet who was marooned in Leningrad during the three-year German siege of the city in World War II. "Our song was not frightened of tragedy."

Suddenly a voice broke in on us, "How well you sing, boys."

We halted in our steps, recognizing the voice of our school director. He was a man of about sixty, with a broad pale face, always clean-shaven, a soldierly bearing, and a deep bass voice. We doffed our school caps and stood at attention like soldiers before an officer. A stern disciplinarian, he never could bear the sight of an unkempt and unwashed student. If ever a boy came to school with dirty ears and uncombed hair, which with my village background I sometimes did, he grew angry and violent. More times than I care to remember he twisted my ears and yanked my hair, shouting *"muzhik!"* making me writhe with pain and shame.

Though we feared him, we also loved him. He was an inspiring teacher, his specialty being literature which he taught us during our fourth, or senior, year. Technicalities meant little to him. It was the content and spirit of a poem, a story, a novel, that fascinated and excited him. An accomplished elocutionist, he could bring tears to our eyes by reciting a Nekrasov poem and make us roar with laughter over a Gogol tale. He, more than any other teacher, though they were all exceptionally competent in language and literature, unlocked for us the treasures of Russia's brilliant nineteenth-century literature. I was not quite fourteen when I graduated from the school, but I had already read some of the major Russian poets and novelists. Turgenev was my favorite novelist, and I fell in love with every one of his heroines. I couldn't imagine girls more romantic, more exquisitely feminine, more brilliant of mind, more sturdy of character—much more so than the men they loved—and more lyrically happy in their love, yet so bravely unhappy in the collapse of that love. Reading Turgenev in those days was more than a literary pleasure; it was a spiritual experience, and the schoolmaster by his eloquent and heartfelt appreciation of the author deepened the nature and the meaning of the experience. He made Turgenev an everlasting part of our developing social sense and our growing emotional life.

So here he was standing before us, the brass buttons of his uniform shining in the twilight, and overawing us with his presence. He came over to me, laid his hand on my shoulder and said, "You must continue your education in America."

"Yes, sir," I replied stiffly.

"Make the most of your American freedom, and don't forget your brokenhearted schoolmaster." His voice shook, though he smiled as he spoke. Firmly he pressed my hand and said warmly, "A happy journey to you and may God bless you." Then turning to the three of us, he added, "Go on, boys, keep on singing. It's

cheering to hear you sing." Bidding us good night he walked
away.

But we couldn't sing any more. We spoke of the great grief
that had come to the stern yet fatherly man. He had two sons.
Both had graduated from the Gymnasium with gold medals and
both had entered the university, the younger, Volodya, having
been admitted to the philosophy faculty of the University of
St. Petersburg.

Volodya had not finished his first year when he was arrested
for belonging to a secret student society. A year later he was released from prison and came home a shattered man. He never
spoke again to anyone, not even to his father and mother. Afternoons I often saw him walking in the little park in back of the
schoolhouse, the gate locked, so nobody could enter nor he
escape. Sometimes he would wave his arms in violent gestures,
as though engaged in vehement controversy with an unseen ad-
versary or with his own troubled self. No words accompanied the
gestures, and whenever a student spoke to him he grew terrified
and fled to the other side of the park.

"Well," said one of my classmates to the other, "who knows
but you and I will someday share the fate of Volodya." Laughingly
he turned to me. "But not you, you lucky devil. I wish I were going
to America."

Some years later one of them migrated to the New World and
settled in a small town in Nebraska. The other, the one who had
said he wished he were going to America, remained in the old
school town, and when I saw him again in 1923, he was an ardent
Bolshevik and a leading political figure in the community. "Remember," he said when I called on him, "the walk we took in the
woods the evening before you left for America? Remember what
I said—that I wished I were going there? I can't tell you how
happy I am that I never had the chance. We have more freedom
now in our Bolshevik Russia than you in your America will ever
have. We are poor now, but someday we shall be richer than
America—we shall be the freest and happiest people in the world."

In those days of the New Economic Policy when private trade
was again legalized, Bolshevik leaders, especially in the provinces,
spoke with ardor of the Revolution as the emancipator of humanity, not only from poverty and want but also from restrictions

that thwarted the unfolding of man's natural gifts and the enjoyment of a full free life, socially, artistically, intellectually, and
above all in sex relations.

In the autumn of 1944, while World War II was still raging, I
revisited the old school town and inquired of the Party Secretary
what had become of my former classmate.

"He—he—well, you'll never see him again."

"Was he killed in the fighting?"

"No, he got into trouble and—well—he disappeared."

Such was the end of the man who had said he was happy he
had never had the chance to emigrate to America.

But I did emigrate and vividly remember the drizzly day in
the autumn of 1905 when, packed into a straw-filled springless
cart that rumbled hub-deep in mud, my mother, brother, two
sisters, and I rolled away from the village of our birth, from the
home of our ancestors. Huddled among the bundles of our scanty
possessions, I had watched familiar faces, houses, fields, forests,
drop behind, certain that I should never see them again. The cart
was shaking my bones and sadness at leaving the old home was
shaking my heart. I cried unabashedly, and then to forget and to
solace myself I kept thinking of the country for which I was
bound. Somehow it was hard to believe that there was such a
country as America anywhere in the world.

But, one day a Danish ship carried us up through the Narrows
and there it was—America! I arrived in New York wearing my
best clothes—my Russian school uniform, black belted tunic, long
trousers, and military cap with a black shiny visor. I must have
been an outlandish sight, especially to children. They stared and
laughed at me, and overnight my oldest brother, who had come
ahead of us and had paid for our ship tickets, changed me into an
American outfit: knee pants, jacket, black stockings, and a soft
cap. Proudly I walked the streets, but inwardly I felt bewilder-
ingly alien, for no two worlds could have been more stupendously
unlike than the mud-sodden village from which I had been uprooted and the towering New York into which I was flung.

Though my four years in a Russian school had enlarged and
enriched my knowledge of the world, it had not prepared me for
the overpowering surprises of New York—the tall buildings, incredibly tall, the gas and electric lights that banished night from

the streets, the horsecars and trolleys that carried one wherever one chose to go and, marvel of marvels, the elevated trains thundering right over one's head. Least of all did rural or town Russia prepare me for the newsstands which sold enormous-sized dailies at a penny each—an unbelievably low price for so much paper. In any muzhik bazaar it would have been worth five times the price as cigarette paper. I marveled at the richness of America where people threw the precious newspapers into ash cans or gutters with no more concern than muzhiks spat out the shells of the pumpkin and sunflower seeds they loved to chew on Sundays and holidays.

Having always associated law with a uniformed official, my happiest impression of the new country, was the absence of uniforms in the streets of New York. It was reassuring to discover that government in the New World did not parade its power in the pomp of silver and golden braid, brass and silver buttons. True, the helmeted and uniformed policeman on the beat was in my early months in the big city a slightly sinister figure. I couldn't quite dissociate him from the overawing *uryadnik,* so whenever I saw him I hurried across the street or dodged around the corner. But in time I ceased associating him with the intimidating and bribe-grasping *uryadnik.*

An older brother and two sisters had preceded us in their migration to America, and when we arrived we settled in with them on the Lower East Side on the fourth floor of a walk-up apartment. We had gas lights, though only when a quarter was put into the slot of the meter. We had running water and even a bathtub. There were eight in our family and to help pay the rent we of course kept boarders, two of them. Soon another sister and her husband came from Russia, so the four rooms were shared by twelve people which caused no distress to anybody, least of all to me, for privacy was no part of my upbringing. Besides, I was so overpowered with curiosity about the big city that the streets lured me irresistibly. They were my first American school. It was in the streets that I saw for the first time Negroes, Chinese, Italians, Hungarians, Irish, others of the multitude of nationalities that made up New York. I had read of these people and now I saw them in the flesh. I yearned to speak to them, to learn all I could about them: how they lived, what foods they ate, what books they read, what they talked about when they were by themselves, what they thought of the peoples among whom they lived, and how they differed from the muzhiks, the Jews, the intellectuals I had known in the Old World. But language was a barrier I couldn't hurdle—not yet. I contented myself with watching and wondering about them—the Chinese in the laundries, the Negroes as day laborers, the Irish as truck drivers, policemen, and saloonkeepers, the Italians as shoe-shiners, ice and coal carriers, peanut venders, and organ-grinders.

One day I passed a Chinese basement laundry. The door was open and I paused to watch a little man with a pigtail at his ironing. He came to the door, smiled, and beckoned me to come in. I smiled back and shook my head. He went back into the shop and returned with a handful of Chinese nuts. He appeared so amiable that I finally followed him into the basement. Smiling and chattering he led me to the rear of the shop, which was cluttered with bags and cases. In dumb show he indicated that he wanted me to help him clean up the place. I worked for about an hour and when we finished he gave me a nickel, the first money I earned in America. I was surprised and overjoyed. In the Russian town where I had gone to school I had helped people lift sacks of grain and load carts of stove wood and they never gave me a kopeck, though they usually rewarded me with a pear or an apple. In America the laborer was worthy of his hire: even a Chinese laundryman paid cash for a service rendered. The heartening realization broke on me that despite my knee pants, I could earn money. Soon I was working as errand boy for a manufacturer of boys' clothing for two and a half dollars a week.

Of all the national groups I observed in the streets, the Italians attracted me the most. They were always friendly and cheerful, always ready to speak to you even if they knew you couldn't understand a word they said. Their hands were as eloquent as their tongues. No other people, it seemed to me, gesticulated as gracefully and as expressively. After I discovered Mott Street I often walked there for the pure pleasure of observing Italians. They were so vibrantly alive that they appeared never to be bored or to harbor grudges against other people. Their fruit and vegetable stands and pushcarts were an exciting and memorable sight; fruits and vegetables I had never seen before piled neatly tier on tier, color on color, not like produce offered for sale to immigrants but like works of art created to delight the passer-by.

Whenever an Italian organ-grinder appeared on the block he brought with him a holiday spirit. The moment he started grinding out a tune, little girls came tumbling out of doorways, shrieking and giggling with delight. Some of them had pennies for the wizened-faced little monkey who accepted the coins with a solemn doff of his tiny red cap. Forming circles, the little girls danced on the sidewalks and into the streets. To the fourteen-year-old immigrant boy they made a pretty scene—none of them ragged or barefooted like little girls in the old Russian village, all clean and neatly dressed, with bright bows on the end of their bobbing pigtails. Though they were children of the slums, tap water, cheap soap, low-priced dress goods which their immigrant mothers sewed into dresses or inexpensive store clothes made them look as attractive as the daughters of merchants and land-lords in the Old Country.

Wonderful little girls! The immigrant boy in his American-style knee pants and long stockings was captivated with them. They were so pretty and so unconscious of the snobberies of the Old World. Wherever their parents came from, whatever their fathers did for a living—tailor, carpenter, plumber, ragpicker, pushcart peddler, storekeeper, or even owner of a tenement—gliding and hopping and circling to the mechanical tune of the hurdy-gurdy, they were equals together. No mother or nursemaid pulled any of them out of their charmed circle of innocence because others were born into the wrong families.

I loved to wander the streets of the Lower East Side and get lost in the adventure. The noisy bustling crowds fascinated me, everyone so feverishly busy. Immigrants mostly, they seemed like a new race in the world, different in manners and behavior from the people I had known on the other side of the ocean. Energetic and purposeful, they were astonishingly informal: well-to-do shopkeepers walked around without coats, sometimes with shirt sleeves rolled up as no member of their profession would deign to do in the scruffy little city where I had gone to school. Overalled janitors, icemen, peddlers tipped their caps to nobody —the very custom was unknown, and so was hand-kissing.

Several blocks away from where we lived was roaring, bustling Hester Street. The pavement was lined with stalls and pushcarts, and men with cribs or baskets suspended on leather straps from their necks pushed their way along, crying their wares—needles, thread, shoelaces, soap, socks—like hawkers in a Russian bazaar. The filthiest section of the neighborhood, it was also the busiest and most exciting. Customers haggled over prices as violently and abusively as muzhiks. Shopkeepers grabbed the arms of passers-by and with torrents of cajolery endeavored to pull them inside their stores, cursing those who escaped their clutching hands. Russian or Polish women, obviously peasants, struggled through the crowds calling for someone to rescue them from clinging Hungarian or Romanian peddlers or shopkeepers whose language they didn't understand. All was bedlam, a cacophony of voices, the Yiddish dialects of Eastern Europe rising above all others. Here the Old World strove loudly against the New with all its undisciplined brashness, a product of the ruthless century-old struggle for survival.

One day I bought a penny piece of chocolate from a Jewish peddler. His Yiddish like mine was corrupted with Russian, and recognizing our common origin he switched to that language. He cursed America for the wretched life he was living. In his native Odessa he had given private lessons in Russian to sons and daughters of the most respectable families in the city—Russians, Jews, Greeks, Georgians, Armenians. His pupils and their fathers bowed and raised their caps or hats when they passed him in the street. He had never wanted to come to America; it was all his wife's fault. She had grown so hysterically fearful of a possible pogrom that he had yielded to her pleas and emigrated. But in America nobody cared to learn Russian, so he was without a profession. Never before in his life had he done menial work, but now he was forced to peddle, to carry heavy baskets twelve hours a day, coming home tired and sweating and aching in every bone, and what was he now? A nobody, a frog in a mud pond, a door mat for others to wipe their feet. Cursed, ever cursed be America!

He was a tragic misfit in the new country. Having no respect for the sweating brow or the calloused hand, he felt lost and degraded. America has never been a land for the non-technical intelligentsia of Eastern Europe. The American rough-and-tumble scramble for survival and success wounds their inflated self-esteem.

The most vexing problem before me in those days was of course the English language. Uncomprehending and envious, I listened to the sounds of the new tongue all around me: children chattering, grownups gossiping, truck drivers swearing; even the Italian bootblack on the corner spouted English and laughed at my blank stare when, despite his supplementary gestures, I failed to understand him.

The street was my English classroom. When American-born boys accepted me as a playmate, I deliberately cultivated the high school students, certain that from them I should learn the language at its purest. Their lessons were not without cost to my self-esteem: once they sent me into a candy store to buy a penny's worth of "son-of-a-bitch"; another time, as we passed an ice cream parlor crowded with girls, they gave me a nickel and told me to go in and ask for five-cents' worth of an obscenity. The girls screamed with shock and the man at the fountain kicked me out onto the sidewalk. My playmates roared with amusement and I felt like crying. Though they never duped me again, they taught me a vocabulary of choice obscenity.

Yet just being with them tuned my ears to the new language. Every day more of the strange sounds took on meaning as words arranged themselves into sentences. During the day I worked as errand boy and evenings and Sundays I played with the boys and studied English. I sweated over a Russian-English dictionary and grammar, often discovering that the dictionary definitions and idiomatic usage were far apart. The new language was a perverse tongue twister, replete with expressions that meant the opposite of what they should. "He is going to die," you said. How absurd! To me it meant he chose to die and what sane person would make such a choice? "Chewing the rag." What a monstrosity! The hungriest muzhik would rather chew wild onions or even birch bark. English was a baffling and maddening tongue.

To hasten familiarity with it, I enrolled in a public night school. The other students were peddlers, shopkeepers, factory workers,

who often fell asleep in class. Instruction was necessarily slow,
too slow for me and I quit night school.

Then an extraordinary thing happened. One evening while
wandering the streets of my neighborhood I passed a building
where a sign announced a lecture on Herbert Spencer. Admission
was free and I walked in. The lecturer was a Scotsman named
Edward King, once a teacher of philosophy, as I subsequently
learned, at Edinburgh University. As I understood only a part
of his lecture, I did not learn much about the philosophy of evolution: still, I enjoyed being in the audience of a man who sounded
so learned. After the lecture a small group gathered around him
to ask questions and to argue and I hung about on the fringes.
King was a short, paunchy man, broad-shouldered, with a massive head, iron-gray hair and thick walrus mustaches. Seeing me
standing there, the only boy in the audience, he beckoned to
me. With kindly interest he asked how I came to attend a lecture
on Herbert Spencer. Hesitantly and awkwardly I replied that
I had come out of curiosity and admitted that my knowledge of
English was so poor I had understood little of what he had said.
Forgetting Herbert Spencer, King proceeded to advise me on the
best way to enlarge my vocabulary. Every day I was to read at
least one page of a book, write down the words I didn't understand and their definitions from my English-Russian dictionary.
Once I finished the page, I was to commit to memory all the
definitions I had written down and read no further until I had
mastered the page. He invited me to come back to his next lecture
the following week when he would have a book for me he thought
I should read. The book was George Eliot's *Adam Bede*, the
first novel I ever read in English.

Thus I set out to acquire a vocabulary. Proudly I would recite my newly learned words to my playmates, and sometimes
they found my accomplishments so amusing that they doubled
up with laughter. They called me "professor" and teased me for
using big words, which, when I strung them together, didn't
mean what I thought they did. I still had to learn the difference
between dictionary and spoken English. I have since studied a
number of foreign languages and not one of them has proved
such a puzzle and torment as the richly idiomatic English tongue.

Subsequently I learned something of the history of the singularly learned and lovable Edward King. A Scotsman with a passion for philosophy, he had settled many years earlier on the East Side and had educated several generations of immigrant intellectuals. The Jewish trade unions and some of his former pupils and followers, who had attained literary or professional prominence, were subsidizing him on a modest scale so he could continue to educate fresh arrivals from the Old Country. After I came to know him well, he invited me to visit his small walk-up apartment in the neighborhood of Jackson Park close to the East River. He had no housekeeper and cooked his own meals or ate in restaurants, usually with a student of yesterday or today. He spent days wandering around old bookshops buying second-hand books that appealed to him even though he knew he would never find the time to read them. Books cluttered his rooms and hallways and whenever I went to see him he talked endlessly of the joy he derived from his collection. His whole life was centered in his books, his lectures, his pupils, old and new.

If my acquaintance with Edward King was one of the happiest experiences of my early immigrant days, my experience with social settlements was one of the most disheartening. Once a playmate took me to the Educational Alliance, and afternoons I often went there to browse through the books in the reading room. I loved to take an armful of books, sit at the table and just turn the pages and look at the illustrations. One evening a new librarian appeared—a slender, gray-haired woman with tight lips and a stern look in her eyes. When she saw me put an armful of books on the table she came over and asked why I took so many books at a time. In my halting English I explained that I loved to look at them, to study the illustrations and read isolated passages. After eyeing me with indecision for a moment, she went back to her desk. Soon she was at my side again.

"Sit up straight, please," she commanded.

Startled, I looked at her with protesting eyes. I had not been aware how I was sitting and now that she had made me conscious of it, I wondered what difference it made to her. But without a word of rejoinder I obeyed. She went away and soon I forgot myself and again propped my head on my hand. In an instant she was back at my side.

"I told you to sit up straight."

This time I ignored her.

Again she repeated her order in a louder voice and the boys and girls at my table looked up as though expecting trouble.

"I like it better this way," I growled.

"You've got to sit up straight," she ordered.

Was I tearing up the books? No. Was I calling her names? No. Why then did she insist that I sit in a position I disliked? Incensed at her arbitrariness I shoved the books off the table, darted out of the room and never again stepped inside the Educational Alliance.

At another time a playmate invited me to go with him to the Eldridge Street Settlement House. Presently I was surrounded by a group of smartly dressed girls older than myself. Smilingly and persistently they put me through an interrogation about myself and my home life. I could not quite make out why they were so set on discovering whether I slept alone or shared a bed with others or whether—as was the case in our family—some of us slept on the floor. They seemed to consider sleeping on the floor a hardship or degradation. In the Old Country I had slept in summer on grass on the ground, in a haymow or on straw on the barn floor and never minded it. The more the girls pried into my private life and the life of others in my family, the more incensed I grew. I felt as though I were in an inquisition chamber. Perhaps they were Junior Leaguers who descended on the slums to sweeten the life of immigrants. Perhaps they were college girls assigned to write a term paper on How the Other Half Lives. Their approach was so tactless that I finally sickened of their questioning and fled the house, never to return.

Years later I happened to be at a dinner party where I met the late Lillian Wald, founder of the Henry Street Settlement. I recounted to her my experience at the Eldridge Street Settlement House. She was quite amused and assured me that at *her* house blunderers like those girls, however well-intentioned, were quickly weeded out of social work. After an evening with that remarkable woman, I regretted that I had not found my way to her house in those days, when her influence would have been of enormous value to me.

When I had been in New York some six months a playmate
called Bert, son of a butcher who lived in the next block and who
was a student at the now defunct Townsend Harris High School,
decided that my English was fluent enough for me to join his
debating club. I had never heard of debating clubs in Russia
and my curiosity was aroused. The club met evenings in a public
school, and though the members were all high school students,
the director, a tall, gray-haired man with a youthful pink face
and an urbane manner, made an exception of me. The first time
he called on me to speak, I was so frightened that I shook and
stammered and the words stuck in my throat. My platform debut
in America was a sorry failure. Embarrassed and humiliated I
expected to be dropped from the club, but the director cheered
me by saying that first failure in public speaking was not uncom-
mon even to American-born boys. He himself had had a similar
experience with his first extemporaneous address. So I stayed in
the club and listened with envy to boys who strode confidently
to the speaker's table and argued their points with a fluency
that seemed forever beyond me. Yet debating excited me. It was
an intellectual exercise that called for quickness of thought,
fluency of speech, economy of words, and I was determined
someday to master it. The debating clubs of boys in knee pants
in the public schools of the East Side in my early immigrant days
were to me a brilliant demonstration of intellectual freedom.
Though the director was there to guide the boys in manner and
procedure, he never attempted to get us to express any opinions
other than our own.

The new language challenged me and I dreamed of the time
when I too would stand at the speaker's table and surprise the
director, the boys, and myself with my eloquence. At last one
evening the director and the boys insisted that the time had come
for me to try again. I froze with panic, but the insistence was so
friendly and the director's suggestion that I take as my subject
the emigration of my family to America appeared so easy to explain that I mustered the courage to rise and walk up to the
speaker's table. I remember looking straight into the director's
eyes and he nodded and smiled encouragement. Suddenly my
tension left me. Words I had been garnering and hoarding
through the months were ready for use. After a brief moment of

uncertainty, they poured out of my lips in a steady stream. Laughter and applause acclaimed me, and I felt that at last I had broken through the barrier of language and that I was no longer an alien. Now I really belonged to the New World in mind and in spirit.

But I assumed too much and rejoiced too soon. I was yet to learn, now with amusement, now with heartache, how little I understood American ways of thinking. Vocabulary and grammar were not enough to penetrate the mystery. All the words in the dictionary could not explain the enthusiasm of my American playmates for baseball, football, basketball, boxing, and other sports. In my Russian school, military drill twice a week was compulsory and we had all loathed it. Sports had no place in our lives. Here they were a subject of intense interest and of heated arguments. Try as I might, I could not whip up emotion over whether Townsend Harris would defeat DeWitt Clinton, or who would win the world series, or whether Jim Jeffries was a greater heavyweight than John Sullivan. I was still an outsider.

American boys even had a special way of scrapping. In my old village, whenever two boys came to blows, the fight quickly developed into a free-for-all, with no holds barred and no rules of combat to respect: fists, fingernails, feet, knees were all fair weapons. The shindy was usually broken by irate fathers or mothers and the reward of valor was often enough the stern application of a bunch of birch rods to our bare behinds.

But here a street fight was conducted strictly according to protocol. The combatants were immediately ringed around by friends and interested passers-by, who might shout encouragement but who never interfered. Only the warning yell "Cheese it, the cop!" broke up the affray, and the combatants either darted away or hastily assumed the attitude of Sunday school innocence.

Girls in America were another mystery. Daughters of immigrants, they were utterly unlike their mothers and unlike the girls I had known in Russia, either in village or town. Even when my English became somewhat fluent I felt we had no common tongue. Their lively chatter and worldly wisdom baffled me and though I wanted to make friends with them, I didn't know how. I always asked the wrong question or gave the wrong answer. Though I wasn't naturally shy, somehow their presence intimidated as much as it excited me. Other boys easily joined in their small talk and in the eternal game of kidding and bantering while I, though envious, stood by tongue-tied and solemn. On the rare occasion when the conversation turned to books and studies and Bert out of politeness would make an effort to draw me in, my interest would liven and I would manage to stammer an embarrassed remark.

The very air of America had affected these daughters of immigrants in a way I could not understand. It was not that they had suddenly assumed equality with boys; the girls I had known in Russia even among muzhiks had never felt inferior to boys, at least until after they married. But these American girls were so much more self-assertive and self-assured. They neither deferred to boys nor feared them. Where the Russian girls, especially school girls, had been direct and literal-minded (they still are) in their relations with boys, their American sisters displayed a feminine guile that baffled and bewildered me. They could twist a boy's words to their advantage with neither hesitancy nor compunction. They always seemed in high spirits and ready with a quick and smart retort, smart at least to my mind. I could not imagine them weeping over Turgenev's doomed heroines as Russian girls did and still do. There was nothing of the earnestness, the tenderness, the social enthusiasms of these heroines about them. Though children of the slums, they appeared so much younger and less mature than did Russian girls of their age, and so powerful was the impact of American civilization on them that they evinced barely a trace of the heritage their fathers and mothers had brought with them from the Old World. They did not even care for the language, Yiddish or whatever, that their parents spoke. They challenged, dismayed, and fascinated me and I felt ages removed from them.

I envied the boys in my neighborhood who were in high school, and I yearned for the day when I too would be admitted to the school, which to me was the equivalent of the Russian gymnasium, the steppingstone to college. The craze of these boys for college had communicated itself to me, but I was baffled by their veneration of medicine as the choicest of all professions in the world. "To be a doctor" was the impassioned ambition of many of them, and I observed that high school girls viewed with special admiration a boy who had set his mind on being a doctor. They esteemed him as something of a hero and were transcendently happy when they had won his attention. The vicissitudes of life in the city, the overcrowding, the filth in the street, the utter absence of greenery except in the one near-by park, were of no moment to these boys. Of course they were city born and city bred. They had never known the wild forests and fields, the swamps and streams, the vast array of birds from crows and blackbirds to storks and swallows, to nightingales and skylarks, that had been my unforgettable and ever-beloved heritage. They didn't have and could not have the feeling for nature that I had brought with me from the far away poverty-stricken Byelorussian village—a feeling that I had now come to regard as one of the most precious rewards Czarist Russia had accorded me. Never would I want to spend all the years of my life in so bleak and unnatural a part of the world as the Lower East Side was in those days. So to hell with being a doctor or a lawyer, the second most popular profession among my playmates, even if at the moment they did bring the pleasure of being a favorite with the most attractive girls in the neighborhood.

When my English was fluent enough for my high school friends to assure me that I would have no trouble in pursuing high school courses, I consulted with them as to which high school would be best for me. I finally decided on the Stuyvesant, and only because it was a manual training school. I loved the idea of acquainting myself with tools so that when the time came to devote myself to my chosen profession, which was agriculture, both my mind and hands would be attuned to mechanical contrivances.

At last the day came when I went to see the principal of the Stuyvesant High School. His name was Dr. Frank Rollins, and when I was ushered into his office, he greeted me with a friendly smile and a firm handshake. I can still see him in his black frock coat, winged collar, the formality of his dress contrasting with the ease of his manner. His eyes were understanding and humorous, and seated beside him I felt surprisingly at ease as I summarized my studies in the Russian school from which I had graduated. Dr. Rollins was astonished at the amount of studying I had crowded into four years. He was particularly impressed with my familiarity with the great Russian poets and novelists as well as with the translations of certain American authors and of Dickens, the only British author I had read in the Russian school.

Looking back to my Russian school years, I marvel at the extraordinarily high academic quality of those Czarist schools, scattered and few as they were in my native Byelorussia and for the most part beyond reach of the masses. The discipline was stern, but the teaching was excellent, inculcating from the very beginning the habits of concentration and intellectual earnestness. In the teaching of literature the Czarist schools had achieved their greatest glory, or maybe my old teachers had a special gift for making us, young as we were, see and feel the wonder and the beauty of great books, or were so fired by the warmth, the indignation, the humanity in them that the students quickly caught their enthusiasm.

Anyway, Dr. Rollins was satisfied that my Russian education more than qualified me for entry into his school. He filled in an admission card and told me to present myself for classes the following Monday morning. When he asked if I had yet decided on my future profession, I answered that I had set my heart on farming. He laughed, not with condescension but with surprise at an East Side immigrant boy's unusual amibition. As I left, Dr. Rollins shook my hand and asked me to drop in on him and let him know how I liked the school and how I was progressing in my studies.

The man's ease and kindliness, the lack of both uniform and pompousness in one so highly placed, buoyed my spirits more than any other experience in this exciting and confusing New World. I had been admitted to what was to me a "Gymnasium" and with no trouble at all. Nobody had asked a single question about my family's social standing, economic condition, or religion; tuition would be free, books, too, would be supplied. I strode down the street feeling as though I had suddenly entered into a new life and a new adventure.

Stuyvesant High School was the first truly American world that opened to me. Here I was privileged to associate with boys who came from all the boroughs of the city, rich and poor, of varied national origin, with but a mere sprinkling of immigrants like myself. They were clean, neatly dressed boys and were gay and boisterous. They rah-rah-ed their heads off at cheering practice, as though determined with their voices alone to bring the fear of the Lord into the opposing team, whether baseball, basketball, football, or track, none of which held the least interest for me. Since I had to work after school hours and on Saturdays, I never went to any games, and I felt convinced that I could digest my food and prepare my lessons on *The Lady of the Lake* and in algebra even if DeWitt Clinton High School trounced Stuyvesant in every encounter they had.

It was not the students as much as the teachers who stirred my imagination. There was nothing of the stiffness and severity of Russian teachers about them. The manual training teachers did not mind soiling their hands with greasy tools or with paint. They showed no feudal disdain of menial work. They never made students aware of a social gulf between them, which made the school a lively and happy community, though not untouched by the petty rivalries, the exuberant roughness, the guileful rogueries that now and then seize teenage boys. From my reading of so much English literature I had become passionately Anglophile, which incensed an Irish lad in my class. He bullied me at every opportunity, and for some time we confined our animosities to sharp verbal exchanges. Then we decided we'd have it out with our fists. Accompanied by a goodly portion of our class, we met to do battle on a vacant lot in the neighborhood. The Irish lad was fast with his fists which I was not, but I had a more powerful punch. He blackened my eyes and I made his nose bleed profusely. Afterward, we were the best of friends, which surprised me because in the Old World, the animosities of boys endured long after they had scratched each other's face and torn the blouse off each other's back.

I soon discovered that in my relationship with teachers my immigrant origin instead of being a liability was a real asset. English was my favorite subject and I couldn't have had more helpful and generous-spirited instructors. I still remember their names: W. Palmer Smith, Hugh C. Laughlin and Dr. Frederick Houk Law. If I wrote a composition that pleased them, they were lavish with praise in their written comments and often spoke to me after class, advising me what books to read and encouraging me to write. Because of my background and Russian education, I was more mature than the average student and the English teachers seemed to have appreciated this because now and then they would engage me in private discussions of the books I had read.

In my sophomore year I won the first prize in the annual short-story contest for second year students. Manuel Komroff, the novelist, whom I knew only by sight then, won the same literary prize for students in the junior class. My story was published in the school magazine and Dr. Law, who was one of the judges was, I thought, as pleased with the award as I was. He counseled me to keep on writing which flattered and uplifted me and for the first time made me doubt the advisability of choosing agriculture as my life work; and the ever-solicitous Dr. Rollins, called me into his office, shook my hand and congratulated me heartily. What a triumph for an immigrant boy!

But that triumph was short-lived. By the time I reached my junior year I grew morbidly discontented with myself, and not only because working long hours in a shop after classes had undermined my health. The New York in which I lived—the Lower East Side—which had so exhilarated me on my arrival, palled on me more and more. The rewards I had won in my early days—the feeling of social equality, the opportunities for education, with no cost to the family, not even for books, above all the gospel of labor with its recognition of the dignity of the "Man with a Hoe," with pick and shovel, with ax and saw—no longer satisfied me. I had assimilated them: they were no longer benefactions bestowed by a benevolent society, but rights and prerogatives in which I too shared, and their acceptance became as much a part of my person as the new language I had learned. School was still an adventure, but outside of school I began to feel lonely and desolate. I had outgrown the New York of the Lower East Side, which was the only New York I knew. The ugly tenement houses swarming with people, the garbage piles in the streets, the rough-and-tumble life of people always rushing and sweating, obsessed with mirages of good fortune, yet despairing of stumbling on a piece of good luck, dismayed me.

I suddenly realized that while I was *in* America, I was not *of* it, not really, not of the immense and alluring America that lay beyond Manhattan Island of which I had read in books and of which "Teddy" Roosevelt, as the boys in the neighborhood affectionately called him, wrote glowingly, but which the tall buildings shut out of my view.

I would explore this America, live in it, mingle with its people, learn to know them, discover how alike and how different they were from the people I had known. More than ever was I resolved to make farming my life work. I longed for trees and brooks, for wild flowers and open skies, for the peace and tranquillity of the land, the real American land, far from the tumult and the filth, the frenzies and obsessions of New York.

At the age of seventeen I fled the city to a farm upstate.

I could not then have foreseen what a boon life and work on an American farm would prove to be in my future career—indeed, as priceless a boon as my childhood and boyhood in a muzhik village.

Chapter 3

A Land to Grow In

◆

On a steep bank over a highway in upstate New York sprawls an old cemetery, very small, about a fifth of an acre in area. All around are hills and fields and in the rear the land slopes into a meadow that sinks down to a wooded swamp towered over by the loftiest hill in the neighborhood. Rusty barbed wire strung on high, wobbly cedar posts keeps pasturing cattle out of the graveyard. Tall maples shadow the grounds and in summer the grass grows lush and wild; dandelions, clover stalks, orchid daisies, now and then wild roses peep furtively out of the grass, and here and there a patch of myrtle, green as the sea, smothers all other growth.

The old cemetery dates back to a time after the War of Independence when pioneers from New England came in oxcarts to make new homes in the wilderness. Prominent on the headstones are the names of Faulkner and Moore, two families that had always been neighbors, if not always friends. The headstones of the Faulkners, fifteen of them, flank the front part of the cemetery and the Moores, five of them, are in the rear. The last Moore to be buried there was James, or Jim, as everybody called him. A slab of marble, square-cornered and about two feet high, rests over the graves of Jim, his father Alford, and his mother Sarah. No pious epitaph is carved into the headstone, only the names and the years of birth and death, Jim's being 1841 to 1926. Jim had hoped to live to a hundred, but nature had the last word. He died at eighty-five, and his proud boast had been that never in his life had he been so sick that he had to miss his "three squares" a day.

Early in March 1908 Jim had written to the Chelsea Employment Agency on the Bowery in New York asking for a young immigrant to work on his farm, offering fifteen dollars a month and keep. I was the applicant selected to be Jim Moore's hired hand. The agency manager was pleased to find a city boy willing to work in the country. He complained that few city boys cared for farm work and questioned me at length to make certain I wouldn't get homesick for dance halls, burlesque shows, Coney Island, and other city pleasures. I assured him he didn't have to have any misgivings. Then he asked whether I could plow land and milk cows. I never had done either, but I had seen my father plow and my mother milk our cow and I was certain that I could do as they did. I left the office of the employment agency with a railroad ticket in my pocket to a village upstate called North Brookfield in Madison County.

At the time I couldn't have known what a providential accident it was that I had applied for a farm job at this particular agency at the time I did. I shall always cherish the memory of Jim Moore. Long after I had left him and to the end of his life, we remained close friends and I often journeyed back to his farm to visit him. Poorly educated though he was, I always think of him as one of the most extraordinary characters I have known and his influence on my impressionable young mind has remained with me to this day. He flung open the doors of a new world for me, taught me a new way of farming, inculcated in me a set of priceless disciplines, introduced me to a new humanity, and gave me insight into an America I never should have discovered had I stayed in the city and even gone to college there. Working for him and living in his home was an education I never could have acquired from school teachers or textbooks, an education that in later years, when I began to write articles and books on Russia, proved a sounder guide to the understanding of some of the whys and wherefores of the Soviet Revolution than all the works of Marx and Engels or Lenin and Stalin.

Yet that spring day in 1908, while I was on the train heading upstate, I wondered about the life that lay ahead of me. What would I eat—would it be the thick soups with big lumps of bread, boiled potato, and porridge, with an occasional slice of raw pig fat, the usual fare of *batraky* (hired hands) on landed estates in the Old Country? And where would I sleep—would it be in a barn, a barracks, a shed, or at best in a kitchen? I kept wondering even more about James Moore, the man who had sent to New York for a farm hand. I could only picture him as a gentleman of leisure like the Russian landlords who wouldn't wear overalls, not even on weekdays.

But the moment I jumped off the milk wagon that had picked me up at the railroad station some two miles away from the farm and glimpsed the shabby house, I realized how far off the mark my speculations had been. It looked nothing like any landlord's mansion I had seen. The two-story clapboarded frame structure, set back from the road and shaded by stately maples, was utterly unimpressive. It had not even been painted. When I stepped inside the door and met my new employer, I was truly amazed. He wore faded and stained bib-overalls and a gray turtle-neck sweater with a big patch on the elbow. I knew at once that this was no gentleman of leisure but a farmer who worked with his hands. The discovery was comforting: it reduced Mr. James Moore to my own humble level of humanity.

All my other preconceptions fell like stalks of rye before a sickle. Instead of being separated from the family, I was made a part of it from the moment I stepped into the house. I shared a room with another hired man, and when he left I had it all to myself, the first time in my life that I had ever enjoyed the luxury of complete privacy. It was a large wallpapered room with three tall windows, one facing the road and looking out on a neighbor's house and land across the way, the other two offering a view of fields and hills and the wooded swamp whose wilderness brought to mind the age-old forests of my childhood.

The farmer's housekeeper (who, I learned later, was his mistress) was a short, slender, pale-faced woman with shining white hair and a pronounced limp. Every day she swept my room and made my bed. When my lamp chimney smoked she washed and polished it. She laundered my clothes, sewed on buttons, darned my socks, and mended barbed-wire tears in my shirts and overalls. When in line of duty I did chores for her—filled the wood box in the kitchen, fetched water from the pump in the woodshed, she would thank me as though I was conferring a special favor on her. The gentle, sweet-tempered though tight-lipped woman couldn't have looked after a son with greater solicitude.

Of course I sat at the same table with Jim and other members of his family. The cooking was new and exotic to me: the dishes quite unlike anything I had tasted in New York or in my old home in Russia. Soup, the stand-by of muzhiks and of immigrants from Russia, rarely appeared on Jim's board, and when it did, it was only a few spoonfuls of hot water in which floated particles of fat and sometimes a few crumbs of toasted bread, a few grains of rice, or bits of potato. A muzhik served such a watery concoction would have flung it, bowl and all, at his wife's head. The slices of bread were so small and thin, and Yankees° ate so little of it that I often wondered why they bothered to put it on the table. So soup and bread, the traditional belly-fillers of Russians, stout foods that often made a meal in themselves, were more shadow than substance, more token than satisfaction on a Yankee farm.

But there were so many other dishes on the table that I soon lost the craving for soup and bread. Meat and vegetables, potatoes and gravy, salads in season, honey from Jim's own hives and an endless variety of corn meal preparations that were new to me: johnnycake, muffins, mush, fritters, rusks, griddlecakes. And there was always a dessert for breakfast as well as dinner and supper, homemade pies, cakes, cookies, doughnuts, or "fried cakes," as we called them at Jim's. A meal without dessert was as unthinkable as potatoes without gravy, biscuits without honey, mush without milk. The astonishing variety of dishes at the farmer's table was a wonder and delight to me.

By prevailing American standards, Jim, who carried a mortgage on his farm, was what Russians would call a *bedniak*—poor man. Yet to a Russian *bedniak*, whose passion for land Lenin would exploit as a weapon of Bolshevik conquest, Jim's board would have been a landlord's luxury. And no Russian today, however high his salary and position, eats as great a variety of foods as we did at Jim's table some sixty years ago! Russia simply does not produce the vast variety of foods that America does, especially in fruits and vegetables, but remains principally a cereal and potato-cabbage-eating country. Khrushchev extolled corn as "the miracle plant," "queen of the field," "milk and meat on the stalk,"

° On the Lower East Side, Anglo-Americans were spoken of as "Yankees," and it is in this sense that I use the word throughout the book.

and with enthusiasm had sought to promote corn and corn products as foods. But even he during his two journeys to America had never discovered the many corn delicacies that I learned to enjoy on a farm in Madison County, New York, a farm which by Soviet Russian standards would have invoked on its hard-working and always cash-poor owner the epithet of "kulak" and would have rendered him subject to liquidation.

All the uncertainty that had oppressed me during my journey from the city into the unknown, vanished overnight. Jim and his housekeeper took me into the family as though I were their son. They accepted me without reservations, with a courtesy and a kindness that touched me, though to Jim it was all as natural as washing his hands before a meal. But to the young immigrant who was still sensitive to the Old World distinctions between class and class and man and man, it was a heartening revelation of daily living in a democratic community. Jim of course was no exception. All the Yankee farmers in the countryside treated their immigrant help, principally newly arrived young peasants from Russia, Poland, the Ukraine, Hungary, with equal regard for their comfort and their persons. This was the custom, in fact the morality of the country, which of course negates the Soviet-Marxist doctrine of perpetual class struggle in the capitalist countryside. Even so brilliant a man as Nikolay Bukharin, one of Lenin's closest associates who on the eve of the Soviet Revolution had spent several months in the United States, was loath to believe me when I once told him of the way I was treated when I had been a *batrak* on an American farm.

Once at suppertime I was served a side dish of corn kernels cooked with green beans in milk. I asked what it was. "Succotash," Jim replied, and the sound of the word roused my curiosity because it was so un-Anglo-Saxon.

"An Indian word," the old farmer explained. "The Indians here ate succotash."

I thought of Hiawatha and the Leatherstocking Tales; here on the table before me was something tangible of the exciting and mysterious world I had read about. Thereafter I pestered Jim for information about Indians who, because of a certain dish I had eaten, had become dramatically real to me. Yes, Jim told me, this had been Indian country until the white man "tooked" it away from them for a pittance. No, there had not been any wars with Indians over land or anything else in this part of the country. Governor George Clinton had bought the land from the Oneida tribe for a mere trifle, and he in turn sold it to new settlers at two shillings (fifty cents) an acre. It had all been forested wilderness, abounding in big and small game. The big game—panther, bear, wolf, otter, wildcat—was all gone, but in the wooded swamp that edged Jim's meadow and pasture, there was still plenty of small game—mink, racoon, weasel, possum, beaver, muskrat. Having no cows and pigs and sheep, the Indians had to hunt and fish for a living and corn was their great staple; they made it into succotash, into mush and cakes, and roasted it on the ear. Since they had no milk, they seasoned their mush with the juice of wild apples. Jim was surprised that I did not know that not only corn, but also beans, potatoes, tomatoes, and tobacco came from Indians on the American continent. He supposed everybody "knowed" it.

I asked when the first white settler came to his countryside. He did not know the exact year they had arrived, except that it was after the War of Independence. They first came to Brookfield, some seven miles away, and held their first town meeting there in 1795. The people had come from New England by oxcart in search of new lands in "the far west," as upstate New York was spoken of in those days. Land was cheap and folks bought a lot of it. Then they laid out roads, built churches, schools, inns, shops, grist and saw mills. "They sure done a mighty pile of work 'fore they got the country civilized."

North Brookfield was settled a few years after the first settlers had come to Brookfield. The hemlock there was so "goddam thick" that the sun was blocked out and so the little hamlet that was started was called "Negro city." And did I know that a Negro from Hartford, outside Utica, and his wife had come to North Brookfield soon after the hamlet had begun? His name was Laban Olby and his wife's name was Jenny. They built a hotel, and the cooking was so good that Jenny was known and admired in the towns all the way to Utica.

Jim's ancestral memories were as spellbinding as the tales of ghosts and goblins I had listened to in the old home in Russia. They peopled the fields and hills and woodlands around me with romantic and heroic figures of the old days and gave me a new sense of the exciting past of the country. And not so distant a past, to a boy of my age. My mother's father had lived to be one hundred and thirteen, so only a lifetime, though an uncommonly long one, separated my arrival from the first town meeting of white New Englanders in the countryside in which I was living.

This grandfather of mine is still a family legend. When he was one hundred and six years old, so the story runs, he fell ill and was pronounced dead. With appropriate ceremonies he was carried in a litter to the cemetery, followed by a mourning family and friends. At the cemetery he suddenly rose up, looked around, cursed the mourners, and walked indignantly away from his own funeral. Seven years later they brought him back to the cemetery, this time to stay. I remember him dimly, a white-haired man, with a tangled white beard and a hearty laugh. In summer he grubbed in the fields. In winter he cobbled shoes. Except for the spell that led to his first journey to the cemetery, he had never been sick in his life.

It was curious to think that while the woods all around Jim's farm were beginning to resound to the blows of pioneer axes, a man I knew was drawing his first breath. What a miracle had been wrought here during the man's lifetime, a miracle that only one like myself, who had traveled the vast distance between the Old and the New Worlds, could vividly appreciate. All his life grandfather had heard muzhiks cry for land even as I had heard them at gatherings in our house in the village of my birth. In the revolution of 1905, they fought for land when for a brief moment of power they put the torch to landlords' mansions and sometimes swung axes over landlords' heads.

The miracle was that here was no landless or land-poor peasantry, no peasantry at all. By no stretch of the imagination could the literate homesteading farmer be called a "peasant" in the old sense of the term. He had all the land he cared to till and sometimes more—land he originally wrested not from a landlord but from nature's own wilderness.

Jim's appearance was as unprepossessing as the slovenly clothes he wore. He was of medium height, bony, and stooped with years of work. The shiny bald spot on the top of his head was fringed with bushy white hair, like an egg in its nest; the backward sweep of his long ears reminded one of a rabbit's. All his waking hours his jaws rotated like a ruminating cow's, and his bristly mustache was yellow with tobacco juice. His gray eyes were large and bulging and shone like lamps out of his gaunt and wrinkled face, giving his person a strength and resoluteness that at first made me uneasy in his presence.

I worked for him about a year and a half and should have stayed longer had he not been such a wretched businessman that month after month, after paying his grain and grocery bills, not always in full, his milk check was spent and he had no money left for my wages. His big commercial crop was hops, the most laborious and expensive crop to grow. But like a Wall Street gambler he always held out for highest prices and eventually had to sell for the lowest. Invariably he incurred a loss that his dairy of twelve cows didn't cover. During my first three months as his farm hand he paid me only three dollars, just enough to buy a pair of work shoes.

The old farmer was without doubt one of the most eccentric men in the countryside, if not in all Madison County. He was famed for his explosive temper, his sharp tongue; his unswerving loyalty to the Democratic party was matched by an implacable hatred of the Republican party. His oddities of speech intrigued me. He used "ye," "yer," and "yourn." For him all forms of the present tense of the verb "to be" were simply "be." He rarely said "a quarter"—the coin was either "two bits" or a "shilling." From him I picked up many an idiom of the man on the land: "go the whole hog," "bring home the bacon," "the hang of things," "bark up the wrong tree," and others.

When in rage the old farmer roared like a lion, and until I got to know him well his roars terrified me. But when in good humor he purred like a well-fed cat. An old-fashioned farmer, he scorned the new agricultural science that was coming out of the Cornell State College of Agriculture in Ithaca. To him college professors were "yahoos" who didn't know whether the bull or the cow gave buttermilk. Year after year he refused to sell his hops with the other farmers when he might make a profit. He would show "them city slickers in New York" that they couldn't cheat him as they did other farmers, only to discover year after year that he was only cheating himself.

He had the simplicity, the audacity, the integrity of the pioneer. He thundered wrath at liars. Once I went back to sleep after he had waked me and showed up in the cow barn late for milking, my excuse being "a splitting headache." Without interrupting his milking he peered up at me and snapped, "Ye hain't got no more headache than the cow I be milkin'." Gloomily I took a stool and went to work. But the old man was not finished with me. The lie rankled and he bided his time until the cows were out of the barn. Upsetting milch cows with angry speeches and aggressive gestures was to him mortal sin. I was cleaning the stable when he suddenly approached me, lifted his milk stool, and cried out in fury: "Ye tell one more lie and, by Jesus, I'll crack yor goddam chicken-brained head so ye'll never tell another as long as ye live."

Afterwards when his temper cooled he lectured to me on the evil of lying, a lecture I never forgot. I had grown up in a civilization where at home and in school discipline was so stern that to escape chastisement children learned to lie as soon as they learned to talk. But Jim cured me. I never again lied to him.

As I look back across the years I have the feeling that a father-son relationship grew up between us. In his young years Jim had been unhappily married and had separated from his wife. His housekeeper had for years been his mistress. He had no children, and young as I was and an orphan, my father having died when I was eleven, he developed an affection for me which I returned. Whenever he went "visitin'" he invited me to go along. He often brought me a bag of peanuts from town. I neither smoked nor chewed tobacco, and when once out of curiosity I asked him for a bite of his plug, he snapped back, "I'll be votin' the Republican ticket 'fore I learn ye the bad habits I got." In time his explosive temper neither frightened nor upset me. It only amused me, and once after one of his blasts of profanity, I laughed and said, "I bet you don't mean a word you're saying." "Ye be goddam right I don't," he flung back.

Whenever I especially provoked him, he would call me "goddam Republican," the most abusive epithet in his vocabulary. He loathed the Republican party as the itinerant evangelists of those days loathed the Devil. He blamed it for all his misfortunes: the low price of milk and hops, the mortgage on his farm, the quack grass in the cornfields, the briars in the pasture that scratched a cow's teats so that she kicked when she was milked. Once a bee stung one of the team of horses I was driving. The horses ran away with me and kicked over a rail fence, upsetting the wagon.

"Ye be a goddam Republican," the old farmer shouted, "or it won't have happened, I tell ye. Them is Democrat horses and don't never run away when they know a Democrat be drivin' them."

"Then your bees," I countered, "must be Republican. One of them stung Bill [one of the horses] and made them both run away."

"Jesus Christ," he struck back, "I hain't never knowed a low-life Republican like ye, blamin' my bees when ye hain't got no-body but yer own damn Republican self to blame."

Though Jim was a profane man he never used the expression "son-of-a-bitch," regarding the epithet "an insult to the bitch." Nor did he ever indulge in sex obscenities. Not that he was puritanical on the subject of sex. In his whippersnapper days, he boasted to me, he had chased plenty of petticoats and "didn't miss a thing." He didn't cavil at a man for his way with a woman, provided, and he was dead earnest about it, "she was willin' to go the limit." To him sex was a private experience which four-letter words vulgarized. "Things that's private hain't ought to be shouted in public," he would say. The sex banter of farmers at a threshing bee once so nauseated him that he roared out, "If it's barnyard filth ye galoots be wantin', ye'd a damnsight better stuff yer gizzards with cow dung."

Since muzhik farming was the only farming I had known, I had everything to unlearn and the old farmer set about educating me to his way. Though his methods were old-fashioned, he was a stern perfectionist. He couldn't tolerate sloppy work, whether in cleaning a tool after it was used, currying and brushing a horse, or turning a straight furrow. In my early days I caused him no end of exasperation, and again and again he belabored me with his favorite epithets: "galoot," "yahoo," "lunkhead," "blackleg Republican." To him a hired man who botched his job in field or barn was not worth his "vittles," another new word to me. But

I was always eager to learn and after I mastered a tool, he was lavish with praise.

Besides, these new tools fascinated and excited me. I had made an abrupt transition from the age of wood, the age of muzhik farming, to the age of steel, the age of American farming. Though in those days the revolution in American agricultural machinery was still in its infancy, it was such a big advance over anything I had known in the old village that handling the new tools was more adventure than work. The tractor and combine had not yet roared into the countryside, but the sulky plow on which a man sat while turning a double furrow, the hay tedder that shook rain out of hay, the horse rake that gathered hay into windrows, the grain drill that seeded evenly and deeply, the binder that automatically reaped and bunched, bound and dropped sheaves, were to me astounding inventions. What toil and sweat and heartbreak they saved the farmer! The muzhik literally grubbed for a living, but in America the machine did the grubbing and far more efficiently than the most skilled hands.

Here the only work women and children did on the farm was to ride the horse rake or drive the team for the horse fork when hay was unloaded into the barn. Manifestly that was one reason the American farm women were so much more feminine and attractive than muzhik women; why they didn't age so soon (alas, how early in life Russian peasant women aged and still age) and were so much more even-tempered and serene. They didn't swear and curse like muzhik women; they never fought with their husbands like muzhik wives; I never heard of them beating their children like muzhik mothers. They were literate and had time to read the paper, magazines, the Sears, Roebuck catalogue, and even novels. They smiled much, laughed a lot, and hardly ever wept, not even at funerals, which in peasant Russia were orgies of lamentation and despair and still are in Soviet villages.

I marveled at the ingenuity that had gone into the construction of the new tools I used and the ease with which I could operate them. Without backbreaking labor they made for more food on the farmers' tables and more produce to sell for cash. Another reason for the material well-being I observed around me was, I concluded, the cheap price at which the pioneers had bought land. Cheap land, as large an acreage as a man chose to carve for himself, and efficient tools to work it with, became guides to my understanding of the new civilization. No books could teach me as much about America as the experience I was having under the watchful eyes of the cantankerous old farmer.

Jim had employed immigrant help before—Polish, Russian, Hungarian peasants; and they were "mean as hell" on livestock, he roared at me when we went down to the barn for my first milking. The memory of them made him livid with rage, and forgetting that I was new and young and already terrified of him, he bellowed at the top of his voice that if he ever caught me beating a cow or lashing a horse, he would stick a pitchfork into me. It was a lesson I badly needed. Kindness to animals had hardly been a part of my upbringing. Unruly animals, horses especially, were mercilessly beaten and dogs were brutally punished on the slightest provocation. Not even the geese that strayed into a grainfield were spared. So the old farmer's stern defense of livestock was a revelation to me. After his temper had cooled, he said, gently this time, "Ye've got to win a cow's confidence, if ye expect to get all the milk out of her, and ye've got to be gentle with a horse if ye expect him to do an honest day's work for ye, and don't ye never forget it." I never have.

Still there were times when the old farmer lost patience with an unruly cow and yelled at her, which in turn made him swear at himself. He was partial to horses and regarded them as the most intelligent of domestic animals. His face brightened when he walked into the barn, and sensing his presence, horses twisted their necks and neighed and snorted and stamped their feet in expectation of their mess of oats or the extra carrot, apple, or lump of sugar he might have for them. If a horse was sick he treated it as tenderly as a child, and when death came to Bill, the old white horse he had raised from a colt, he asked me to dig as "decent" a grave for Bill as for "a human." After I had covered the body with dirt he stood there gazing at the fresh mound of dark earth, not saying a word, not even chewing, a silent, solemn, stricken man.

But bees roused his tenderest sentiments. After supper or on Sunday morning we often sat on a bench under a tree or lay on the grass in the orchard where he kept his hives, while he discoursed with warmth of the miracle they performed. Had they not pollinated plants and trees, he assured me, humans would have starved to death and "don't ye think they wouldn't." The food they manufactured nobody since the days of Adam could duplicate, and they sealed their combs so tight with wax that not a drop of honey leaked out "no matter how ye held it and how many times ye turned it upside down and downside up." And when the queen was getting old they got themselves a new queen by feeding eggs a special jelly, that was how smart they were. There was nothing and nobody under the sun as decent as bees. They never shirked work like humans, never cheated like humans, never loafed like humans, never wasted anything like humans; and when cold weather came on, the worker bees stung and killed the loafing drones and threw them out of the hive so they wouldn't have to be fed. God outdid himself in creating the bee, a beautiful little thing as brave as a panther and with more wisdom than any human that ever lived.

If I was stung by a bee he would swear at me for not knowing how to get along with them. If he was stung, he would swear at himself for forgetting to be gentle and mannerly with them. A bee never stung anybody, he assured me, out of a wish to hurt or kill—only out of disgust at your being in his way, or thinking you wanted to do him harm, when he was working his head off to make for you the finest food in the world. The old farmer would never tolerate any criticism of bees. To him they were sacrosanct. To a neighbor enraged by the pain of a sting on the eyelid he shouted, "A hell of a lot ye got to complain of. When a bee stings ye, he's the one who dies but ye go on living, ye low-life Republican pup!"

The nine-mile swamp is the wildest stretch of nature in all Madison County. Once it had been the hideout of the notorious Loomis gang, a farm family whose skill and audacity in horse-stealing had terrified the countryside. Several books, fiction and non-fiction, have been written about the depredations of the Loomis gang.

Jim owned a modest acreage in the wooded swamp and, at the time I worked for him, its big timber was still one of the glories of the region. At the first opportunity I made my way into its green somnolent depths. The trees stood so tall and close, the

underbrush grew so dense, that to walk into that wilderness was
to enter another world, a hushed solitary place through whose
green roof the sun rarely penetrated or only in driblets. There
were no paths there and, warned by Jim of treacherous sinkholes,
I leaped from hummock to hummock, often getting entwined in
vines and creepers and scratched by briars. But it was home-
coming after hard city pavements and walls of brick and steel and
stone; it was the world I had been yearning for when I tramped
the streets of the Lower East Side, which had shut all greenery
out of my sight. It was a part of the America I had always imagined existed outside of New York and a part too of my childhood.
Only the birches here were disappointing. They were yellow,
stunted and scrubby, crowded and choked by the mighty ash and
beech, cedar, and balsam and by the tall white pine. Birches here
grew in grudging sufferance of the stronger trees, like a muzhik's
stepchild.

Jim cherished "them white pine" of his so highly that, though
hard pressed for cash, he all but spat in the face of lumbermen
who offered to buy the trees. He cursed farmers who sold their
woods for "filthy Republican" dollars. To him the big timber in
the swamp was sacred, not only because it protected land from
erosion and kept streams from drying up, but because, like his
bees, it fed some deep hunger in him for the beauty and glory
his life had failed to provide. To put an ax to those mighty pine
was a crime and a sacrilege.

Wandering alone in that green gloom was an eerie experience. The old fears and superstitions of my childhood stirred
in me again, reviving memories of the *rusalka* and the elves. I
wouldn't have sworn that unseen eyes were not watching me
from behind the leafy or evergreen tangle. Sometimes I took
a strange pleasure in the revival of those old fears, as children
do when they frighten themselves; and sometimes they would
become so strong that I would rush out of the silent wood into
the sunny fields as though pursued by some unseen and fearsome spirit.

Apart from the wooded swamp there was nothing in the lay of
the land to remind me of the Russian countryside I had known,
monotonously flat or swampy beyond the forest. Here rolling
hills, green with grass and crops and woods, sank into lush val-

leys, then rose and fell again into lowland field and meadow. Never had I seen a land of such wide horizons. Mornings before milking I watched the blue mists fade along the edge of the world as the sun rose; evenings I watched them gather when it set. There were no nightingales, skylarks, or storks, but there were plenty of other birds. Wild flowers grew in fields and along roadsides, and wild-growing berries—strawberries, redberries, currants, raspberries, blackberries—were there for anyone to gather, without paying a fee to the state or to some landlord. I picked endless quarts of them, in baskets, in empty cans, in Jim's broadbrimmed old straw hat, for pies and shortcake, for jams and preserves.

The land here was not only beautiful but rich in nature's gifts to man other than wild berries. Once I picked a leafy sorrel stalk in a pasture. The leaf was small, the taste bitter, not as winy as the wild Russian sorrel I had picked for Mother. It was news to Jim that in Russia it was a favorite ingredient of soup. It was news to me in turn that young dandelion, milkweed, mustard plant, and cowslips, when boiled, made a fine dish of greens. I picked messes of them for the housekeeper. They were so abundant that most of them went to seed—so much free food going to waste! In Russia hardly a blade of the precious sorrel or wild onion escaped the searching eyes of women and children. Nothing ever went to waste, not a wormy apple or pear, not an overgrown yellowed cucumber. Russians ate every edible plant and fruit, however battered and overripe. They still do.

Chapter 4

Thanksgiving and Country Bounty

◆

In the Russian countryside, autumn was the most dismal season of the year. The word-of-mouth calendar (published ones we never saw) assured us that the interval between summer and winter lasted for three months, but we were never aware of it. Overnight, it seemed, the nightingale, the skylark, the stork, other summer birds deserted us, leaving us to the raucous caws of the black crows.

We exulted when the birch leaves turned fawn-colored and golden in the early weeks of autumn. But the exultation didn't last long. The pretty leaves withered and fluttered to the ground and so did the more sturdy leaves of the oak. Cold winds tore at our thatched roofs. Rains splashed down; street and road turned into mud in which horses and wagons got mired. Mornings we no longer heard the shepherd's trumpet calling on housewives to let cows out of yards so they could be driven to pasture. Even if there was still grass to graze, the pasture grew so boggy that there was danger of cows sinking to their bellies so that they would have to be pulled out with ropes and poles and a team of horses.

Then one morning we would awake and see frost patterns on the windows or snow swirling outdoors. Winter had come, howling through the forest; unwanted dogs were driven from homes to save feeding them. Straying wolves added to the terrors of the forest and to the uncertainties of life.

But upstate New York autumn was the most enchanting season of the year. Here nature didn't mock the calendar as it did in the countryside of my childhood. The time between summer and winter passed in a blaze of glory, and the cycle of growth and ripening came to a triumphant and exhilarating climax. I loved the upstate autumn more than any season of the year.

It might announce its arrival with a thundershower, which after the sultry August dog days you welcomed with a glad heart. Creeks swelled and water for cows and horses was no longer a worry or a problem. Meadows and pastures regained their luxuriance; second-growth clover freshened with life and you debated whether to let it stand for a second cutting or to turn the cows on it and reap the immediate reward of an augmented flow of milk that comes when cows feed on green clover, if only for a part of the day.

A day or so after the rain you woke one morning to behold a spectacular sight: a solitary maple in some front yard or at the foot of a hill dressed in a new garment of cloth-of-gold, shining in the sun. Each day the maples grew more dazzling in their new dress of bronze, copper, gold, and some in scarlet so flaming that they seemed afire. The clumps of sumac turned rich crimson and the homely and brambly blackberry glowed fiery red. The beech, the basswood, the elm, the butternut shone richly in wood and field. Against the somber green of hemlock and cedar, of pine and balsam, the turning trees, most conspicuously the maple, made a fairyland of brilliance and beauty. Never in my life had I seen anything so entrancing. Nowhere was there a hint of the melancholy that the silver birch in the raw Russian autumn roused in muzhik and poet, in the song of the one, in the verse of the other.

Roadsides and pastures shimmered with the brightness of blossoming wild flowers: the golden-petaled, black-eyed Susan, the purple heart-leaved aster, the ever-present goldenrod, the gangly white-spudded carrot, the white and pink clover. Even the spiny-leaved thistle, which, like the coarse-leaved burdock was the farmer's pet aversion, reared a crest of purple as soft as silk, the only thing on the pestiferous plant the hand could touch with delight and the eyes could for once admire.

There were foggy mornings and rainy days in autumn. At dawn when I went to pasture for the cows I often saw pockets of white haze in the dips of the land. They vanished with the rise of the sun, and with the heat and haze gone from the air the sun was more brilliant than in summer. I could see faraway hills in all their seasonal splendor. The skies were the bluest of the year, the clouds the fleeciest, the air the freshest and so crisp that one walked briskly, felt a new strength in the body and a new cheer in the heart. And so it seemed did the wild creatures one saw: chipmunks flitted along rail fences with a louder and gayer chatter; squirrels bounded through oaks and butternuts with a fresh and exuberant audacity; and the usually nocturnal racoon— a "hog" for corn, tomatoes, and sweet apples—boldly prowled by daylight in the garden, cornfield and orchard. Once on a Sunday afternoon, I almost stumbled on one in the hillside orchard of a neighbor. Apple in mouth he bounded up a tree and clung to the bark like a cat. I stood under the tree and watched. He never moved, never looked down, never let go of the apple. I didn't call the farmer. I didn't want him to shoot the racoon.

Only the woodchuck, fat from a summer's lush feeding and no longer protected by tall timothy and redtop or clover, seemed more wary. He stuck closer to his hole, stood on his haunches more often, ready to dart into his earthy darkness at the least sign of danger. It was a wonderful time to hunt the grizzled reddish-brown marmot, and he seemed to sense it and was too wily to fall easy prey to bullet or fang.

In the crisp and pungent air you worked with a new zest, the work itself—gathering the fruit of spring and summer sweat— heightening the zest. You cut corn and shucked it, leaving the field yellow with pumpkin, a yellow that enriched the beauty and the brilliance of the autumn landscape. Then you dug potatoes and other root crops and picked apples, the cleanest and to me the most pleasant work on the farm. I hadn't known before that apples were picked by hand: muzhiks always shook them down— to save time, I suppose, though what they did with the time they saved, I never knew. But then muzhiks didn't mind if apples got bruised and battered. They rarely stored them for winter use as the Yankee farmers did. They quartered and dried them on the hot bricks inside the huge brick oven. But here every apple was plucked by hand, the wormy and rot-spotted ones thrown to the ground for pigs and cows. Standing on a ladder cushioned by the branches of the tree, the aroma of the fruit sweetening the air I breathed, reaching out for an apple at a time, was more play than work.

Then came the cutting of the cabbage, the green and the red, and the harvest was in. By Thanksgiving autumn was over. Nature's riotous pageantry was spent. The wood lots were dark and somber, meadow and pasture were withered and browned by frost. No bees buzzed; with plenty of honey inside the straw-packed hives, they withdrew to the dark and warm solitude of winter life.

With the bees tucked away, the only chore left was banking the house with horse manure to keep frost out of the cellar, and when you walked into the deep stone-walled, spacious cavern under the house with lamp or lantern, the light gleamed on a rich-colored and heart-lifting scene.

I know of nothing in those days that was more joy-giving and more comforting than the old-fashioned farmer's cellar at the onset of winter. Potatoes lay heaped in the largest bin, green cabbage in a small one, red cabbage in still another small bin, then the beets, the turnips, the carrots, the parsnips, the pump-kins, the green winter squash, each separate from the other, each different in size, shape, color, taste, smell, the fragrance of earth still clinging to all of them. Then came the apples—the greenings, the Baldwins, the russets, the Northern Spies, the pound sweets, the largest of all and so beautiful in their cream-colored skins that they were saved for Sundays or when company came.

To me the Northern Spy was (and still is) king of the orchard, the choicest of all apples I have tasted anywhere in the world. Large, round, small-stemmed, crimson-cheeked with shades of yellow and green, it was hard and winy in the picking season. With the passage of time it grew more tender and juicy, its yellow-ish fine-grained flesh staying firm into May and even June. It lent itself superbly to every possible use—eating raw, cooking, baking—to anything an imaginative farm wife could concoct out of apples. No other baked apple was so savory, no other gave such tang to pie, tasted so refreshing when eaten raw before bedtime. Why this most serviceable and delicious apple has come into dis-favor in New York and other cities, I never understood until an Italian fruit dealer who shares my ardor for it explained it to me: "It doesn't look beautiful." Valiantly he has been battling for the cause of the Northern Spy, a losing, profitless battle. Why an apple should be judged by appeal to the eye rather than the palate is a mystery I cannot fathom. Though while not as shapely as the Western apple, the Northern Spy with its roundness, its smooth and tender skin, its rich coloring, has a beauty all its own, even as has the upright frost-defying tree on which it grows.

The back wall of the old-fashioned farm cellar was a special eye-filling sight. From floor to ceiling it was lined with shelves of home-preserved fruits and vegetables: jams, jellies, relishes, preserves, pickles, all in glass jars. By light of lantern the jars of strawberry, blackberry, raspberry, peach, crab apples, cherry, tomato, cucumber, sparkled with color—green, red, yellow, brown, green—like jewels in an emperor's treasury. But nowhere was there a single jar of sauerkraut, whereas in the old Russian village we stored barrels of it. These Yankees seemed to have no taste for sour or acid foods; they seldom bothered to pick the currants and gooseberries that grew wild in pasture and on roadside. Everything had to be sweet, even the pickled cucumbers, which to me were never pickled but only sweetened, and the finger-length size of the vegetable that the Yankee housewife favored for her jars, always amused me. I couldn't imagine a Russian peasant woman today having the heart to pluck one so small when in a few more days it would be many times larger and offer so many more mouthfuls of food. I couldn't think of an East Side housewife in those days who wouldn't lift her nose with contempt at a pushcart peddler who might shout the glories of such puny green things, each no more than a single mouthful, hardly a good mouthful. But then Yankees disdained the cucumber, some of them even believed they poisoned the blood, an absurd idea to me. How many a meal of dark rye bread and green or pickled cucumber I had eaten in my boyhood days!

Take the cucumber away from Russia and the people, I am certain, will grieve more than if they were suddenly deprived of all the Sputniks their scientists could shoot into space. Freshly plucked and green, soaked in brine until yellow, it assuages the burn of vodka in the gullet; it freshens the taste of salt herring and spicy sausage, favorite breakfast foods; it livens the taste of fish, fresh or salted, and of meat—fowl, game, pork, beef, mutton; it flavors and thickens soup, especially the cold summer soup; and if you come on evil times and can afford neither meat nor fish nor dairy foods, you eagerly reach for it to make the dark rye bread more palatable. Millions and millions of peasants under the Czars counted themselves lucky when, in times of scarcity or famine, they could lay their hands on a green or pickled cucumber to go with what bread they had, even when the bread was a mixture of rye flour, dried grasses, and crumbled bark. And so have millions and millions of peasants and city folk in the Russia of the Soviets during the famine years in the twenties and the early thirties and again during the disastrous drought in 1946. No other vegetable in the vast Soviet empire is so relished, so popular, and so indispensable.

But to return to the farmer's cellar as I knew it in the years before the furnace and the deep freeze. It was the richest and most colorful larder I had seen, stowed not only with fruits and vegetables but with a barrel of salt pork, another of salt beef, with smoked hams hung from the ceiling and with casks of cider on wooden platforms. Everything that grew on land, bush, and tree, that came from stable and pigpen was there, neatly arranged, awaiting your need and your pleasure.

So let winter come; let the blizzard whistle and howl; let the frost nip the nose and numb the hands; let "them New York bankers"—a favorite butt of Jim's ridicule—scheme for new ways to cheat the hayseed on the price of milk and hops. Your airy and roomy cellar was beyond the reach of any schemer and any enemy. You mightn't have a dollar in the bank, but you knew you would always have three tasty and ample square meals a day; you would eat as well as any city slicker; better, you thought, than most of them, with cookies and doughnuts and even apple pie for breakfast. Your cellar was your treasure house of abundance, even as the cordwood and the chunks of hemlock and apple tree in the woodshed were your assurance of fireside comfort all winter long. Your cellar made you unbeholden to anybody for your living and gave you a sense of independence as vigorous as any man on earth could ever know.

Europeans who write so easily of Americans as hopeless conformists, all cut and trimmed to the same pattern in speech, thought, manner, would discover the error of their assumptions were they to take a single Sunday dinner with an American farmer. If there is a more "cussed" individualist anywhere in the world I have yet to meet him, even among the English. I still have to hear an upstate New York farmer talk of "keeping up with the Joneses." It would seem ludicrous to him if anybody were to suggest the importance of impressing his neighbors. He is his own "Jones" and lets the world know it. And where else can one find such original characters as in the rural America of yesterday, bookless philosophers whose eccentricities lent a warmth and gaiety and drama to the rural scene?

I celebrated my first rural Thanksgiving in America on Jim's farm, and it was as happy an occasion there as I had yet known. The feast marked the liberation from the most arduous work of the year and the gathering in of every last bit of the harvest. We relaxed in contentment, knowing that for months now we need no longer worry over the uncertainties of the weather nor fret over the demands of crops.

Snow flurries whitened the outside world, winter was closing in, but the wood stove in the large sitting room kept us snug and warm while we waited for dinner. We had scrubbed and combed ourselves as for a Sunday morning and dressed in our Sunday suits. The cat purred beside the crackling fire and the lazy dog snoozed at Jim's feet as we sat and chatted in pleasant idleness. Dinner we knew would be late; the housekeeper had warned us that the feast would take a long time to prepare; she had been at work in the kitchen since daylight. No, we weren't going to have the traditional turkey I had heard of; this was not turkey-raising country and a man like Jim had to think of his cash. Why spend money on turkey when there were fat hens in the coop and pork chops from a freshly butchered pig in the cellar?

So we sat by the stove, Jim and I, savoring the rich aromas that were exhaled from the kitchen and enjoying our sweet laziness with no thought of outside intrusion on our tranquil festivity. I again reminded the tobacco-chewing farmer that with our field work over, with only morning and evening chores to do, I would no longer postpone enrollment in the village union school. Jim had always been heartily in favor of my continuing my education, though as always he mocked my idea of going to the Cornell State College of Agriculture to learn scientific farming. He was certain the professors would "unlearn" me all the good farming a dirt farmer like himself had "learned" me. But I was too young, too ambitious to be talked out of my dream of enrolling at Cornell.

Suddenly there was a knock on the door, and I was sent to see who it was. Before me stood a stranger, a tall, lean, straight-backed man, with a long narrow face wrinkled like a dried plum; a winged collar and black bow tie showed under his black shabby overcoat and in one hand he carried a stout cedar staff. I took him for a preacher, for only preachers wore collars and ties like his. He inquired if Jim was at home. I called Jim.

"Good to see you, Zeke," Jim said politely but without enthusiasm.

When he took off his overcoat I knew he was no preacher. He wore a cutaway frock coat and striped trousers, both old and rumpled, the coat spotted with food stains. The elder of the Baptist church and the itinerant evangelists who now and then preached from its pulpit never affected cutaways and their frock coats were always clean.

There was something mysterious about this stranger in his stained, seedy gentleman's attire who had so unexpectedly turned up with the apparent purpose of sharing our holiday dinner. Russians thought nothing of inviting themselves to other people's tables, but I had never known a Yankee to do so. Yankees never dropped in casually, for an unexpected guest might prove an embarrassment to the housekeeper.

It turned out that Zeke was a distant cousin of Jim's whom he had not seen in years. We all sat down by the stove and Zeke put out his hands to warm them. As if in apology for his unexpected arrival he told Jim that since he was pushing nigh eighty he had decided to pay him a visit, and Jim coolly but deferentially invited him to stay for a few days. Zeke replied that he was making the circuit of what relatives he had left and didn't think he would have time to stay longer than overnight, but he would give consideration to his cousin's kindly invitation. Yet the man had neither bag nor suitcase, and I wondered how he could have set out on a circuit of visits with no thought of flannel nightshirt, a change of underwear or even a freshly laundered handkerchief. After all, he was a Yankee, and Yankees weren't muzhiks. However poor they might be, they didn't as far as I knew disregard personal cleanliness and comfort.

Zeke talked in a slow, halting, bass voice, his face solemn, his eyes half shut as though weighing every word he said. He was sorry, he moaned, to see the brave and free United States go to the dogs. People had become so dishonest that there was nobody a decent citizen like himself could trust any more. He had had a widowed housekeeper and she turned out to be a thief, stealing his eggs and sugar and potatoes. He had had a tenant on his farm who turned out to be a robber. It was the war that had corrupted people, meaning, as I learned on inquiry, not the Spanish-American but the Civil War. The North, Zeke held forth, had won the war, and he was glad of it, but it had destroyed the moral fiber of the people. The good old days when a citizen could trust a neighbor were gone and it made a man like him in the twilight of his life sick to the stomach to think of it.

Ignoring his cousin's charge, Jim reminded him that after all he had no cause for worry, because he had more than enough money saved up to live in comfort even if he lived to be a hundred or more. The mention of money made Zeke start as though he had been struck an unexpected blow. Recovering, he deplored his cousin's being so gullible as to believe the fables about his supposed wealth when in truth he was one of the poorest men in New York State. Jim remarked dryly that he wished he were so poor.

Finally we were called to dinner. The housekeeper's lengthy preparations resulted in a sample of everything in the cellar appearing on the table. We gorged on roast chicken and pork chops, potatoes and gravy, hot biscuits and honey, side dishes of beets, boiled onions, parsnips, and pickles, the inevitable cole-slaw. For dessert there were pumpkin and mince pies. Jim and I helped ourselves to a slice of each, but Zeke managed only a cut of the mince. Everything was washed down by cider, still too young to be fermented. We ate slowly, talked and talked and the dinner must have lasted several hours.

After dinner Zeke, groaning with surfeit, stretched himself out on the couch. With closed eyes he kept muttering complaints about the stories of his supposed wealth, insisting that he would in all probability end his days in the poorhouse. By the time Jim and I left to do the milking he was gently snoring.

Out in the barn Jim exploded. There wasn't a damned word of truth in his cousin's protest of poverty. The Yahoo Republican, always wearing his highfalutin livery so folks would think he was a gentleman, had so much money that he couldn't count it. Not trusting banks—in which Jim allowed he was right—he had buried his cash all over the premises; and after he died nobody would know where to find it, unless the woodchucks dug it out. The scallawag was paying visits to his kin, not because of family sentiment, but because he was too stingy to buy his own meals. That was the kind of good-for-nothing, low-lived blackleg Republican he was, complaining all the time that folks were indecent when all his life he never had learned the meaning of the word decency. Jim vowed he would lash into Zeke and give him a piece of his mind when he got back to the house.

But when we returned from milking Zeke was gone. The housekeeper explained that when he woke from his nap he had put on his overcoat, picked up his stick, thanked her briefly for the dinner, and walked out of the door, leaving no message for his host. No, he hadn't said where he was off to. Jim fumed with rage. Here he was all set to give his frock-coated cousin a hot tongue-lashing and the rascal had simply vanished. He should have known, Jim railed, that was what would happen once the subject of the buried money was raised. He should have known better than to wait until after milking to give the Republican galoot a piece of his mind. The scummy tightwad had smelled a rat and taken to his heels. The old farmer couldn't forgive himself for underestimating his cousin's shrewdness in ducking away from the lambasting that awaited him.

I, too, regretted to have missed the verbal fireworks between the two extraordinary rural eccentrics.

After Thanksgiving I enrolled in the North Brookfield union school, which was a combination of grammar school and the first three years of high school. Except for mathematics and third-year English I did not fit into any of the classes, and the English teacher soon discovered that I was too advanced to be in her third-year class. Only about twenty-one years of age, she was a devoted teacher, and without my suggesting it she gave a special English and an advanced German course with myself as the only pupil. She was not required to burden herself with the extra work, nor was she being paid for it. But she seemed glad to help the immigrant farm hand prepare himself for college.

Once more I was busy from dawn until bedtime. At Jim's there was no stove in my big room upstairs, so I read and studied in the sitting room. The housekeeper sat at one end of the table cutting and sewing snips of cloth together for a patchwork quilt and I sat at the other end bent over my books, while Jim in his ancient rocker by the fireside read his favorite literature, William Jennings Bryan's *Commoner* and the new Sears, Roebuck catalogue. There was scarcely any conversation and in the stillness of the room Jim's frequent squirts of tobacco juice sounded like the crack of a whip. But when the party-line telephone rang, Bryan's fervent disciple instantly sprang to his feet, made a rush for the telephone on the rear wall, and stuck the receiver into his ear, hearing as he often said the click of other telephones lifted off their hooks. However long the conversation, the old man listened to the end and then told us who said what about whom, with comments, sometimes acidulous, on what he had overheard.

A farmer never neglects his stomach. During those long winter evenings we pampered ours. Maybe it was consciousness of the food-stocked cellar underneath that roused our appetites. Milk and cookies or doughnuts did not seem to fit the winter atmosphere, so we popped corn, and there was only one way to do it: to put the kernels into a wire basket and hold it over the open wood fire in the kitchen. One shook the basket lightly over the leaping tongues of flame until the kernels burst into a white bloom like freshly falling snow flakes. No farmer woman would desecrate the flavor with cooking oil. Butter made them so much more fragrant and appetizing. To this day I am never tempted by popcorn sold in the lobbies of movie houses. The electric popper and the cooking oil rob it of the aroma and the flavor of the popcorn I remember.

But munching handful after handful of the popcorn invited thirst, and so one went down to the cellar for a platter of apples and a pitcher of cider made from one's own apples in the lumbering press in the village. Unlike supermarket cider it had not undergone pasteurization and no "preservatives" had been added. If it went to one's head a little, it loosened the tongue for lively conversation such as no store cider could bring to a man's lips in a million years. When company came or when I went visiting, I could always count on the evening of lively chatter while munching popcorn, gulping cider, and eating apples.

I shall always remember the sense of well-being those long winter evenings brought, when the lamplight fell on heaped bowls of popcorn and gleamed on glasses of cider and piles of Northern Spies.

Chapter 5

The Baptists

◆►

Only recently, after listening to my reminiscences of those far-off times, a friend said to me, "I'll bet the Baptists immersed you; you're a crypto-Baptist." Though the Baptists didn't immerse me, there was some truth in the remark. I always speak with affection of the small white-painted wooden Baptist church in the village of North Brookfield that gave me so much of the best of the America of those days. Whenever I return to the upstate village and walk by the little house of worship, I experience a twinge of nostalgia for the days when I joined my lusty voice in the stately old hymns. It served me well at a period in my life when mind and heart were in perpetual struggle over the riddles and realities of the new civilization, so unlike the civilization out of which I had come. Though I was accepted and welcomed inside its doors, not even the Reverend Mattison, the elder, ever pressed conversion on me. A visiting evangelist once attempted it, but finally gave me up as hopeless.

North Brookfield was a small village rimmed around with green hills and woodlands. I remember the majestic elm that grew tall and beautiful there, the long, sparsely inhabited street from the railroad station to the square broke at the square into a scatter of little streets, as the upright trunk of the elm broke into a scatter of branches. The streets bore no names, nor did the square. There were only about sixty families in the village and everybody knew everybody else, as people did in my old Byelorussian village. There were neither street lights nor sidewalks here, except those that had been privately laid. Two creeks that never dried up murmured through the square, and these, with the hills that sheltered the village, the trees that shaded it, made it one of the most beautiful communities in that extraordinarily scenic part of upstate New York. There was still a touch of wildness about the place, lent by the patches of wild flowers that grew on vacant lots and along the roadsides.

At the time I came there it was still the age of the horse and buggy. Kerosene lamps lighted the houses and lanterns lighted the barns; the cast-iron stove and the spittoon were features of the general store, the post office, the railroad station, and of course the saloon. The rural church in those days was more than a house of worship; it was the center of communal life, of all "social doings." It was an extension of the home and the school, enriching the life of both. In North Brookfield it breathed not only cheer and good fellowship into the community for young and old, but also culture. Its "literary programs" drew packed audiences and were the talk of village and countryside. The church welcomed the stranger with warmth. In the city the immigrant might be a "foreigner," but not at the Baptist church of North Brookfield. He was one of the community, be he Baptist or not. With my irrepressible curiosity about the people among whom I had come to work and live, it was only natural that I should gravitate into its orbit.

I knew nothing of Baptists or their faith; in fact, I had never been inside a Protestant church before. In the hymn singing I found something that had been especially missing from my life. Here was the one place in the unmusical world in which I was living where people sang, and I fervently joined them. "Rock of Ages" moved me deeply as a song and a poem. It was beauty and sadness, glory and hope.

But the elder's sermons were something else. People spoke of him as a powerful preacher, and I was ready to be impressed by his sermons. Only I wasn't. Elder Mattison, blessed be his memory, was a short, plump man with a massive head and a pale face. He walked with a light, springy step and radiated cheer and good will wherever he went. But I soon learned to think of him as two persons in one: in the pulpit he was the prophet of a God of vengeance; he thundered threats of brimstone and hellfire on the heads of sinners who allowed themselves to be enticed by the Devil into smoking, chewing tobacco, card playing, swearing, dancing, and drinking spirituous beverages. There was no salvation for you if you as much as wet your lips with beer. Out of the pulpit, the elder was a lovable man, an amiable hand-shaker, a delightful storyteller. Even the village drunks spoke well of him, and his thunderbolts bounced lightly off their tough hides.

Nor were they the only ones who made light of his hellfire sermons; at the milk station and in the general store I often heard Baptists, invariably men, poke good-humored fun at his fulminations. Jim, a man of faith who knew his Bible, never went to church. His excuse was that he didn't want a preacher to make him too good for this world. Besides, he once assured me, he knew more about hellfire than all the preachers in the United States. The flaming pit was for roasting Republicans, and since he was a Democrat, the gates of heaven would be thrown wide open to him by St. Peter himself.

As for me, I had come from a civilization in which smoking (chewing tobacco was unknown), card playing, swearing, even vodka drinking were never counted as sins, and dancing on Sundays and holidays was the highpoint of folk festivity. So the elder's sermons sounded strange and even amusing. Out of the pulpit the man was so joyful and charitable that I marveled over his obsession with sin and damnation.

The boldest defiance of the elder's crusade against the Devil and all his works and ways came from a woman of eighty who kept house for the German bachelor-farmer for whom I worked after I left Jim. The old lady who had not been in church in a long time, was an inveterate pipe-smoker; of this the elder of course disapproved. One day she fell ill and we mistakenly thought she had contracted pneumonia, spoken of in those days as a "killer." When word of her illness reached the elder he hurried by horse and buggy to minister to her spiritual needs. He found her shivering and sweating, but her mind was clear and alert. The elder treated her to an elevating discourse on man's mortality and earnestly urged her to make peace with God and renounce the sins of the flesh, in her case pipe smoking. The old lady protested that she didn't know she had been out of peace with God, who had always been good to her. Besides, she had never found a single word in the Bible against pipe smoking. But the elder stoutly maintained that smoking was a sin which would drag an otherwise blameless soul like herself down to hellfire.

"Well, Elder," she replied, "if I be goin' to hell I won't need to buy no matches for my pipe."

Astonished at her audacity, I asked her afterwards how she had dared to speak so boldly to the elder.

"Us Baptists," she replied, "is the most ornery Protestant folk you ever come across."

She was certainly the most "ornery" Baptist I knew. But whether Baptists as a group were "the most ornery Protestant folk" I still cannot say. Then they were the only Protestants I knew, and I was profoundly impressed by their singularly liberal approach to religion, as I learned about it from observation and from talks with the postmaster, a pillar of the church. They were bound, the postmaster explained to me, by the acceptance of Jesus Christ as their Lord and of the Bible as a divinely inspired book. But they had no hierarchy. They tolerated no intrusion on their beliefs and church affairs. They didn't even have an official creed that held them to a particular set of principles or dogmas. I was more than astonished when he told me that they elected their minister, and if he proved unsatisfactory, they dismissed him, just as a farmer got rid of an unsatisfactory hired hand. At the time I had not heard of John Locke, the English philosopher, and had not read his tribute to Baptists as being "the first propounders of absolute liberty, just and true liberty, equal and impartial liberty."

The audacious old woman who refused to be intimidated by the elder into abandoning pipe smoking, seemed, as I now think of her, a living embodiment of these words, of which of course she had never heard. Her mother, she told me, had smoked a pipe and so had her grandmother, and she saw no reason why she should deny herself the pleasure just because the elder thought it a sin. Clearly, it was not only the Baptist faith as she interpreted it, but also the sturdy spirit of independence of her pioneer ancestors that had made her as "ornery" as she was. In any event, she had her own ideas of sin, and so did other Baptists in the community. They seemed as unconcerned about hellfire as was the sharp-tongued octogenarian. At least they didn't talk about it. The elder's spine-chilling fulminations didn't spoil their appetite for the Sunday hot chicken-and-biscuits dinner, not even of Miss Schutz, the gaunt, gray-haired, elderly spinster who was the most pious soul in the congregation. They seemed more keenly aware of the rational and practical aspects of their religion than of the fearsome interpretations of their elder. Every man was answerable to his own conscience, so I gathered from hearing them speak, which was precisely what my mother had taught me about the Jewish religion.

What I liked best about the Baptists in North Brookfield was that they didn't wrangle over religion with non-Baptists. They accorded others the same right to their beliefs that they demanded for themselves. If they imagined themselves superior or more blessed than those of a different faith, they never made me aware of it. Had I been a communicant of their church they couldn't have been more friendly and hospitable toward me than they were. Actually, with the exception of one elderly man who was morbidly anti-Catholic and who was no Baptist, they were as well disposed toward the few Methodists and Catholics in the community as toward me. Somehow the bitter intolerances and violent passions of Baptists in other parts of the country, where even Baptist ministers joined the Ku Klux Klan, never touched them. The foreman of the railroad section was a devout Catholic, while his wife was an active member of the Baptist congregation. There were several other mixed marriages, harmonious and happy, in which neither partner had changed faith.

The elder's Sunday school class for young people was known all over the countryside for the extraordinary part it played in the social and cultural life of the community. Never before had the little church managed to build up as large and celebrated a Sunday school class of young people as it had since the Reverend Mattison had become the minister. I had first heard of it from the Quaker high school student who had once helped me lift my horse and milk wagon out of a creek into which I had tipped over. He spoke of the wonderful times young people were having at the class socials, which he had often attended, though he belonged not to the Baptist church but to the Quaker Meetinghouse up on what was known as York Hill. So when the elder himself invited me to join his Sunday school class I gladly accepted the invitation. I regarded it as a fresh adventure in living and a fresh opportunity to make myself a part of the community which I had come to accept more and more as a new home.

To me the class was an education in social relationships, especially with girls. If my learning was slow and painful it wasn't the elder's fault. A sociable and warm-hearted man, he provided me with every opportunity to meet and mix with people of my own age and with older folk at the social doings of the church. There were the monthly Ladies' Aid suppers, where for twenty-five cents one could eat his fill of home-smoked ham and home-roasted chicken and potato salad and jams and preserves and cake and doughnuts and cookies, and drink all the oversugared lemonade he chose and coffee, too, if he wanted it. Then there was the annual oyster supper for the elder; the rich steaming stew climaxed by tempting home-baked pies and cakes. I always marveled at the cheapness of these memorable meals, to which traveling salesmen never failed to come. Farmers might rant at the city slickers who robbed them of decent cash returns on their milk and their hops, but when it came to "vittles," and not only at the church suppers, they ate like kings of the earth.

To the young immigrant among them, their rich boards, laden with the fruits of their own lands, was the realization of the muzhik's dream of a time when land and its fruits would be his and not the landlord's or in the grasp of the state as it now is under the Soviet government. The church suppers were occasions for the most genial good-fellowship I had known. People dressed as for Sunday services, and non-Baptists were as welcome as members of the church. Even Catholics came, and the frock-coated elder hovered around welcoming everybody with a warm handshake and a friendly greeting. Despite his fundamentalist doctrine, he was everybody's brother. On these occasions his humanity warmed us all, Baptist and non-Baptist alike.

Though his grammar was as weak as his religious convictions were strong, he felt it his duty to bring literary edification to the farm folk roundabout. In those days elocution and debates were popular features of rural life and the elder saw to it that I was not left out of his assiduously planned programs. He coaxed me into reciting poems, stories, and participating in debates. Once he prevailed on me to act as lawyer in a mock breach-of-promise trial in which he took the part of the other lawyer.

In all these activities I felt at ease with farm girls and I could hold my own in any group gathering with them, even as I did in the union school in which I had enrolled. It was only when I found myself alone with a girl that I grew tongue-tied, imagining myself to be too serious and too lacking in liveliness to entertain or even to interest her. I cursed myself for my ineptitude, but it seemed there was nothing I could do about it.

For the young people the most popular gatherings were the socials of the Sunday school class, held biweekly and in rotation in the homes of the members. In summer we drove to the socials in hayracks, in winter in sleighs, and I always looked forward to these evenings of recitations and chatter, of games and sandwiches, of hot chocolate and cake. The elder usually drove with us; he never dampened our jollity; quite the contrary, he was always the life of the party. For me there was the added incentive of being in the presence of girls.

I liked the farm girls much better than the city girls I had known. Less sophisticated than the New York girls, they were more approachable. Whatever their European origin in the long ago, time and place and a homogeneous culture had obliterated all traces of their ancestry. They were delicately built and fresh of face, with complexions that any city girl would envy. Their manners were at once more reserved and more direct than those of the New York girls; their voices were softer; their laughter spiced innocence with coquetry. Conscious of their femininity, they didn't flaunt it. No advertising agency had yet glamorized the bosom, and if the farm girls' dress didn't deliberately emphasize it, neither did they seem to take particular pains to hide it. They took no liberties with nature, one way or another. Nor did they make their likes or dislikes of certain boys obvious as I had known city girls to do. They never forgot their good manners.

I was particularly captivated by their freedom with boys, and I observed that their lively informality did not trespass decorum. The institution of chaperones was in vogue, but I had never heard of it in the farm country—not until I went to college did I discover its importance in the social life of young people. Farm boys played with girls as freely as boys and girls did in a Russian village or on New York's East Side. Farm mothers trusted their daughters and the boys who took them buggy riding or drove them to some social event. Lapses in sexual behavior did of course occur. Once a pretty girl, no member of the Sunday school class, became pregnant by a married man. When the physician who examined her inquired who the man was, she bluntly replied that it was none of his business. Quietly she moved to another and much larger community, where she was unknown and brought up her child alone.

In another instance a young man who never came to the Sunday school class but who frequently attended the socials, climbed by ladder into his sweetheart's bedroom and climbed into bed with her. Soon afterwards he married the girl; no shot gun was brandished over his head and it was a happy marriage. Though their transgression was known, they didn't forfeit the regard of their friends or the community. Actually, except for the elder and some of the older women of the congregation, "tripping up" a girl was looked upon as more unlucky than sinful, though such occurrences were rare. Girls had their "steadies" and married young, soon after they were out of high school or of equivalent age. Marriage was of course deemed inviolate and divorce was deprecated, though not unknown.

The most puzzling feature of the socials of the Sunday school class was that often, under the eyes of the elder, boys and girls played "post office," "spin-the-platter," and other kissing games, all new to me. The elder disapproved mightily of dancing—the embrace was all too likely to arouse the sinful desires of the flesh. Yet he never voiced a word of objection to kissing games, not even to post office, when boys and girls kissed each other in a dark bedroom with the door shut. I puzzled long over the paradox in the man's character. As for myself, though fired by the thought of the forfeited or invited kisses in the dark room, I remained timidly and cautiously aloof, a not-so-innocent bystander.

But how did the good elder, guardian of our morals, explain his inconsistency? I put the question to him and he gave me a straightforward answer. "There's nothing wrong in kissing games, my boy," he replied chuckling. "I used to play them myself when I was a boy."

Once, on my arrival from the milk station, as I was unloading the empty cans onto a stand immediately outside the barnyard gate, my Quaker friend drove by with a girl beside him. I had seen the girl in the elder's Sunday school class but had never spoken to her. She was about sixteen or seventeen, a girl with a wide mouth, sparkling white teeth, and lively blue eyes. "I suppose," said the Quaker boy, "you know Paulette." The girl smiled on me and said she had seen me in church. "Well," said the Quaker, "Paulette wants to tell you something." "Yes," said the girl, "you were not in church last Sunday and I thought I would tell you that Elder Mattison will preach a special sermon for young people. I hope you can come." I told her I would. We exchanged a few pleasantries and that was enough to make me feel I was in love with her. Ever afterwards I watched her dumbly in Sunday school, but never dared to walk home with her after class for fear I would bore her. But while I milked the cows I often day-dreamed, imagining myself in long romantic scenes with her in which I was impressive and persuasive.

Oh, if only these farm girls loved poetry like Russian girls! Though I left Russia at an age when I was just becoming seriously aware of girls, I had already learned that the best way to communicate with a girl who had roused your "exalted emotions" was to send her a poem, preferably one of your own composition. Sometimes the girl responded with a poem of her own, one that might or might not be encouraging. But the farm culture did not instill a love of poetry in its boys and girls as Russian culture did under the Czars and as it still does under the Soviets. It would, therefore, I concluded, be futile to address a poem to Paulette, however ardent my desire to communicate the sentiments she had wakened in me.

Then an unexpected thing happened. One winter evening the Sunday school class stopped for me in a hay-packed sleigh on the way to a social in a distant farmhouse. As all the seats were taken, I had to stand up and hold on as best I could to the rack. Girls were sitting in boys' laps—the lucky dogs! If only I could be so fortunate with Paulette, the girl of my heart. As if in answer to my prayer, she got out of her seat, invited me to take it and plumped into my lap. My cup was full, but I found myself bereft of speech.

Jim had heard of the incident over the party-line telephone and teased me for "sparking" with the Baptist girl. Sparking was just what I had not done. I had muffed the golden chance and was furious with myself. I then hit on a bold tactic. At Sunday evening services the boys always sat in the rear pews, so they could slip out ahead of the congregation and wait for the girls to come out. Then each would take his favorite girl by the arm and walk off with her into the dark street. The girl I loved, though popular, had no "steady." My plan was to go to the evening services, which I rarely attended, and capture her at the church door.

Tormented by expectation, I hardly heard a word of the elder's sermon, and at the proper moment I slipped away and took my station outside. I saw her in the doorway and my heart thumped violently. But by the time I mustered the courage to approach her, another boy had his arm in hers. They passed me and strolled off together into the darkness.

Chapter 6

Character and Characters

◆

In the Russian village Sunday was the liveliest day of the week. It was a day of feasting and drinking, of song and dance; the music of fiddle, accordion, and tambourine resounded until late in the night.

In the American countryside Sunday was the dreariest day of the week. The quiet of the Sabbath, a bleak feature of New England puritanism, lay heavy on farm and village. On the farm the routine was always the same: morning chores, the weekly shave with straight-edged razor; the most thorough scrubbing of hands, neck, and face of the week; then breakfast; then church if you felt like going, which most men didn't; then the heartiest meal of the week, often with ice cream on the pie if you could prevail on the hired man to crank the freezer, which no farmer I ever worked for had any trouble in doing; after dinner—sleep, so sound that the ringing of the party-line telephone failed to arouse you to the pleasure of eavesdropping on the gossip. In the evening, after chores came supper, usually a bowl of bread and milk or corn mush with syrup and cake, too, if you wanted it.

On Sunday the village was as lifeless and drowsy as the farm. Only cats and dogs appeared in the quiet streets. Even young people succumbed to the Sabbath lethargy; rarely did a boy take a girl for a buggy ride then. Life seemed suspended in that Sabbath torpor.

But on Saturday evenings the village was at its liveliest. The long church shed and the square were jammed with horses and buggies. Farmers, their wives, and hired men came to town for shopping and a good time. The hired men usually made a beeline for the saloon. Though it was a small village with a population of about three hundred and a sparsely settled countryside, its three saloons did a flourishing business.

The crowds in the saloons attested only too flagrantly to the futility of the elder's crusade against whiskey, beer, and hard cider. I knew Baptists who wouldn't be caught dead in a saloon, but who carted their apples to the mill and drank their own cider all winter long, however hard it turned. The resourceful Jim had contrived a formula of his own which sweetened his cider to his taste without sacrificing any of the kick. He mixed it with milk and mustard, which turned it into a pale nectarous drink. Finding that it suited my taste too I once helped myself to a pitcherful in the cellar and took it with me to the hop yard. It was as delicious as the freshly tapped birch sap I had drunk in my childhood, and I slowly emptied the whole pitcher. Soon my head whirled and I lay down on a pile of hop poles that I was supposed to be setting into the ground. Never again did the old farmer allow me to drink more than a glassful of the deceptively mild cider with the kick of a mule.

Inquisitive about the Yankee countrymen, so different from the people I had known in the Russian village or on the East Side, I often walked to the village on Saturday evenings and loitered about wherever people congregated—the post office, the general store, the bologna basement, and occasionally the saloon.

The bologna basement became my favorite hangout; its main attraction was the ponderous, bearded, red-lidded proprietor. His name was Ely and he was the most refreshingly amiable personage in the whole countryside. I shall always remember his adroitness in rescuing me from an embarrassing predicament with the owner of the general store when I was still new in the village. I had gone to buy a pair of thick-soled work shoes, and finding one to my liking, I asked the pale-faced, taciturn, squeaky-voiced storekeeper how much it was. Three dollars, he said. True to the tradition of the Russian bazaar and the East Side market place, I bargained. I offered two dollars, fully expecting that we would split the difference. But to my dismay the man thrust the shoes back on the shelf and turned his back on me in disdain.

As I stood there wondering why he behaved so strangely, I heard a voice say, "D'you like them shoes?" I turned to meet the smile of a tall, portly, bearded man, who introduced himself as the village constable. He said he "kind of liked to help folks" when they needed help. "Them shoes is as cheap as you can get," he assured me, and I replied that I was ready to buy them for the price asked. "Come over here, John," he called to the storekeeper, "I sold your shoes for you." He gave a delightful little laugh—"he-he-he"—like the bleating of a lamb. This was the first time I met Ely Hibbard.

He was pushing "three score and ten," as he expressed it, and had been constable since he was a young man, young enough to have participated in the arrest of the "Loomis lady," wife of the head of the notorious gang of horse thieves, who are still a legend in Madison and adjacent counties. He was so ponderous and moved so slowly that I wondered how he could arrest anybody who might try to resist him, but his boast was that nobody ever did. "I can slip them handcuffs onto a man so fast he just don't know what's happened to him," he declared, smiling proudly, never imagining the deep humiliation that lay ahead.

Ely was called to the saloon one evening when a stranger took one too many and became violent. With his usual dexterity Ely slipped on the handcuffs, but as the obstreperous drunk still "thrashed around," the constable clamped leg irons on him. Then he padlocked the stranger in one of the two cells he had built in his horse barn. It was Ely's custom to keep a drunk over night until he sobered up, then to serve him a hearty breakfast and let him go. The breakfast was at his own expense and prepared by himself, since he was a widower. When in the morning Ely, carrying a tray loaded with griddlecakes, ham and eggs, and coffee, walked into the horse barn, he found the heavy cherry-wood door of the cell open and his prisoner gone.

Never before had anything like that happened, and what irked the constable most was the disappearance of his only pair of leg irons. For the police officer of a small and peaceful community, he possessed a respectable arsenal: a cane gun from Civil War days, an old revolver, three pairs of handcuffs, and the prized leg irons. Though he searched for the irons every place he could think of, they were nowhere to be found.

Months later he sold the manure pile behind the horse barn to a farmer who, while loading it into the wagon, struck his fork against something metallic. There deep in the manure pile were the missing leg irons. Ely admitted that the rapscallion had outsmarted him good and proper; who would have thought of searching in the manure pile! For days he soaked the rusty shackles in kerosene and buffed them with sand and emery, but rust still clung to them. "It's sort of indecent to put them rusty irons on a man," he protested. He did it just the same.

His salary as constable, he told me, didn't begin to cover his groceries, so in his spare time he "rived" shingles out of hemlock logs and sold them. But his chief source of income was his famed bologna basement, where he sold thick slices of bologna, crackers included, for a nickel, two hard-boiled eggs in the shell for the same price. He also sold cigars and chewing tobacco, and week-ends he tempted the appetites of inland folk with clams and oysters. On Saturdays he popped corn and placed a deep dishpan full of it on a side table for customers to help themselves free. Invariably his fat cat curled up to sleep on the bed of warm pop-corn, but nobody minded this, nor did the cat mind having its bed gradually eaten away from under it.

I soon discovered that the estimable officer of the law also sold hard cider "under the hat"—without a license—to trustworthy customers in the back room of his basement. On Saturday eve-nings whenever I went to the village I dropped in for a fill of bologna, Yankee-farmer conversation, and a glass of illegal cider. No women went to the basement; only men gathered there, so it partook of the nature of a men's club. To me the talk of the men was always engrossing, not only because of the subjects discussed, but also because of those which never came up, that weren't a part of the every day life and thought of the Yankee farmers, as they had been of farm folk in my old home in Russia.

I never heard them discuss the problem of land, for land was no problem; they often owned more acres than they could cul-tivate. They never told ghost stories or fairy tales—superstition was no longer a part of their culture. They never accused anybody of stealing a sheaf of grain or a sack of potatoes or a bosomful of apples; their stables, barns, bins, chicken coops and milkhouses were rarely locked; there were no thieves to lock them against. They never showed one another letters from sons in the army and never speculated on which nation would be the next enemy; no farmer's son in those days was mustered into army service and no threat of war haunted America as it did old Russia, the Russia that was *always* hungry for conquests, as is Russia today.

In Ely's basement I never heard anybody wail his heart out over the prohibitive dowries extorted from a daughter's parents; dowries were unknown. Nor did I ever hear anybody rail against fate as muzhiks did; with their vigorous sense of personal responsibility, the Yankee farmers never blamed their misfortunes on some dark malign power or on God. "God helps those who help themselves" was their creed. The problems, the aspirations, the spirit of the Yankee farmers were a world apart from those of Russian village folk. They still are.

Serious conversation in the basement was concerned with practical, everyday affairs—cows, crops, the price of produce, and the social gossip of the countryside. Though literate, these Yankees never wrestled with ideas, indulged in no soul searching. I never heard them discuss a book, music, art—these seemed to have no place in their life. Unlike the immigrant tailors I was to know later in Carl Baum's shop in Hamilton, world ideas and world movements didn't excite them. They were men of action; coolheaded and easy-tempered, rarely given to quarreling or to excitement, not even over politics, not much anyway. With the exception of Jim, a tobacco-chewing crony of his, and a few Irishmen, they were Republicans to the marrow of their bones. Politics was rarely a subject of dispute or concern. It was a game to be played, a diversion to be enjoyed, not always as exciting as pitching horseshoes.

However spirited the talk in the bologna basement, it rarely turned ribald and when it did, Ely would cut it short with a tactful admonition and with his bleating "he-he-he." Schoolboys, he reminded customers, often dropped in for a mess of clams or oysters and he would as soon they didn't get an earful of raw talk on his premises. Folks with a taste for such talk could go to the saloon a few doors away, where they would have plenty of company—"he-he-he!"

They would, indeed! In those days a farm or village woman would no more think of entering a saloon than of living in a brothel. Free from feminine restraint, men used explicit language when discussing "petticoats." No word was taboo, no story too lurid. After dropping in there a few times I found myself acquiring a vocabulary that would have burned the ears of those East Side boys who had first taught me American obscenities.

One evening after stuffing myself with Ely's bologna, I went to the saloon for a glass of beer. At the end of the bar a group of young men were gossiping about a farmer's widow noted for her shrewd eye to a bargain and to a handsome man. I knew the widow. She was plump and fortyish and I often saw her driving her milk wagon, always wearing an enormous black hat. She was known as "a hot petticoat," and the gossips were speculating on why she had discharged her Polish hired man, who was a handsome buck. It couldn't have been, they agreed, because he lolled in the shade when he should have been hoeing corn or hilling potatoes. He was a hard-working and trustworthy hired hand. They finally decided she got rid of him because she had drained him "clean out of sap." The talk was gay and ribald, the speakers boasting about their prowess to more than meet the sexual demands of "the hottest petticoat" around.

Muzhiks couldn't have spoken more unrestrainedly. Yet there was a difference between these men and muzhiks: in the presence of women they would never utter a single profane or obscene word, even when drunk. These upstate farmers had inherited a tradition of chivalry that had never reached the illiterate muzhiks. To the credit of the Soviets it should be recorded that they have striven to cleanse the speech of peasants and factory workers of the frequent mother obscenities that had spiced the talk I used to hear in my boyhood.

Yankees loved banter and anecdotes. They would tease one another just to raise a guffaw, a style of conversation new to me, as new as the chatter and banter of the American-born boys and girls on New York's old East Side. In those days there was something in American civilization—an air of optimism and a lack of a sense of tragedy—that evoked a spirit of levity and an avoidance of seriousness which I had never felt in Russia, Czarist or Soviet. I admired these farmers for their gift of endlessly joshing one another and envied them a little too. Their sense of the absurd in human experience amused and challenged me.

But what most interested and enlightened me were their discussions of character as the true measure of a man. The subject cropped up continually in the elder's sermons, in the speech of women, in the gossip of men in the general store, the saloon, the bologna basement, the milk station, and even in Jim's profane tirades against Republicans.

One Saturday evening I dropped into the saloon and noticed a man standing at the further end of the bar, a glass of whiskey before him and a faraway look in his eyes. His flabby cheeks were darkened by thick stubble and despite the dry warm weather he wore knee-high rubber boots. An ancient and battered felt hat added to his look of decrepitude though on closer inspection I judged him to be about thirty. Uninterested in the people around him, he maintained a brooding silence. A lonely man, I thought, perhaps sick. Later in the bologna basement I found out from Ely that he was the son of a retired doctor, one of the most respected and affluent farmers in the village; he stood to inherit a prosperous farm and a select herd of Holsteins. No, Ely explained, he wasn't exactly sick; he just couldn't leave whiskey alone.

"Trouble with him," ventured a farmer, "he was born with a silver spoon in his mouth and don't know enough to hang on to it."

"When his old man goes," another put in, "that'll be the end of him. Sure's you live he'll drink up everything, down to them rubber boots he's wearin' rain or shine. He ain't got no more character than a woodchuck."

"Not as much I'd say," someone else said.

A silver spoon was no guarantee of character. A man was what he made of himself; he couldn't walk through life in the reflected glory of his father. The father might pass on to him his possessions but not the virtues that made for character, and it was character that earned the respect of others.

Ely knew Zeke, Jim's frock-coated miser-cousin, and dismissed him too as a good-for-nothing "human" with not a grain of character to him. Men like Zeke would never trouble to build schools and churches after land was cleared and would as soon leave people as heathen and ignorant as the Indians were. No, misers, like liars, never did the country any good, so Ely avowed, and the farmers heartily agreed.

And poor Jim! Once in a moment of exasperation he reproached me for not having as much character as the rabbit we had scared away from the cold spring that fed the water tank in the milk house. Yet he himself, frugal and hard-working as he was, didn't measure up to the popular concept of the term; a man of character paid his debts and Jim didn't. He held back his hops when he should have sold them; neither would he sell his pine to meet his obligations, that was how "cussed" he was. Yet it was this very "cussedness" that made Jim somewhat of a hero to me, a man who wouldn't sacrifice a principle and wouldn't deprive himself of the beautiful sight of his pines for all the money in the world.

But here was John, an immigrant of German peasant stock, just literate enough to sign his name. John managed the farm of a native son who worked on a railroad in some distant part of the country, and the farm prospered. Though John occasionally indulged in beer, he didn't squander his money on booze or "petticoats." He put it in the bank or loaned it out on farm mortgages. He never ran into debt, never made a promise he didn't keep, never refused to do a favor for a neighbor, and was always polite to women. So John, the semi-literate German peasant, was spoken of as a man of character.

And so were his three brothers who lived in the countryside. When they came to Madison County they, like John, took jobs as farm workers. They saved their money and finally bought farms of their own and prospered. I worked for one of the brothers. He was so illiterate that I attended to his business and personal correspondence. But like John and his two other brothers he was an excellent farmer. He never failed to pay a hired man his wages on time and settled his bills for grain and groceries as soon as he got his milk check. His word was law unto himself and others. He never made a promise that he didn't keep. And he, too, like all his brothers was always polite to women. So despite his illiteracy and his foreign origin, the Yankee farmers spoke of him as a man of "character."

Still more illuminating was the attitude of the Yankees toward a certain Lithuanian peasant, an immigrant from Russia, who had Anglicized his name to Charles. Father of a large family, he bought a neglected hill farm and within a few years brought the weed-grown, bush-choked fields to green fertility and stocked his barn with a herd of Holsteins. He spoke broken English and could neither read nor write; his signature was all he could manage. His children attended school in a neighboring village. A

modest, soft-spoken man, he so impressed his Baptist neighbors
with his character and integrity that despite his illiteracy and
his Roman Catholic faith, they elected him a member of the
Board of Education.

Unlike the uptowners I had observed in New York City, these
Yankees had no sense of social exclusiveness. I never heard any of
them speak of "first families," of "best families," of "society." I
knew men who were mocked for "carrying a chip on their shoulders," but I never heard anyone relate the chip to national origin.
Neither in North Brookfield nor in neighboring villages did I
hear of anyone derided for coming from the "wrong side of the
tracks."

The local weekly paper devoted pages to news and gossip
about the township's residents. But it featured no social elite as
did the metropolitan press. If a Yankee farmer broke a leg he
didn't get more space than the Hungarian or Polish hired hand
who broke an arm. A member of the elder's Sunday school class
came from a *Mayflower* family, a fact I learned many years later
when he casually mentioned it. He showed me the genealogy
which for years he had been quietly and painstakingly compiling.
To this day very few people in the village know of his ancestral
origin—or would care much if they did.

By prevailing standards I was not lacking in character, as I
soon learned. I might indulge in a glass of beer, but I had no
taste for whiskey, and no farmer who ever employed me needed
to worry about my sleeping off a jag instead of showing up for
milking on Sunday or Monday morning. I was no spendthrift and
I didn't run into debt. If I didn't put money in the bank while I
worked for Jim, it was because the old fellow was always "plumb
up against it" and couldn't pay me my wages. I had learned to
plow a straight furrow, to be gentle with livestock, to pull a saw,
swing an ax, and handle farm tools with a fair degree of compe-
tence. If my employer was called away on business to the city or
for jury duty to the county seat, he knew he wouldn't need to fret
over anything going amiss in his absence.

My peculiarities were a source of amusement to neighbors. On
warm sunny days I plowed barefoot and stripped to the waist,
which no Yankee farmer would think of doing. But I liked the
feel of moist earth underfoot and the warmth of the sun on my

body, though out of respect for womenfolk I never neglected to put on my shoes and shirt before returning to the house, which I never would have thought of doing in a Russian village. Summer and winter, in rain and blizzard, I never wore a cap. On the coldest days I didn't bundle up in muffler and overcoat; the Sears, Roebuck jacket kept me comfortable. Somehow I rarely found time to go to the barbershop and my thick bushy hair stood out like a golliwogg's. Farmers joshed me for my peculiarities but didn't attribute them to lack of character. Neither did the womenfolk on the farms where I worked. I didn't smoke nor chew, so didn't mess up my bed with cigarette ashes and the floor with tobacco spit. Nor did I need to be reminded to fetch wood or to fill the water buckets. Farm women spoke of me as a "hired man of exemplary character." Yet, when I reflected on it, the local concept of the term, didn't evoke my enthusiasm. There was something calculating and cold about it. It was like speaking of a tree only as a source of wood and shade. It missed, I felt, much of the inner life of man—his intellect, his imagination, his very heart. It made misfits of non-conformists, who to me were always fascinating, while some respected citizens were often insufferable dullards.

There was Terry, for example, a young Irish lawyer from a near-by village, whom I occasionally saw in the saloon or the bologna basement. He was tall, handsome, reddish-haired, with a gay laugh and a sparkling wit. After a few years of successful practice his calls at the saloon grew longer and more frequent where whiskey heightened his eloquence and sharpened his wit. Finally he was to be found more often in the bar than in his office and sociability took precedence over legal briefs. Farmers charged that he had bartered away his character for whiskey and gab and took their legal business elsewhere.

Yet to me his conversation was more than "gab." Once he told me that no man could pretend to be educated if he hadn't read Mark Twain, Dickens, and Shakespeare. Another time, when I met him on the train to Utica, he held me spellbound with a discourse on *Huckleberry Finn* and *David Copperfield*. He had a taste for good books and a gift of language that neither farmer nor professor nor minister could match. He was the one real intellectual in the township, and how could I deny him the quality of character? There were other ways, I thought, of demonstrating this quality than those the Yankee farmers recognized.

Then there was young Leonard, son of a neighbor. He was some five years older than myself and lived with his father on the edge of the forested swamp. He was tall and strong and when hard pressed for money he would hire out to a farmer or take a job on the railroad section as a common laborer. With hoe and pitchfork, ax and saw, pick and shovel, he could hold his own with any man; but hard work wasn't in his blood. He never stayed long on a job. What was considered even worse, the money he earned went for hunting traps and whiskey rather than for a Sunday suit. He was no habitual drunkard; he could go for weeks without touching beer or whiskey. But when he dropped into the saloon his good nature got the better of him and he treated everybody in sight until his money was gone. He never regretted these splurges either.

The forested wilderness that stretched behind his house was Leonard's one great passion in life. He knew everything about it and loved it all—the trees, the flowers, the birds, the animals, the green river that flowed silently through the trees. Sometimes on Sundays I went prowling with him through the swamp. The unstirring air there was warm and steamy, full of the fresh smells of moist earth, the acrid aroma of rotting logs, and the sweet odors of growing and blossoming things. In this mysterious world Leonard was a new man: the smells, the sounds, the silences, the lights and the shadows exhilarated him. He told me the names of every tree and plant, of every bird and animal, and talked about them as knowledgeably as a farmer talked about crops and cattle. As we pushed our way through fat reeds and tangled vines, past burred bushes and lofty trees and leaped over treacherous sink holes, he spoke like a poet of the realities and mysteries of the wilderness and of its unending cycle of life and death. From him I learned more about the nine-mile swamp than from anybody I knew.

In winter he trapped for fur and cut Christmas trees, not always on his own land. He was king of the swamp and nobody really missed the balsam saplings he cut down; there were too many of them anyway. Big trees he never touched. His most articulate detractors admitted he was "as honest as the day."

He knew the ways of muskrat, mink, beaver, coon, weasel, fox, opossum, and spoke of them with all the elation of a boy. He laughed at the stupidity of the mink, who always betrayed himself in the snow by taking the same course back and forth from hunting. But he admired the little beast for his fussy taste in bait: no carrion for him—fresh fish and fresh chicken, especially the leg, tempted him to the trap.

The racoon's gluttony and childlike curiosity about shiny objects amused Leonard too. The bugger was always on the prowl for a free feed, and if it weren't for his irresistible urge to examine anything shining, he wouldn't be easy to trap. But he was a clean cuss and plenty smart too. He licked his fur like a cat and washed everything he ate, even the fish he pulled out of the river; and when cornered by a dog he could climb a tree like a squirrel, plunge into the river, swim away like a fish, break up his scent, and make a fool of the dog. The coon was such an amusing little critter he really hated to kill it. But fur was fur and he had to think of that, the same as farmers thought of the apples and the potatoes they sold.

But Leonard never had a single good word for the weasel— the bloodiest beast in the swamp—who lived on blood the same as cattle lived on grass. It was nothing for the bloodsucker to kill fifteen chickens in a single hencoop. That was why it always made him feel good to see the little monster in a trap. He didn't weigh any more than a pound and a half, but he was as bold as a bear and when he got real mad he would as soon tackle a man as a rabbit. And he was so strong he could drag a rabbit three times as heavy as himself. The only good thing he would say for the bloody bugger was that it kept him in tobacco all winter. "I buy all my tobacco from them weasel furs I sell."

Yet folks spoke of Leonard as a man who lacked character, who wasted his strength and frittered away his years on do-nothing foolishness. To Jim he was "a loafing pup," and his own father, whose capacity for whiskey was curbed by the fear of losing his job driving the school bus, bemoaned his fecklessness. But Leonard never cared what folks said about him. Again and again he told me that he hated cows because day in and day out, Sundays and holidays, they kept a man chained like a dog to the cow barn. He preferred the freedom of the wooded swamp to the rewards of conventional effort.

I last saw him shortly before he died when he was over seventy years old. The years had mellowed him so that he no longer shot for the sake of shooting as he had done in his younger years.

"No, sir," he confessed, "I hain't killed a squirrel or a crow in years. And I wouldn't shoot a woodchuck neither unless he got into my garden. Let them live. It kind of makes me feel good to see crows in the horse chestnut in front of my house. Crows you know gets tame if you don't scare them. Squirrels are the same. They come right over if they know you ain't going to harm them. No, sir, I don't want crows and squirrels to be afraid of me no more."

He still lived on the edge of the swamp, still fetched his water from a spring on a near-by hill, and still trapped for fur and cut Christmas trees. His one deep regret was that nearly all the big timber in the swamp had been cut.

"Won't it grow again?" I asked.

"I don't hardly think so. Something has gotten into the swamp so the white pine don't grow cones no more and if there ain't no cones there ain't going to be no trees. The big timber you seen when you worked around here ain't never going to come back."

I swept my eyes over the swamp from where we stood in back of Leonard's house. It still looked thick and dark and jungly. "It's always going to be like that," he said, "that rich muck there ain't going to dry up and things ain't going to stop growing. Yes, sir, it's going to be plenty wild. But the big timber is finished and there ain't nothing anybody can do about it. But I ain't complaining. I got lots of fur out of it in my lifetime and I still do. Got a mink the other day—a beauty. Come in, I'll show it to you."

We walked into the house and suspended from a wire strung across the room hung a fresh pelt stretched tight over a little board, still raw and smelly. Leonard turned it round and round, caressing the deep soft fur.

"She's a beauty, she sure is," he said, his eyes twinkling with triumph. After more than half a century of trapping he still thrilled to the reward of the hunt.

"But you still don't wear a Sunday suit," I teased. "I've never seen you in one yet."

He grinned at me. "Well, sir," he said, "I do sometimes. Now I do." His face suddenly grew solemn.

"On Sundays?"

"When I go to a funeral. A fellow's got to show respect for a friend he ain't going to see no more."

We sat down and talked and suddenly he gave a bright laugh.

"Did I ever tell you what my great-grandfather done when he first come here?"

I shook my head. In all the years I had known him he had never mentioned the forebear who was the original settler of his family.

"Well, sir, when he first come here he staked himself nine square miles of as good timberland as the Indians ever seen. But he wasn't much on work. He lived off hunting and fishing like he was an Indian. Once in a while he'd burn logs for charcoal and sell it. He cleared maybe eight acres. But he was a bear for liquor, couldn't do without it, and bit by bit he traded his timberland for liquor until he got it all drunk up. That's what he done, and from all I heard about him, he ain't never regretted it."

Neither, I thought, did his great-grandson. A rugged and unpretentious man, a cheerful companion, steeped in the lore of wood and wild life as no man I have known upstate, a freehearted spender when he got a check for pelts or Christmas trees, Leonard never regretted the healthy, carefree, adventurous life he lived. He felt the presence, the power, the wonder, the beauty of nature as few men ever did.

Then there was the genial miser Mert who bought a large upland farm with a big house several miles outside of the village. He had been a school teacher, a profession he had long ago abandoned for trading in Wall Street. Shrewdly he reinvested his dividends until he became a rich man, the richest in the countryside.

His first appearance in the village was something of a sensation. He announced to the storekeeper that he never bought butter—margarine was good enough for him; nor would he buy fresh meat—salt pork was cheaper; he wouldn't even smell Ely's clams and oysters—ciscoes, the cheapest salt fish, would do for him. He made it clear to anybody who cared to listen that he wouldn't spend a penny on anything he could get along without.

He was so stingy he wouldn't buy new tools, invest in fertilizer, or hire a helper on his farm. In consequence, some of his richest fields were turning to scrub.

"When are you going to get yourself a hired man," a neighbor once twitted him, "and get some decent crops off your land?"

"When you see rabbits grow wings and fly like birds," he tartly replied.

He was known as a tightwad who wouldn't take a breath if the air weren't free. People poked fun at him, but there was neither malice nor censure in their jests. A man had a right to hoard money if that was what made him happy. Then a small but telling incident occurred in the store that invoked widespread scorn of the man. He and the woman who lived with him had come in with a box of eggs which they bartered for groceries. When the woman heard that a penny change was coming to them she picked up a peppermint stick and asked to have it for the penny.

"You know I can't afford it," he snapped.

Meekly she put the peppermint stick back in the box on the counter. The story of the incident echoed through the country-side and people laughed at him harder than ever, now with scorn rather than with amusement. The man was not only a crackpot but a contemptible one—denying his woman a stick of peppermint!

Though he was a miser, Mert was no recluse. Quite the con-trary, he had an extraordinary zest for sociability; he was always ready to talk, to argue, to ridicule spendthrifts. His door was never closed to callers, and I shall never forget the friendly smile he gave me the first time I went to see him. He was a handsome man, tall, erect, with a dignified bearing and with an air of radiant self-composure. He wore old slippers, a work shirt, and faded jeans patched on the knees.

He ushered me into the kitchen, which was living room and office as well, and my nose wrinkled from the sour smells of by-gone meals. I had never before seen a farmer's home so cluttered with decrepit furniture, battered pots and pans, or that reeked so with squalor. With courtly hospitality he sat me down on a wobbly chair and treated me to a lecture on making money in the stock market and his own shrewdness in investing. It always made him feel good to go out to the mailbox on the road and find envelopes with dividend checks in them. Of course he never cashed the checks. He was not like other folks, who threw their money about like chips of wood. The trouble with Americans was that they no longer knew the value of a dollar. But he knew, and that was why he reinvested his dividends in securities. That was what I should do, for a man was never too young to dip his hand into the Wall Street pile and build up a pile of his own. He had started with his first salary check as a teacher and had been at it ever since, getting more joy out of life than any of his detractors. On and on he talked, while his smile, his glances, the play of his handsome features betrayed an inward rapture at his accomplishment. His English was that of a cultivated man, free from the "hain'ts," double negatives, colloquialisms of country folk. It seemed incredible that such a man would make the acquisition of money the overpowering passion of his life.

Once I put some questions to him.

"D'you ever go to a doctor?"

"Certainly not. Doctors don't know anything."

"What d'you do when you're sick?"

"I've never been sick a day in my life."

"Not even a headache or a stomach-ache?"

"I wouldn't say that. Bicarbonate of soda and castor oil are all the medicines a man needs, and they don't cost much. I wouldn't waste a nickel on doctors."

"What d'you do when you have a toothache?"

"I rinse my mouth with kerosene and save dentist bills; remember next time you have a toothache."

I laughed. Not even muzhiks, who through the centuries have accumulated a vast lore of homemade remedies for every conceivable ailment, ever thought of kerosene as a cure for toothache. Vodka was infinitely more palatable.

I apologized for asking so many personal questions.

"Don't apologize," he said with a wave of his long arm. "Ask any questions you please. I'm always glad to tell folks what I think."

"Very well," I said. "Why d'you love money more than anything else in life, more than good food, good clothes, more even than a new coat of paint for your house?"

"I'll answer your question," he replied without a moment's hesitation. "If the folks who inherit my money enjoy spending it as much as I've enjoyed saving it, they'll have a mighty good time."

I probed him further, but it was of no use. He was what he was, with an overriding passion for money which he didn't even care how his heirs would spend. He was playing a game, the one great game in his life, and nothing else mattered. The world laughed at him, but he laughed at the world. Yet he was a man of dignity and charm, with a courtly manner, a pleasant smile, a gay twinkle in his fine blue eyes and a hearty laugh. I didn't pretend to understand him, but through the years on all my journeys upstate, I enjoyed talking to him and always marveled at his utter frankness about himself and his delight in his accomplishment. Though the farmers said he lacked character, he was one of the most memorable characters I have known.

Quite different was a farmer called Ezra, widely respected as a man of outstanding character. He was of course industrious and thrifty. He never touched whiskey or beer and never ran into debt. He was the most unlikely candidate for the poorhouse in the whole county. A man of his word, he never made a promise that he didn't keep. He was an exemplary father and husband, and his white-bonneted, blue-aproned wife was the acme of courtesy and gentility. Anybody who passed his house could hardly fail to turn for a second look, so beautifully did it stand out from the grove of trees that sheltered it—a symmetrically built two-story frame structure, with an elevated porch, a gabled roof, always gleaming with blue and white paint. His front yard sparkled with neatness and so did his barns and toolsheds.

But he was the most unneighborly Yankee I knew. He never visited anybody, and I never knew or heard of him inviting anybody to his house for a meal or a chat. He never swapped tools or chores with his closest neighbor. Whenever I saw him in the post office or the store, he was always in a hurry to finish his business and drive off home, as though he feared somebody might draw him into conversation. On Election Day, when sociability prevailed, he would dash into the polling place, vote the Republican ticket, and dash back to his farm.

Nor was he a man of courage, as I discovered one Sunday morning as I was coming home from church. He hailed me from his porch as I passed by and asked if I could spare a minute of my time. Surprised and curious, I went to his gate and waited for him to come down. Without opening the gate, he reached over and handed me a large ripe apple, then stood there a moment, peering at me with his sharp sun-squinted gray eyes until he could bring himself to speak. Finally he asked if I would oblige him by coming over the next afternoon with a pitchfork and help with his threshing. I was amused and astonished that he would make the request of me instead of the man for whom I worked. This wasn't the custom of the country. I therefore suggested that he go with me and speak to Jim. He protested that he didn't feel like doing it. Would I do it for him? He would pay for my help.

"That blackleg Republican," Jim shot out gruffly after I told him what the farmer wanted. "He hain't got the guts to come himself. He be afraid I'd ask him to help do my threshing and he'd no more do that than vote the Democrat ticket. But ye go jest the same."

To me it seemed ironic that people should regard Ezra as a man of character but not Jim. Why not Jim? They were a fairminded people, with deep-rooted convictions, a hardheaded sense of justice, and considerable tolerance of ordinary mortal frailties. Yet here their judgment was, I thought, singularly one-sided and narrow-spirited. Why?

The answer came to me quite unexpectedly.

I had heard so much of Round Top, the highest hill in the township from whose peak one could look into seven counties, that one Sunday afternoon I set out to climb it. I crossed through fields and pastures, orchards and woodlands, up hill and down dale to get to Round Top by a shortcut. At last I found myself on the summit, a three-acre meadow, freshly mowed and sweetsmelling. In the valley from which I had come the sun was scorching, but here a strong chill breeze from the north cooled my sweat-drenched body.

I had never before climbed so high; I seemed to be standing on the very top of a vast green world that rolled on and on to the distant circle of the horizon. At every turn I saw tree-crowned hills rising through walls of mist that concealed towns and villages. Here and there I could see cattle grazing on a hilly pasture, and a moving speck in the far distance became a miniature horse and buggy rolling along a thread of road. Man seemed lost in the vastness of this rich and beautiful world.

I had listened to stories of the pioneers who came in oxcarts to carve out farmsteads in the forested wilderness. I wondered how they had dared; surely they had never looked down from Round Top on the country they proposed to settle, or they would have gone back to New England: the task seemed so titanic.

But they had not gone back, and here at my feet were the homes and the farms of their descendants. I too was a happy beneficiary of the miraculous achievement of free men in a free world. All this they had given us out of the strength of their hands and their hearts.

Men like the witty lawyer, the engaging miser, the genial trapper and his great-grandfather who had drunk up nine square miles of primeval timberland never could have accomplished the prodigious task. They never would have attempted it. They lent color and charm, drama and comedy to the human scene, and I responded to them more sensitively, I think, than to any other Yankees I knew. Romantics and idlers, they were incapable of preserving their ancestors' hard-won fields and pastures from the encroachments of weeds and underbrush. Earnest, sweating toil, honesty of purpose, reliability of word, integrity of action, scruple in the handling and spending of money, diligent attention to the task at hand—these were the qualities that made for character.

You might or might not go to church; you might or might not accept Christ as your savior; you might live with a woman out of wedlock; you might not even pretend to love your neighbor as yourself (nobody did anyway); you might even shut yourself off from him; you might have been born with a silver spoon in your mouth or as poor as the proverbial church mouse; you might be a Yankee from way back or only an illiterate German or Lithuanian peasant—all these were of no special consequence, matters of accident, and neither made nor unmade character. But if you lacked the qualities that converted a wilderness into a blooming land and kept it blooming, you forfeited all claim to character.

If there was nothing of romantic idealism in their conception of character, nothing that recognized man's inner travail and sense of splendor, yet to me there was drama in their struggles. They had met a challenge and they had won, as the view from Round Top attested.

Chapter 7

The Great Reward

◄►

The day the springless, straw-filled peasant cart carried me away from the mud-sodden Byelorussian village of my birth, I wept with anguish. My ancestors had lived there for centuries, had become intimately intertwined with the life and culture of our lowly, talkative, hospitable muzhik neighbors. Now I was leaving it, the only home I had known. Though my mother, brother, and sisters were with me, I felt the desolation of the uprooted. Despite poverty, mud, bribe-extorting Czarist officials, I had loved the old home with a fierce primitive emotion, and leaving it was like tearing something out of my very soul.

Our tenement flat on the Lower East Side in New York with its conveniences of hot- and cold-water taps, gas jets, and flush toilets was no compensation for what I had lost. You couldn't get to love a tenement flat; it was not home. We never stayed long in one flat anyway. That was the way it was in the big city. People moved from house to house, from one neighborhood to another, never missing the old place, glad perhaps never to have to see it again.

In the big city people were as rootless as tumbleweeds, as flitting as birds. Today's friend might vanish overnight and be gone forever. You felt a sudden void within yourself but there was nothing you could do about it. You were one of a crowd you rubbed shoulders with, strangers about whom you wondered but who vanished as suddenly as they appeared. You yearned for an attachment to something outside of yourself and the yearning remained unsatisfied. You were an alien, belonging nowhere, attached to nothing, alone. Even though you lived with your family, there was no fireside at which to warm the cold inner emptiness.

It was not until after I had been in the farm country for nearly three years, that I realized how truly homeless and alone I had felt in the city slums. On the farm home was home, though the country and the people were new to me. The moment I walked into a farmhouse every sight and sound and smell assured me that I was in a home. Though I was living with strangers, people whose ways were at first as alien to me as mine to them, I felt that I was living in a home, and not only because I was treated like a member of the family. The solidly built, spacious upstate farmhouses had an air of intimacy and permanence that bespoke home, and that gave the stranger, even an immigrant like myself, a feeling of acceptance. You knew the houses had been there a long time and that the people who lived in them wouldn't pack up and move away tomorrow or next week. The friends you made you knew you would see again.

The sturdy elm on the lawn, the maple and basswood that shaded the porch had been planted by some ancestor in the faith that his progeny would take comfort from them. Inside the houses there might be chairs, mirrors, chinaware brought to the spot in pioneer wagons. There were family Bibles, their yellowing flyleaves recording births, marriages, deaths that went back a century or more. Here was a sense of continuity of home life, a bond with the past, a link with the future. Consciousness of it filled the void I had known, whatever the psychological or social reasons—the peculiarities of my temperament or my old heritage— that had created the void. I was no longer the restless, discontented, rootless immigrant, constantly at war with himself and the world that surrounded him. I was breathing a new atmosphere, growing attuned to new surroundings, getting anchored in a new land. I was amazed how quickly the physical and moral ills I had known in the big city passed away, leaving me healthy and strong for farm work.

Shortly before the conclusion of World War II, on my return from Russia as correspondent of the now defunct New York *Herald Tribune*, I went back to North Brookfield to visit old friends. One of them, who had been in school with me and had since become one of the most successful dairy farmers in New York State, asked why I kept coming back—I who had traveled the world over, had written books, and doubtless had plenty of friends more interesting than mere farmers in a remote part of the hill country upstate.

"Because," I answered, "it makes me feel good to get back. I feel more at home right here than in any place in the world."

Some sixty years have passed since the memorable evening when I boarded a Lackawanna day coach at Hoboken for the long journey into the unknown. I couldn't then have realized how warmly attached I should become to the rustic place I was bound for, or that the rest of my busy and wandering life I was always to think of it as home, though I have neither kin nor house nor property there.

Whenever I return from some far away country, I am overcome by an irresistible urge to go back. Once there, I tramp across familiar fields, through old wood lots, down winding dirt roads or cowpaths, up and down hill, and drop in on some old friend from the elder's Sunday school class or the union school. I never write or telephone that I am coming, as I would do in the city. I just come, and doors are always open and there is always time for leisurely old-fashioned visits. We may or may not engage in discussion of cosmic matters. We may give ourselves only to small talk—local gossip, events in the countryside since my last visit, everyday farm affairs. We may reminisce of old times and bring back to life the horse-and-buggy age. There is no lack of subjects for animated conversation, and I never leave without feeling stimulated and freshened.

So if a place has been home to you and if the people there make you feel at home, you find it impossible not to go back. You have come to know places that are sometimes only names on the map to your old friends, and they know that you have lived in a wider world of ideas, events, adventures than theirs, but no gulf divides you. There is always the bond of youthful years, of beginnings together, school lessons and literary programs, of hymn singing and Ladies' Aid suppers, of sleigh rides and socials, of the remarkable elder with his savage sense of sin and his tender heart, of sentimental infatuations and exuberant conceits, of distressful uncertainties and happy triumphs, and of course of the place itself: meadows and cornfields, rolling pastures and misted wood lots ruddy in the setting sun, of elm and maple—of shaded white houses, of red or white barns and silos, of yelping dogs who understand the friendly gesture, who respond to the friendly word. These are the things that count, that remain timeless in a changing world, that neither superhighways nor television nor all the new kitchen gadgetry can blot out of mind.

The recovery of the sense of home, which I had lost when I left the village in Russia, was only one of the rewards of my years as a farm hand. In New York City there were so many Americans, uptown and downtown and across the river in Brooklyn, that I never really came to know any one of them. Forbidding walls shut me out.

In the upstate country there were no walls between farm and farm, nor between people. Here was no leisure class living off accumulated wealth, no social distinctions, no society of sables and diamonds, of Social Register, of exclusive clubs. Here even the well-to-do farmer milked cows, plowed land, shoveled manure, and did the chores along with the hired man. Living among these people, talking to them in the easy sociability of the general store, Ely's basement, the saloon, the milk station, or in chance encounters on the road and at church socials, I learned to know the descendants of the men whose hands had hewn a place for themselves out of the wilderness and through them to understand something of the people who had conquered a continent. I learned to appreciate the dignity of the women, the unaffected friendliness and spirit of independence of the girls, the comradely intimacy between parents and children and the unforced good fellowship in family life. I was impressed with the sturdy self-assertiveness of the men and their extraordinary chivalry toward women. There was nothing about the farmers in North Brookfield to remind me of the peasants I had been born among, except that they too sweated on land. In *The Great Gatsby* Scott Fitzgerald observes that "Americans . . . have always been obstinate about not being peasantry." I think I understand the author's meaning perhaps more profoundly than the native-born citizen.

Never having suffered from feudalism, political repression, or a hidebound caste system, these upstate farmers had never known the agonizing land hunger of the Russian peasantry, with all its accompanying fears and hatreds. Owners of their own land even when it was mortgaged, they possessed their own souls, and they neither feared nor kowtowed to anybody. They were free to speak their minds on any subject, to associate with whomever they would, to respect their Presidents or to scorn them as Jim did both Theodore Roosevelt and William Howard Taft because they were Republicans.

Though they reverenced God, I doubt that they feared Him. Whatever He was to the elder, to them He was no God of wrath and vengeance. I never heard them refer to Him as an ever-watchful Being noting their slightest peccadilloes or as an omnipresent policeman ready to pounce on them for their trespasses. Their relationship to the Deity was a private matter that needed no mediation by elder or minister—a relationship I understood. They shouldered the blame for their own weaknesses and misfortunes, as I too learned to do. Unlike the self-pitying muzhiks, who continually cried aloud to Heaven for help and mercy, they faced their problems with quiet assurance.

Some prayed and some didn't. Some said grace before a meal and some didn't. But rare was the man or woman who judged his neighbor by his outward piety or his adherence to theological doctrine. They seemed to be as practical and rational in their faith as in their farm work and their family life, in their kindness to animals and their decency to hired men. They mocked liars and hated cheats, though not all of them were beyond lying and cheating. But they never turned their backs on a man for smoking, playing cards, drinking hard cider and whiskey, all mortal sins to the highly articulate elder.

Never having lived under a feudal order, these upstate farmers formed something of a classless society. The term "folks" which has no equivalent in Russian, was new to me; it bespoke their sense of equality. Rich and poor, good farmer and loafer, drunk and teetotaler, preacher and professor, blacksmith and shopkeeper, immigrant and Yankee—all were "folks." The term may be snickered at by city intellectuals, but to me as to anyone who has ever worked on farms, it has always seemed to express a living reality. In the city, where you may never step inside your neighbor's door, its use sounds hollow; television announcers and performers who address their audiences as "folks" repel me with their hearty insincerity. But in a rural community it conveys a genuine sentiment of friendliness and equality.

One of the most educating aspects of the rural community was the fact that social approbation was conditioned not by possessions, antecedents, racial or national origin, but by character grounded in the commonly accepted virtues of politeness to women, integrity in personal relations, industriousness, and efficiency in work. Any man who was credited with character, even if he was an illiterate immigrant, had no reason to feel social inferiority. Up on Quaker Hill, a small community of predominantly Quaker farmers, there lived a Polish family by the name of Kleek. I knew George Kleek, the stocky walrus-mustached head of the family. He spoke broken English, could barely read or write, but was known as a man of character; so were the four German brothers I mentioned earlier, as well as the few Lithuanian farmers in the neighborhood. They were all excellent farmers, men of unimpeachable integrity, who never swore in front of a woman. The Yankees accepted them as equals; and their children and grandchildren have long since married into Yankee stock.

These immigrant farmers quickly lost the sense of social inferiority they had brought from the Old Country. The same was true of me. The sense of inferiority that had haunted me during the time I lived in the slums passed completely. I was flattered when farm people spoke of me as a young fellow of character, and in the years to come a snub would have no more power over me than it would have had over Jim or any other farmer around North Brookfield.

The comparisons continually forced on me between the rural Russia and rural America proved in the long run more enlightening than all the lessons I learned from American history books. At the time I had no thought of a writing career, my ambition being to study at Cornell State Agricultural College and finally to farm my own land. Yet had I deliberately set out to prepare myself for a career of writing about Russia and the Bolshevik Revolution I could not have gone to a better school than Jim Moore's farm.

Following the plow or sitting on a sulky, riding a binder, a horse rake, a hay tedder, a mowing machine, I grasped the significance of modern tools in man's struggle with the stubbornness and hazards of nature. I was never to forget the difference it made to a society whether men plowed their own acres or a feudal lord's fields, whether they scratched the earth with "a sharp stick," as Westerners call the Persian or the Arab peasant's iron-pointed plow, or cut deep into it with blades of steel.

To me a plow became more than an instrument of tillage, a stand of grain more than a crop to harvest. The make of the tool and the condition of the crop revealed the farmer and the farmer revealed the civilization in which he functioned. A chicken was more than a bird in the pot; a pig more than pork chops; a glimpse of the animals in any barnyard in any country on earth through the eyes of an upstate farmer became a precious guide to understanding the culture that produced them.

Had I never had the experience on the American farm, with its impact on my mind and imagination, I doubt that I ever should have won the attention of editors and publishers. The fact is editors ignored me until I began writing of people who lived and worked on the land. I firmly believe that a direct experience of the problems of land workers, a knowledge of crop raising and the care of livestock offer priceless and indispensable insights to journalists and diplomats who set out to explore the dynamics of Communism and the appeal it can make to the deprived and discontented peoples of Asia, Africa, and South America. Without playing on the despair and desperation of land-hungry peasants, whose toil and sweat fattened a landlord's fields more often than their own, if they had fields of their own, neither Lenin nor Mao Tse-tung could have risen to power, though once in power, the party they headed didn't hesitate to shatter the peasant's most cherished dream—individual land-holding.

But neither Lenin nor Mao Tse-tung could have stirred up the least excitement among farmers like Jim Moore, though by prevailing standards he was no man of affluence, always cash poor, always mortgaged. No Marxism-Leninism would have won the ear of a farmer like him or even of those poorer than he. By Russian standards Jim would have been branded a "kulak" and would have been liquidated if only because he employed hired labor. Actually, I never knew a kulak anywhere in Russia who cultivated as large an acreage as Jim did, milked as many cows (twelve), or was so well supplied with agricultural implements.

I could never make even as brilliant a Bolshevik as Nikolay Bukharin understand the vast gulf that separated the heritage and the character of the American farmer, as I knew him, from the heritage and character of the land-hungry Russian muzhik who until 1861 had borne the yoke of serfdom for some three centuries. Possessed of small holdings of land or none at all, the muzhik was vulnerable to the Bolshevik promise of free land, while the landowning American farmer, with his superior tools and superior methods of farming and his highly individualized self, could never respond to any Bolshevik promise. Lenin never understood it, neither did Trotsky nor Stalin.

The people in my new country, self-confident and self-reliant, were as untouched by any *Weltschmerz* as by "philosophical questioning doubt," which Tolstoy had rated among the highest human qualities. At the time I had not read Tolstoy's words, but even if I had, it would not have lessened my admiration for the spirit of affirmation and optimism of the people around me. So powerful was the impact of this spirit on me that less salutary features of the upstate rural civilization, such as the lack of intellectual stimulation, never dismayed me.

In contrast to Yankee practicality and optimism, I often contemplated the heroes of my beloved Turgenev, and the images of the "soulful" do-nothing Rudin and of the "soulless" man of action Bazarov rose before me in all their beautiful futility and gloomy grandeur. Both longed for a life of worthy allegiances. Rudin mesmerized his drawing-room listeners with his eloquent eulogies on the glories of a dedicated life, while Bazarov scandalized his listeners with stinging ridicule of everything Rudin revered. Both were victims of their own delusions; in the inhospitable social soil of Czarist Russia they could reap only frustration and defeat. Seeing them from the vantage point of the American countryside, they seemed pale ineffectual spirits, impotent to cope with the realities of their time and place. With arbitrary mercifulness Turgenev removes Bazarov from the scene of his hopeless rebellion by a convenient case of fatal typhoid.

To me one of the most admirable traits of the upstate Yankees was self-control. The quality was poignantly revealed to me at the first funeral I attended there. A lively handsome boy, one of the elder's Sunday school class, died from pneumonia. The funeral was held in his father's farmhouse, and when I arrived the parlor was already crowded. To my amazement all the mourners were dressed in their Sunday best and nobody was weeping. A luncheon was served and people sat about eating sandwiches and cakes and drinking coffee and conversing quietly, in controlled voices. I alone did not eat and could hardly speak; I was too conscious of the casket in the next room. An Old-World primitive terror of death gripped my heart.

During the service that followed the lunch there was choked sobbing, but no hysterical moaning or wailing, as though the bereaved found it unseemly to make a demonstration of their deepest feelings before others. I had not imagined that there were people anywhere in the world who were capable of such supreme mastery of their emotions.

There must be iron in the blood of these people, I thought. In the face of death they were solemn but not stricken; they bore their grief with touching dignity. When misfortune struck, they neither raged against fate nor allowed it to overwhelm them; always they were masters of themselves. I was amazed that even women bore their sorrows with fortitude. If the father of a family died, his widow didn't give way to despair nor did she teach the children self-pity for their orphaned state, as my mother had taught her children after my father died. When the shock was over, home life flowed on as tranquilly as before, and with a renewal of hope and cheer.

Among the muzhiks and the Jews death had been a shattering disaster, a funeral an occasion of self-torture and harrowing laments. The sociability of a Yankee funeral would have seemed sacrilege, an insult to the dead. But these Yankees lived life on its sunny surface, unaware of any abyss. Their concern was with things, with what they could grasp, manage, control with their own hands and their own intelligence. The dark places of the soul were not for them. They faced calamity so serenely that I often wondered if they had any sense of tragedy such as I had acquired from my life in a Russian village and from Russian fiction.

Pneumonia claimed another victim, the wife of a farmer who lived on Quaker Hill. It was early winter and Jim and I walked to the funeral over a snow-swept road in the face of a biting wind. People had come for miles around, crowding the sitting room for the welcome midday meal. The services were held in the meetinghouse, comfortably warmed by a potbellied stove: the living were not to be slighted, a funeral was no penitential event. Like the Baptists, the Quakers showed respect for the dead in terms of simple, sincere, solemn everyday behavior, with no hint of dramatic tribal ritual.

During the services in the meetinghouse I sat beside my Quaker friend, the high school student. When the moment came for mourners to file by the uncovered casket for a last look at the dead woman, he rose to go, but I didn't follow him. I couldn't bring myself to do as others were doing, look calmly on that still face in the coffin. Perhaps they thought me unfeeling, unmannerly, I do not know. I was not unfeeling: only my feelings were different from theirs. I was still haunted by a primitive horror. Yet the longer I worked on farms, the more I was turning into somebody different from what I had been, I was losing the sense of differentness between myself and the people around me. In time, as I was growing into a new self, I lost my old primitive terror of death.

Chapter 8

The Immigrant as Freshman

◆

I was twenty. For nearly three years I had worked on farms, the most fruitful and happiest years I had known in the new country. During the winter months when the land was frozen and there was no field work to do, I attended the North Brookfield union school which covered only three years of high school. Under the guidance of one of the teachers I studied fourth-year subjects and creditably passed Regents' examinations in all of them. Now I thought I was ready for college and eagerly looked forward to enrolling in the Cornell State College of Agriculture.

I filed an application, submitted my Regents' certificate of credits, and with mounting suspense waited for a reply. When it finally arrived the light went out of my eyes. It appeared that I lacked the required number of credits and was rejected. My farming experience failed to count in my favor. The curt impersonal words made a mockery of my ambition. But I soon braced up. I wouldn't be so easily rebuffed. I wrote the registrar assuring him that I would find it no burden to pursue extra courses and work off my conditions during freshman year. Again rejection. The registrar was firm; rules were rules and he could make no exception. He advised me to study for a year in the high school of a near-by town and come to Cornell the following autumn unencumbered with conditions.

The prospect of another year in classes with boys and girls younger and less mature than myself distressed me. At that time a year seemed an age—an age to lose only because the registrar, to my mind, was a stonyhearted man. But I would touch his heart, and why not? The Yankee teachers and school principals I had known had been kindly and helpful—Dr. Rollins of Stuyvesant, a select high school in New York, had admitted me without a

scrap of paper attesting to my studies in the Russian school. He
trusted my word. Why then wouldn't the Cornell registrar trust
my assurance that I would clear conditions in my first year in
addition to carrying the prescribed courses? So I wrote the registrar once more, this time a pleading letter. It didn't do any good.
The rejection was summary.

In my despair I went to see Elder Mattison who was a master
at cheering people in distress. The elder offered more than solace:
apply, he advised, for admission to Colgate University, which
was only some nine miles away. Of course, Colgate was a liberal
arts college, but a year there would be more rewarding than a
year at a high school, and then if I still wished to study agriculture
at Cornell, I could be certain of acceptance. A Baptist college
like Colgate, the elder assured me, would treat my application
with "proper Christian understanding." Besides, Hamilton, the
town where Colgate was, was so near that weekends and vacations I could come over to visit "home folks," go to the socials
of the Sunday school class, and have a good time with the boys
and girls I knew so well.

The world suddenly brightened. It brightened even more when
the elder told me that there were dairy farms all around Hamilton where an experienced farmhand like myself should have no
difficulty in finding board and room in exchange for help with
morning and evening chores. I left the elder's house in high
spirits.

Dr. John Greene, Colgate's dean of admissions, wrote a friendly
though discouraging letter. He did not think it advisable for
me to enter college with more than the allowable of conditions.
But there was something in the language and spirit of the letter
that made me feel the dean might reverse his decision if he knew
about my background. I wrote again. Promptly the dean replied
that if I was so eager to enter college he would allow me the
opportunity to prove myself. I rushed with the letter to the Baptist parsonage, and I can still see the pale-faced elder beam with
triumph as he proudly declared, "I was sure Colgate would do
that, absolutely sure they would show proper Christian understanding of your problem."

Toward the end of September 1911, several weeks after college
started, I arrived in Hamilton with a small trunk packed with

books and my Sears, Roebuck clothes. It was early afternoon and I immediately went to see the dean.

Dr. Greene, or "Johnny," as students called him, was a bald-headed man with a fringe of white hair encircling a gleaming skull. His forehead was so wide that the slope of his lean cheeks gave his face a triangular shape. It was a very expressive face, lighted up by shrewd and penetrating eyes. He spoke in a soft, muffled voice as though there was an obstruction in his throat. His informality at once put me at ease. He shook my hand warmly, and then and there we worked out a schedule of my courses.

The details of my enrollment over, I wandered around the campus. Under the mellow autumn light the wide close-cropped lawns, still untouched by frost, shimmered like carpets of the softest emerald, sloping down from the gray limestone buildings on the crest of the hill. The tall trees turning russet and gold and the yellowing willows bending to their reflections in the little lake made the path along the bank and up the hill a place of quiet beauty, fit, I thought, for contemplative strolls and scholarly meditations. Nothing grew wild here: man had set unruly nature in order to suit his own purposes; no goldenrod or asters or thistles had been allowed to seed themselves along the edges of the willow walk or any other paths; no fallen twigs or branches cluttered the lawns. Never in my life had I seen grounds as immaculately kept as this campus. For my rustic tastes and love of wild nature it was all too elegant, too subdued. I felt as overawed as a muzhik in a landlord's drawing room.

Then following a random road off the campus I started my search for work on a farm. One farmer directed me to another, until I came on a man who told me that his neighbor down the road was looking for a student to help him do chores for board and room.

The neighbor's name was Irving Bronson and he lived alone in a two-story clapboarded, red-painted house about a mile away from the college. He met me at the door, a tall man with a massive head set on a scrawny neck like an apple on its stem. A man of about sixty or over, his bushy brows shadowed his big, unmoving gray eyes and thick tufts of hair grew out of his ears. I explained to him the purpose of my call and without saying a word he motioned me into the sitting room and pointed to a chair. I sat down and he disappeared in the kitchen. Soon he returned with a panful of steaming baked apples.

"D'you like baked apples?"

It was a relief to hear him speak. We ate the apples and between bites I told him of my farming experience. But not a word came out of my listener, though now and then he would steal an appraising glance at me. After we had our fill of the apples, I waited for him to announce his decision. Instead, he sat with bowed head and pinched the lobe of his ear. I didn't know what to make of him and concluded that despite his hospitality he didn't care to engage me. But when I rose to go he looked up with surprise and drawled, "You might hitch up the horse to the milk wagon and bring over your things."

A strange man, I thought; perhaps sick, perhaps lonely, or perhaps just plain lazy. But his character was of no consequence now that I was assured of earning my room and board.

Bronson was an incredibly slow worker, and whenever he went to empty a pail of milk into the can, he would tarry, pinch his ear, groan, and stare at the floor. He walked with leisurely steps and spoke in a languid voice, as though motion and speech were distasteful to him. My attempt to engage him in conversation in the barn failed. He didn't ask me a single question about myself nor vouchsafe a word of information about himself. He seemed to live in a locked world of his own, more absorbing than the one outside.

For supper he fried thick slices of ham, warmed up potatoes and gravy, and brought out another pan of baked apples; this time the pan was large, and I was glad of it, for I too had a passion for baked apples. In an effort to be sociable, I remarked, "I love baked apples." His only reply was a jerk of the head, a stare, and a grunt. I gave up my hopes of communicating with him as man to man.

After supper I went upstairs to my room. It was a small, low-ceilinged room, furnished farm-fashion with an old wooden bed, a little table, a chair, a bowl and pitcher, and the inevitable kerosene lamp. I piled my books on the table and forgetting my inarticulate employer gave myself to the enjoyment of my new status in life: I was now a college student—a dream fulfilled.

I was happy I didn't have to leave the green hills of Madison County to continue my education. Still, though North Brookfield was not far away, I was in another America, the America of books and learning, of students and professors, where I could face intellectual challenges the farm never provided. On the farm I had had a rewarding experience in living, in adapting myself to a new civilization, a new people, as salty and earthy as any I could hope to encounter in the new land. Now ahead of me lay an experience in the things of the mind, and even if it were to last only one year, until I was able to overcome the resistance of the stubborn Cornell registrar with my scholastic accomplishments, it would be an exciting adventure. With these reflections I blew out the lamp, slipped into the chilly bed, and fell asleep.

I awoke suddenly. Someone was singing; through the darkness came the strains of a familiar hymn. I thought I was dreaming. But no; loud and clear the sounds came up the stairs. At this late hour the somnolent and taciturn farmer had come to life and was singing hymns. My curiosity aroused, I got out of bed and went downstairs to see what was happening. Bronson was sitting at the table with a winter coat over his ankle-length flannel nightshirt, an open hymn book before him. He did not hear me enter, and I stood by the door watching, puzzled by his peculiar behavior—rising out of bed in the depth of night to sing hymns, with a fervor that contrasted strangely with his earlier behavior.

After he finished the hymn he noticed my presence. Without saying a word he went into the next room, came back with another hymnal which he pressed into my hand and motioned me to sit down, obviously expecting me to join in the singing. I was more amused than impressed, and not wishing to offend the man, I sang with him, one hymn after another. We concluded with "Nearer My God to Thee," which I associated with funerals, and then he recited a long prayer in a voice charged with emotion, the words a plaintive plea for forgiveness of sin and for succor. I concluded that he suffered from some inner torment and was fearful of death.

Yet when he sat up, he sighed with relief and rubbed his hands with satisfaction, as though refreshed and strengthened. Hymn singing and praying had manifestly cheered him. Then he walked into the kitchen and I was not surprised to see him return with

the pan of apples left over from supper. This time we finished
the apples.

My first day in college gave me a few hours of anxiety until I
was rescued by a gallant fellow freshman.

I thought I had so well assimilated the folkways of farm and
village that I could cope with whatever contingency might arise
in college. But I had reckoned without the tribalism of American students in those days. On the farm and in the village a
man could do as he pleased, cut his hair regularly or take his
time about it, and I always took my time. There was no barber in
North Brookfield and I knew farmers whose wives had to cajole
or scold them into submitting to their shears. That college students might not countenance a taste for long hair had never
occurred to me. But the moment I entered my first class, my
golliwogg hair drew curious stares. I felt disconcerted and in
my ignorance I assumed it was because I was a newcomer. But
the stares didn't abate, and I thought it rude of my classmates to
subject me to such disturbing attention.

Suddenly one of the students came up. He was a striking looking young man with shining blond hair, a high prominent forehead, deep-blue eyes, and a friendly smile. He introduced
himself as Bernard Clausen, and welcomed me to the class. I felt
relieved. The clean-cut appearance of the friendly student, his
easy manner, his soft voice so attracted me that I forgot the rude
stares.

But during recess another classmate drew me aside and whispered an ominous message: if I didn't hurry downtown to the
barbershop and cut my hair short, the TNEs would cut it for me.

"Who are the TNEs?" I asked.

To my consternation I learned that they were a secret sophomore society that dealt roughly with freshmen who violated college customs or otherwise incurred their displeasure. To impress
me he spelled out in detail the fearful nature of their vengeance,
which was inescapable. Hide where I would after dark, they
would find me. They would hack off my hair, thrash me black
and blue, and toss me into the cold lake.

Then he asked if I had yet gotten my freshman cap. He showed me his, a gray beanie with a green button on top, hardly large enough to cover a kitten's head. Yes, I must immediately get one, my classmate warned, or I wouldn't escape sophomore retribution.

I was shocked and scared. My preconceptions of college were rudely shattered. I had pictured it as a place where the intellectual youth of the country—as students were regarded in Europe and especially in Czarist Russia—gathered to pursue their studies in a cloistered atmosphere of high thinking and serious living, and here were the TNEs, a self-appointed gendarmerie, enforcing the observance of absurd and humiliating customs on helpless freshmen. Had I come to the wrong college? My classmate assured me it was no different in other colleges, only I mustn't take matters too seriously; he didn't—no freshman did. I was amazed at his unconcern with what was to me an atrocious perversion of the American spirit as I had come to understand it in the farm country, where a man would raise his pitchfork at anybody who threatened to beat the devil out of him if he didn't cut his hair.

Despite the forewarning of my new friends, I decided the barber could wait; I had classes to attend and I wouldn't cut them on my first day at college. As it turned out I was glad I didn't miss my class in freshman rhetoric; it was the high point of my first day as a student.

When I took my place in the packed classroom, I saw a sign on the wall above the professor's desk which read:

THESE ARE EVIDENCES OF AN EDUCATION:

Correctness in the use of the mother tongue
Refined and gentle manners
The power and habit of reflection
The power of growth
The power to do.

As I waited for the professor I wondered that the sophomore TNEs should have remained untouched by this admonition to use refined and gentle manners. Who were they anyway, brazenly to defy one of the professor's tests of an educated man?

When the professor—Ralph W. Thomas, or "Tommy," as students called him—entered the room, chatter subsided, and unlike my previous class not a whisper disturbed the attentive silence. The professor seemed to have cast a spell over the students. Yet there was nothing distinctive or impressive about his appearance. He was short and paunchy, with broad shoulders and a thick neck; he waddled as he walked, though his steps were brisk. He looked more like a self-indulgent businessman than an academic. But the moment he began to speak I sensed something of his appeal—a smooth and resonant voice, an instrument with which to express a wide range of emotions. As the lesson proceeded I grew aware of other engaging qualities in the man: a gentle wit and an extraordinary memory for passages of poetry or prose to illustrate his points. He rarely referred to the textbook—Genung's *Rhetoric*—which, when I read it, proved a dull treatise on a fascinating subject. But Tommy infused into it the breath of life. More than instilling in his students an appreciation of "correctness in the mother tongue," he strove to impart to them his own love of its beauties. He made me think of the Russian master who had held us breathless with his expositions and recitations. I left the class reassured that absurd sophomores did not set the tone of college life.

Still, when classes were over for the day, I hurried downtown to the barbershop. Timian, the barber, greeted me with a hearty laugh. "You're just in time, boy," he said, as though he had already heard about a new freshman in dire need of his professional attention. As swiftly as gossip traveled over the party-line telephone back on the farm, news of me and my predicament had flashed from the hill to the town. While slashing handfuls of hair from my head, the barber regaled me with a lurid description of the TNEs tonsorial technique, and when I arose shorn he complimented me on my more decorous appearance. But observing that I had no freshman cap, he reminded me that I wasn't safe yet. I assured him that I was on my way to equip myself with the absurd symbol of freshman humility.

The cap was so light on my head that I had no way of knowing whether it had blown off or not, so I walked back to the farm holding it in place with one hand.

When I reached the farm Bronson was feeding corn to hens. There was a guinea hen with purplish-gray plumage in the flock which he had tamed to keep close to him at feeding time so he could favor it with a special handout of corn. My sudden appearance scared it off and the farmer signaled me away. He obviously had a special affection for the beautifully feathered fowl.

When he returned to the house he sat down and gave me an inquiring look as though surprised at my changed appearance. "Now," I said, "I'm a regular freshman."

He made no comment but continued to contemplate me as though he were seeing me for the first time. I wondered what was on his mind, but didn't ask him. At milking time he appeared in no hurry to get to the barn, and when I picked up the pail and strainer and started for the door, he motioned me to wait. I did and finally he asked in his slow drawling voice whether I'd like to work full days on Saturdays helping him to draw hay and corn to the barn and cut winter wood. He would pay me seven and a half dollars a month beside my board and room. Gratefully I accepted the offer. Now I would have some spending money without drawing on my meager savings.

As I look back to those times it occurs to me that long before the Bolsheviks appeared on the world scene, the American college, as it revealed itself to me, had created the mass man; and long before the Bolsheviks had glorified the collective society, the American college had perfected it, complete with songs, slogans, mass meetings, banners, rituals, an ideology and a mystique of its own. The essence of the mystique was college spirit, and the first lesson drummed into newcomers like myself was that Colgate spirit was unmatched by that of any other college, least of all by Syracuse University, Colgate's most bitter football foe—not mere rival, but *foe*, whom a loyal son of Colgate was duty bound to hate (Syracuse coeds excepted), at least until the annual football match was over. Colgate might honorably lose a game to West Point, even (the Lord forbid) to Cornell, but never, never must it suffer the ignominy of a walloping by Syracuse. No freshman must ever forget this.

But during the football season of 1911 the athletic feud between the two universities of central New York resulted in a break in diplomatic relations; no game was scheduled between them. Instead, the big game was to be played with Trinity College, a mere rival, not an ancient enemy. Under the circumstances the cheer leaders were going to find it difficult to rouse the Colgate rooters to their accustomed pitch of frenzy on the great day. But they were going to have a good try at it anyway.

An immigrant from the swamplands of Byelorussia could only think the "rah-rah-rahs," the "zim-boom-bahs" a kind of mass madness. My own blood ran cool, and it amazed me that college men and academics should behave this way. Such Dionysiac howling and such frenzied cavorting were no part of any picture I had ever formed of life in the halls of higher learning. Still, it was another aspect of my new world and I tried to understand it.

I was glad to be living off campus, a mile or so away on a quiet farm where I could be my own man, not a member of a collective that demanded every student's conformity and enforced it if necessary by the paddles of the vigilant TNEs that fell hard on an aberrant's behind. Out at Bronson's I was away from all that and safe from those punitive paddles.

Chapter 9

Another America

◆▸

I had expected college to be different. I could not help comparing my classmates with the Russian students of Czarist times, with their hunger for ideas, their veneration of art and literature. The son of my old schoolmaster had gone mad from the punishment he had suffered for his political opinions.

American youths, like those of other Anglo-Saxon countries, knew nothing of such stresses and torments. "The Russian universities," according to E. H. Carr, one-time editor of the London *Times*, noted for his scholarly studies of the Soviet Revolution, "in contrast to Anglo-Saxon tradition, have always been the home of advanced ideas." I should have remembered all I had learned about the type of humanity that had conquered the New York wilderness and the psychological heritage it left of an ideal of character that stressed the pre-eminence of practical accomplishment.

But I still lacked the perspective to apply my knowledge of the American countryside to the American college. I had dissociated the one from the other, which ill prepared me for the new order of things that confronted me in college.

Yet the new scene fascinated me once I recovered from my initial disillusionment, not of course with teachers, but with students. The process of unlearning my preconceptions of college life became a rewarding though often a painful and embarrassing experience.

To begin with, I soon discovered that there was nothing lofty about the vocabulary of the American college man, as I had imagined there would be. Food, for example: on the farm it was "vittles," here it was "grub." I had grubbed hills of hops on the farm and couldn't for the life of me relate the grubbing I had done on the land to the new meaning of the word. Once in the college commons I heard a student ask another to pass him "the goo." He meant the bowl of gravy. Nobody on the farm ever called gravy "goo." Nor had I heard farmers use the expressions "by gravy" and "by jingo," favorite expletives here.

On the farm, refreshments were a "bite" of this or that. Here refreshments were "tunk." Why tunk? Nobody could explain it. Nor was Webster's dictionary any help. On the farm when men were by themselves they spoke of a sexy woman as "some petticoat." Here she was "some chicken" or "some lulu."

Literature was "lit," mathematics was "math," a professor was a "prof," and the president was "prexy"! Studying was "boning," a tedious chore. An easy course was a "snap" or a "lark," suggestive of no particular strain on the mind; and heaven forbid that a student should admit he studied hard. He would be called a "grind" or a "bookworm."

After I had been in college some weeks, a classmate said to me, "Gee, you're a highbrow."

"Why d'you say that?" I asked, taking it as a compliment.

"You ask so many questions," he answered in a tone of voice that implied no commendation. The charge was true. I doubt if my record for asking questions in class during the freshman year was ever equaled. In our ensuing discussion it became clear to me that "highbrow" was no epithet of which to be proud. However, I continued to ask questions.

And what could I make of a classmate who was so elated by praise from one of his professors that he boasted joyfully he had "put the professor's eye out"?

One afternoon as I walked down the willow path with a junior, I saw a professor limping along ahead of us on a metal leg. "Who is he?" I asked. "Cooky cutter" was the reply. I was shocked to hear a professor referred to so disrespectfully, as I knew what a cooky cutter was, and I was puzzled as to why he should be called one. The explanation was simple—his metal leg cut circles in the ground as he walked. But didn't the professor resent his nickname? Not at all. Once a freshman addressed him as "Professor Cook," and the professor laughed when he told about it to his students and colleagues.

The head of the chemistry department was a solemn-faced,

gray-haired, soft-spoken man, an accomplished scientist whose textbooks were widely used. He was an excellent teacher, and students responded to his personal interest in their work. Yet they nicknamed him "Hog," which was only a good-humored allusion to his prominent jowls.

The head of the physics department, who was a consultant to General Electric, was a little man with sloping shoulders, a whining voice, and an inconsequential manner; he was nicknamed "Icky," after Ichabod Crane. Once when I was working in the professor's garden, I was surprised to hear him use the nickname himself: "Students who try to bluff in class soon find out they can't fool Icky." And nobody did. When two well-known basketball players on the varsity team signed up for one of his courses, he invited them after the first session to come to his office. "I understand you boys play basketball?" he inquired. The students nodded. "Well," he warned them, "nobody can be a success at both basketball and physics. That's all."

There was an unsmiling mathematics professor who made students sweat for their marks, called "Twister." The dignified professor of public speaking who insisted on the precise enunciation of every syllable in every word was nicknamed "Precisely," pronounced slowly and with great precision. And so it went: no reverence for age, position, or accomplishment, but pride in irreverence, glee over cutting anybody down to size, now with genuine affection, now with downright coarseness, though never with malice or spite.

Inevitably in my early months in college I found myself in tilts with fellow students. Once after a lecture in chapel by a visiting professor, I heard a student express his judgment of the lecturer's ideas as "bullshit." I was shocked, not at the expression, my vocabulary having already been enriched with barnyard words, but by the affront to the lecturer, whom the president had introduced as a distinguished "scholar," a hallowed word to me.

I remonstrated with the student. At first he was amused, then as I grew a little heated he cut short the argument by saying, "Come, come, be human!"

Living a mile away from the campus, I never came to know any student intimately, not even the handsome and gifted Bernard Clausen, who in time became my closest friend, or the others whose brilliance in the classroom had roused my admiration. Nor were they easy to know. Their jollity seemed to mask their real selves, though I could only judge them by what I saw of them in the classroom and from our casual encounters.

The more I saw of them, the more paradoxical they appeared. They were and weren't what I judged them to be. They pretended to be frivolous when they were serious, as though being serious was an offense against good taste. Disdainful of dress or demeanor that was different or conspicuous, they yet admired a student who showed marks of leadership or was outstanding in his studies. Even when they studied hard, as some of them did, they would not admit it, lest they be called "grind" or "bookworm." The freshman handbook those days openly counseled, "Don't be a grind. Get into college activities"—meaning activities outside of the classroom, divorced from books and studies. Yet my classmates were proud of their high marks and of their professors' praise of their scholastic achievements.

I vividly remember the first intercollegiate debate I attended. It was a great age of intercollegiate debates and oratorical contests, the only kinds of competition I enjoyed. I loved the clash of minds, whatever the subject under discussion.

On my way to the village opera house—which had never witnessed an operatic performance in all the years of its existence—where the debate was held, I wondered if many students would turn out for the event, a highbrow affair to my mind. Yet by the time the chairman and the speakers appeared on the platform the house was crowded. Students came as for an athletic contest, and during the debate they warmly applauded points scored by the visiting speakers.

The Colgate team won the contest, and when the decision of the judges was announced, the opera house thundered with applause. Though this was a contest between highbrows, the students were as jubilant as at a football game.

And what could I make of the adulation bordering on idolatry of Dr. William Henry Crawshaw, or "Craw," as he was familiarly called, head of the department of English literature? He had taught generations of college men, and none of them had ever ridiculed his eccentricities. Students said that a man forfeited the best Colgate had if he missed Craw's course in Shakespeare.

I could only conclude that while students might frown on intellectual activity for its own sake, they looked up to any man who had attained scholarly distinction.

And there was still another baffling paradox. One Saturday evening I walked to the village to see a movie. It was an installment of *The Perils of Pauline* and drew students like a football game. In the course of the picture, they grew wildly unruly. They clapped and whistled, stamped their feet and yelled. Calls for quiet from older people were drowned in renewed bursts of tumult. I was shocked; children would behave better. What made these privileged young Americans forget their maturity and their good manners?

Yet at student meetings they were models of decorum and self-discipline. Nobody interrupted the chairman or the speaker. Disagreements, however sharp, were courteously presented. The other man's opinions were attentively listened to. The majority vote decided the issue, and the minority acquiesced. It was democracy in spirit and action, a lesson in self-government, which the Lower East Side intellectuals had not yet learned. The few lecture meetings I had attended on the East Side were invariably accompanied by loud disorder and impassioned wrangling which the chairman was often at a loss to control.

After I had been in college for several months, I was invited by classmates to a Saturday evening bull session, deliberately planned, so one of the planners subsequently revealed, to force me into expounding my favorite heresies so they could have some fun with me. But when the baiting started I suspected mischief and adroitly diverted attention from myself by telling them about Jim, the farmer-Democrat who blamed all the ills of the world on the Republicans. My would-be inquisitors forgot the purpose of the gathering as I told one story after another. Finally I related the incident of Jim's newly freshened Holstein heifer. Mistrustful of the creature, I had declined to break her into milking, so after lambasting me for having no more guts than a yahoo Republican, the old man proceeded to do the chore himself. He had almost finished when a cat leaped down from the haymow and scared the heifer, who in panic kicked the pail of milk clear over Jim's head. The old man was so infuriated that he clobbered her with his stool, shouting at the top of his voice, "Stand still, you goddam Republican!" My classmates guffawed delightedly, and so did I, though not at the recollection of Jim's wrath, but at my social triumph. I wasn't as "weird" as they had imagined. I had moments when I could be as "human" as they.

But I wasn't always. One afternoon as I was walking to the farm I caught up with a freshman on the road. As we talked, the subject of fraternity initiations came up, on which my companion appeared to be an authority. He described the nature of the ceremony, the jests, the taunts, the pranks, often climaxed by a paddling on the behind, that the initiate underwent.

"Why are the initiations so cruel?" I asked.

"So a fellow wouldn't get the idea he was a big shot in college because he was a big shot in high school."

"D'you approve of it?"

"Of course."

"D'you mean you'd actually stand for it?"

"I guess I'll have to."

He was pledged to a fraternity and the ordeal of the initiation didn't faze him. I knew I would hate it, and he laughed when I said so. I thought him insensitive, and in spite of the prestige a fraternity pin conferred, I can't say that I envied him. Hazing has since been outlawed by Colgate and many other colleges all over the country. But in my day it was a distinctive feature of college tribalism, which to me was a form of youthful sadism.

And how unkind students could be to those who incurred their disapprobation! They didn't criticize, reprimand, or laugh at him to his face. They were too polite to be openly offensive. They did worse, they ignored him. Outside of classes he lived in a social void, or, since misery loves company, he consorted with other outcasts. With rare exceptions, students never tried to understand the man not cut to their pattern. They just didn't bother with him.

But if a student was a "good fellow," he never lacked friends, whoever he might be—banker's, baker's, farmer's, factory worker's son; so affluent that he wore Brooks Brothers' clothes or so poor that after classes he slipped into overalls and chopped wood or shoveled coal for a living. They seemed without consciousness of class or caste. I knew students who waited on table in fraternity houses, but the members of the fraternity neither patronized nor snubbed the waiters, nor did the waiters toady to the men they waited on. There was no social stigma attached to being a waiter; it was just one way of getting an education. It was the man who tried to play the "big shot" who was scorned and sooner or later cut down to size.

Of course if a student came from a rich or privileged family, he might more readily be "tapped" for membership to one of the more select fraternities than the student of poor or humble origin. But even then he didn't escape the indignity of a hazing.

I still wonder how I struggled through those early months without incurring the resentment and opprobrium that by tribal standards I so richly merited. Though I didn't go around spoiling for an argument, I never concealed my opinions (except from sophomores) whenever there was chance to air them. Of course, after classes I was not seen much on the campus or in the village —there were chores to be done and after them, study—so my association with students was limited. In Tommy's rhetoric class I had made an impression on teacher and classmates, and however sharp the witticisms against the "grind" and the "highbrow," students had a healthy respect for a classmate who had the right answers.

Perhaps there was a particular reason for the friendly attitude of students toward me. I was an immigrant, one of only two on the campus, a Persian and myself, and both in the freshman class, and I was expected to be different. It was not that students had sympathy for me: to them sympathy was a feminine weakness. But an immigrant couldn't be supposed to know better than to act the way I did. And so instead of being outraged by my "queer" opinions on freshman rights and sophomore barbarousness, at my derision of football spirit and other orthodoxies, students were only amused. I could get away with the murder of their sacred cows and they would laugh at the slaughter.

In contrast to many an American campus today, the campus I knew sixty years ago seems to have been actually a place of refuge for all but a tiny minority of students from the troubles and turbulence of the world outside.

Meanwhile, I clung fast to my purpose, which was to get an education. Homework was no particular burden. Evenings on the farm were long and peaceful, wonderful evenings for studying and reading in my room or by the fireside downstairs, with a platter of Northern Spies, raw or baked, always on the table. Now and then Bronson would be seized by his passion for hymn singing, but I never again joined him. I read omnivorously, my association of reading with education being a heritage of my Russian school years.

I had discovered Thomas Hardy while browsing around in a second-hand bookshop in Utica during my first year on the farm. Hardy's Turgenev-like love of nature, his masterful depiction of rural folk, his temperamental kinship with Russian novelists drew me to him. I still read him more than any other English novelist. I also came upon Ibsen, of whom I had heard on New York's East Side. Mark Twain's *Prince and the Pauper* had been a favorite in my boyhood, so I read his other works. Jack London and James Fenimore Cooper were the two other American authors I had read in boyhood, so I read more of them, never tiring of London but quickly losing my liking for Cooper. Poe, George Eliot, Dickens, Thackeray, Balzac, Zola were other favorites. I never tired of reading, and I wondered why so many students stuck to their textbooks which so often bored them, to the exclusion of great books.

Almost by accident I wakened to a fresh appreciation of the King James Bible. Bronson was a Baptist and he never missed a Sunday service. I preferred to stay home and read and to prepare a special Sunday dinner that would vary the monotony of Bronson's cooking. But I had heard so much about Professor Thomas's Sunday school class of college men that one Sunday morning I drove with Bronson to church.

The minister's sermon was a disappointing performance. A highly educated man, he had neither the voice, the gift of language, the talent for the apt illustration to rouse my interest. I contrasted him with the unscholarly elder in North Brookfield: an old-fashioned type of preacher, the elder never allowed an audience to slip away from him. His superlative platform manner, his booming voice, his gift for storytelling, his humor, even his obsession with hellfire, held his congregation spellbound. But the minister in the college town was plainly a bore. I sat beside Bronson and he snoozed through most of the sermon as did other

worshipers. But when the service was over a second congregation occupied the pews, a large audience of college students.
Professor Thomas, or "Tommy," waddled toward the pulpit—
he never mounted it—spoke a few preliminary words on the
Bible as literature, then read the first chapter of the Book of Job.
Never in classroom had I known the master elocutionist so
carried away as he was now. He was God, he was Satan, now one
messenger, now another, and now the scourged but uncowed and
unbowed Job. Never in my life had I heard anything so moving;
the words rolled out like thunder, murmured like a brook,
moaned like the wind, and died like an echo. The magic of his
voice fitted the magic of the text, the language majestically simple, beautifully rhythmic, poetry and music stirring the ear, the
tragedy and triumph of man in his battle between good and evil,
long to remember and to ponder. Not a student stirred in his
seat or lifted his eyes off the professor. Ever since, I have thought
of him as more than a teacher of rhetoric and of the college men's
Sunday school class. He was one of the great gifts of the college to
its students.

I began to attend the professor's Sunday school class regularly
and the King James Bible became a book to keep by my side.
Years later when I made my frequent visits to Russia, I never
failed to put it in my bag. In Moscow, if it was not Walter
Duranty of the New York *Times*, an inveterate collector of Bibles,
who walked off with my copy of the Book, there was always
some Russian author who managed to appropriate it. The late
Alexander Afinogenov (killed by a German bomb in Moscow
in 1941), one of the most gifted Soviet playwrights, after reading several pages of it in my hotel room, borrowed it for a few
days, which in Russia might mean a few months, a few years, or
eternity.

It wasn't until the spring of 1942, when I went to Russia as a
war correspondent, that I saw it again in the deceased playwright's library in Peredelkino, outside of Moscow, where he had
a dacha. His widow, American born, showed it to me and told
me how often her husband had turned to it during the darkest
year of his life. *Pravda* had denounced him as an "enemy of the
people," and he and his family withdrew to the country. He never
knew when the night would come that a knock on the door would

summon him, perhaps to death from a bullet in the back of his head, the Soviet way of executing political offenders. During those anxious and wakeful nights, one of the books he, a Party member and an atheist, read for forgetfulness and comfort was the Bible he had borrowed from me five years earlier and never returned. I shall always be glad he didn't.

Chapter 10

The Campus Intelligentsia

◄►

One morning when Bronson was feeding the chickens, he missed his beloved guinea hen. He searched all over the farm and did not find it. I milked all the cows, and when I came in to breakfast he announced in a slow, shaking voice that a fox had no doubt gotten away with the missing bird. He was so grief-stricken that he could not eat. He just sat there, dark-faced and brooding. With the best of intentions I suggested that after all the guinea hen would sooner or later have ended up on the Sunday dinner table. "Don't say that," he cried out. More tactfully I reminded him that if he missed the bird so much he could buy another. He glared at me fiercely and muttered something under his breath. Clearly the vanished guinea hen had left a void that nothing could fill, and I wondered whether its disappearance had heightened the man's fear of death.

My suspicion deepened when night after night my sleep was disturbed by his hymn singing. As he never paid me for the extra work I did, I decided to quit the farm and move to the village. From classmates who worked their way through college too I learned that even in winter there were jobs to be had in the village, clearing snow from sidewalks, tending furnace, chopping wood. In spring there was always work for students with farming experience on some near-by farm or planting some professor's or businessman's garden. The standard wage was twenty cents an hour and I figured that if I worked only three hours a day and half or all day Saturday I could earn a large part of my living.

From an elderly invalid widow in the village I rented a room with kitchen privileges for four dollars a month. I would save money by boarding myself as so many other students were doing.

I gave Bronson a week's notice and reminded him of the wages he owed me. He didn't say anything. But while I was at classes he flung my books and clothes into my trunk, drove to town, and dumped the trunk on the porch of my new lodging. When I came back to the farm I found myself evicted. Bronson offered no explanation and promised to pay the money he owed me as soon as he received his next milk check. He still owes me the money. Soon afterwards he sold the farm and moved away and that was the last I heard of him.

Once settled in the village I felt grateful to the fox that had eaten the guinea hen and hastened my release from the farm. I was beginning a new life, no longer burdened by time-consuming chores seven days a week. I was surprised at how cheaply I could live by making my own meals. Food prices in those times seem incredible now: a quart of milk, fresh from the cow, cost five cents; eggs, fresh from the nest, twenty cents a dozen; butter, twenty-five cents a pound; a five-pound bag of corn meal for mush, which I ate with milk and molasses, twenty cents; beans, which I had learned to bake while in North Brookfield, as cheap as corn meal; ground meat, fifteen cents a pound; cookies from the bakery, a penny apiece, and a whole pie, ten cents; apples for baking cost nothing—a farmer offered me a bushel of Northern Spies for sorting his apples.

I lived comfortably on some three dollars a week. Nowadays milk alone would cost more than half as much as I spent on all my groceries, including an occasional molasses cookie and a piece of apple pie.

Living closer to the campus, I had time to visit back and forth with students. I was learning more and more about them. What especially interested me was that here even sons of farmers and ministers rarely judged a man in terms of "character." Instead, they judged him by his personality. I never had heard farmers or the elder appraise anyone in terms of personality.

Personality didn't necessarily have to do with character, nor with looks, nor the way a man dressed; the varsity letter on his sweater didn't automatically confer it on him. Nor did family origin, wealth, or scholastic standing. Either a fellow had personality or he didn't. If he had it, fraternities might compete for his membership.

No dictionary defined "personality" to fit the sense in which the students used it. "He is not much to look at," a girl was quoted as saying about a student, "but how he can turn on the personality"; or "she may not be so cute," a student said about a girl, "but she's a personality kid."

As nearly as I understood the term, it was expressive of something inside a fellow that shone out of his face, that vibrated in his voice, that breathed out of his manner, of the way he walked, stood, shook hands, smiled, talked and impressed and attracted people, including, of course, girls. It was not charm either. Charm was supposedly a feminine attribute and no student would use the word to describe another.

The one Negro in my class, a theological student and son of a poor Baptist minister in Alabama, was admired for his personality. The son of a wealthy brewer, handsome and a flashy dresser, didn't earn the accolade. Neither did a mathematics shark nor a celebrated football player. And so it went.

"A funny thing about Clausen," a classmate said to me. "He has so much personality he can join any fraternity he wants, but he won't do it."

"Why not?"

"He doesn't believe in fraternities. He doesn't think it is right for some students to enjoy privileges denied to others."

At the time I was not interested in fraternities. The fraternity men I knew never behaved like privileged persons in classroom or on the campus. In their houses they might eat better food than I did, hold weekend parties to which they invited out-of-town girls, an enviable privilege in a small and isolated man's college, but in their attitude toward me they behaved like anybody else. Nobody spoke of any fraternity or any group of students as "the right crowd." The "right" and "wrong crowd" Owen Johnson writes of in his *Stover at Yale* were virtually unknown in the rural college of Madison County, for the simple reason that most of the students came from farms and small towns and were innocent of the social distinctions and snobberies of the metropolis or of the self-assumed superiorities of the wealthy and elite in the smaller communities.

But that so exceptionally brilliant and personable a student as Clausen, who cheered for the team as enthusiastically as anyone, should out of moral considerations challenge the fraternity system didn't fit the pattern of conformity that I had ascribed to college men. Here was a rebel.

I cultivated Clausen and soon discovered that he was exceptional in other ways. Son of a Binghamton physician of German origin, he grew up in a home that cherished some of the finest aspects of German civilization. Students might frown on the reading of novels and poetry as "feminine" diversions, but Clausen read both. He loved music, another supposedly "feminine" indulgence. (Why this sensitiveness to "feminine" contamination in a country where men and women were such "good pals," more so than in any country in the world, I couldn't begin to fathom.) Nor was Clausen ashamed of sentiment, still another supposedly "feminine" weakness. On our hikes across hills and fields, he spoke of a favorite poem or novel as feelingly as a Russian student might. Profoundly religious, never missing a Sunday service, he was preparing for the ministry, and though a fervent Baptist, he was above sectarianism. Nor did he draw boundaries between religion and other fields of human knowledge; ideas wherever they came from never clashed with but only enriched his religious thinking. His intellectual interests were broader than mine and I admired and envied his lucid and vivid speech. He had the gift of easily and cheerfully identifying himself with others. On Saturdays we often hiked to North Brookfield and visited my farm friends. He always felt at home with them, readily fell in with their interests, their chatter, though he had never in his life hitched up a horse or handled a hoe. To me he was the ideal college student, the youth who was constantly exploring the world about him and exploring himself and others in the process.

Lionel Edie, who until his ultimely death had attained distinction as an economic analyst whose list of clients read like a *Who's Who* in American finance and industry, was another classmate who impressed me with the diversity of his intellectual interests, though unlike Clausen, he was unmoved by imaginative works and scoffed at fine writing as "pure bosh." A farmer's son who earned his living as a tree surgeon, he was all for facts and logic. Interested in politics and economics, he analyzed and discussed these subjects with the calm and sobriety with which he examined diseased trees. He was pure intellect, and there wasn't a political and economic issue in American life, however remote from class studies, that didn't engage his attention or on which he shrank from expressing his decisive views. He might have been preparing to be a future congressman or senator, so ready was he to defend his opinions against any and all challengers. Yet he had a great sense of fun and a liking for practical jokes. A visit to his room combined fun with serious discussion.

A still greater surprise was a classmate by the name of Ellwood Gates, who years later became head of the German department at Colgate. Light-haired and blue-eyed, he looked so slight and young and shy that I thought knee pants would be more fitting for him than trousers. Though brilliant in classroom work, he was so quiet-voiced, so unassuming, so withdrawn, that I imagined him to be unsociable or to feel out of place among older students.

One Sunday evening as we were coming out together from a travel lecture before the Christian Endeavor Society of the Baptist church, he suggested we go for a walk. We discussed the lecture, courses, professors, and the recent Colgate-Trinity game. I told him I had had no desire to see it. To my astonishment he said that neither had he. He said that on the day of the game, in answer to a friend's insistence that he show up in the cheering section, he replied with one word, "Bunk!" and had gone off to work on his family farm some six miles away from the campus.

I wasn't the only heretic in college. Though Gates loved football as I didn't—not yet—he wasn't swept into the emotional frenzy that seized the campus during the season. He did his own thinking, even about such a sacrosanct institution as football. When I remarked that students must have thought me a pain in the neck because of my unconventional views, he replied, "Don't you think it; you're yeast in the porridge."

Then I met the greatest rebel of them all. He was a junior named Tom Healy, now an eminent Wall Street lawyer. Students were allowed to browse at will in the stacks of the library, and often when I went there, I would see Healy standing before a stack so deeply absorbed in a book that though I was curious about him I didn't dare to speak to him. He never sat at a table by the window like other students, preferring to do his reading leaning against a stack, as though the immediate proximity to books heightened his pleasure. Here, I thought, was a dedicated bookworm, openly defying opprobrium and seemingly determined to read through the library stack by stack, as farmers hoed a cornfield row by row.

One day we got to talking. A pale-faced, loose-jointed youth, he was as careless of attire as I was; his hand was as soft as a girl's, his cinnamon-colored hair straggled over his forehead, and his deep-blue eyes sparkled with a boyish mischievousness. He too was "agin" many things in college and didn't care who knew it. He was against physical exercise, against working one's way through college, against trigonometry, which he took twice and flunked twice; and for two years had engaged in a one man strike against compulsory chapel attendance, the first time this had ever happened since the founding of the college. He had come to Colgate, he contended, to cultivate his mind and didn't need anybody's help to look after his soul. To his bitter regret he had to abandon the strike because he had forfeited so many credits that his graduation was in jeopardy. He assured me that though he now attended chapel services, he never sang any hymns and never recited the Lord's Prayer—in his heart, he was still on strike!

Once I came to know my fellow students outside the classroom, I discovered that some of them, though a small minority, reached out for ideas beyond the campus and beyond the classroom. Like the rest, they had their practical goals in life, but their aspirations went beyond material satisfactions and social pleasures.

I am writing these lines at a time when disturbances in colleges all over the country have stirred students and professors into a reappraisal of higher education in America. "The blunt fact is," writes James H. Bollington, professor of history at Princeton, "that liberal education is dead. Its humanistic heartbeat has failed and rigor mortis is setting in throughout the giant educational system." (*Life*, May 24, 1968). Further on, the professor quotes the editor of the Columbia *Spectator* as saying, "We have just not been given the passionate sense of the excitement of intellectual life around here." The professor also quotes a columnist of the *Michigan Daily* (Michigan University): "This institution has dismally failed to inculcate in most of its undergraduates, at least, anything approaching an intellectual appetite."

However justified these remarks, the fact is that there always was in every American college, a minority, however small, of intellectually restless and inquiring students who revered the things of the mind as much as did European students.

Having discovered this minority on the campus, life became more interesting and more exciting. Meanwhile, I was clearing my entrance requirements and was getting high marks in my courses. The dean was pleased, and I felt grateful to him for having set aside technicalities and admitted me to college. Best of all, the president awarded me a scholarship for my tuition, which was only sixty dollars a year. (Tuition is $2250 now.) Also, I was beginning to doubt the wisdom of transferring to Cornell the next autumn, though I still could think of no career that would be as satisfying as farming.

Then one day Tommy called me into his office. I was both pleased and apprehensive as I stood before him, and observing my uneasiness he pushed a chair my way and invited me to sit down. He asked what I planned to do when I left college and I told him I had set my mind on an agricultural career. For a few minutes he didn't say anything, but I saw him leafing the pages of my latest composition.

"D'you like reading?" he asked.

"Yes, very much," I answered. He asked what books I read and I told him.

Then he complimented me on my compositions—I always had something to say and said it clearly and concretely. Of course, he went on, I had had an unusually rich experience, having come from a Russian village to New York, then to an upstate farm, and now to college, and subjects for compositions obviously came easily. Someday, he continued, it might be worth considering my experience as subject for a book. But I must go on reading, and I must enroll in Dr. Crawshaw's courses in English literature. Reading the great books would help me in my writing. Of course, farming was an honorable occupation. But it was sweating work, and if some day I would toil as hard with pen and paper, I might turn out a manuscript that would be accepted for publication.

I walked out of Tommy's office with my head in a whirl. To be a writer, to have a book published under my own name—my imagination soared and soared. But no, it was impossible, no mat-

ter how rich and varied my life experience. And yet—the irony
of it—the Cornell registrar hadn't considered me fit for the higher
learning about cows and corn! What a joke on him, and how
wise the Baptist elder had been to steer me to a college that
would show "proper Christian understanding" of my problem.

But could Tommy really have meant what he had said? How
could I doubt his words—he a learned man and a senator in Albany, a Republican senator, too serious and too busy a man to invite me into his office and plant a new idea in my mind, if he
didn't mean it? An intoxicating idea, which had never even occurred to me. No, Tommy couldn't have been deluding me. But
I did like farming, and must I really abandon all thought of an
agricultural career? I had faith enough in myself to feel certain
of success in farming. But in writing I was certain of nothing. All
Tommy had said was that if I sweated over pen and paper as I
would over plow and hoe, I might achieve the reward of publication. No assurance and no guarantee, and a hard road ahead.
A wild idea but it haunted me, and my once firm resolve to study
agriculture was shaken.

Then one Sunday Dr. Crawshaw substituted for Tommy as
teacher of the college men's Sunday school class. This was the first
time I heard him and it proved a decisive moment in my life.

The head of the department of English literature was outwardly
unprepossessing. He walked all shrunken together as though he
were perpetually cold. Of medium height, pale-faced, round-
shouldered, with a narrow chest, he had a quick shuffling gait
as though in a hurry to get under cover and seclude himself
from the world. Other professors walked sociably with students
down the shaded willow path and the village sidewalks; Craw
rarely did. When I learned that his hearing was so seriously im-
paired that conversation in the street was difficult, I understood
the reason for his aloofness. But in chapel he bore no resemblance
to the shrunken being who seemed always in a hurry to be off
by himself. The bared head made all the difference in his appearance. It was large and shapely, crowned with a mass of
thick dark reddish-glinted hair neatly brushed back, not a strand
out of place. There was an air of repose about his handsome
sensitive face, the full reddish mustache and the neatly trimmed
Vandyke beard giving it a somberness that was softened by his

fine eyes. Yet there was nothing particularly distinguished about him, nothing to suggest the great scholar and the campus idol.

On that Sunday he was more the teacher of literature than gospel expositor. Like Tommy, he made us conscious of the Bible as literature, illustrating his interpretations with readings from the Old and the New Testament. It was an enthralling performance.

Craw was not the robust man that Tommy was. His voice was thinner, but with deeper organlike overtones in the lower range. He was not as theatrical as Tommy and gestured less, but he had a greater ability to project emotion. He was the more polished and poetic elocutionist. I doubt if he could make as much drama of the first chapter of the Book of Job as Tommy did, but what a poem he made of the Lord's Prayer, which I remember with particular vividness. We recited it daily in chapel until it had become a routine, spiritless exercise. But the moment Craw uttered "Our Father," he imparted new meaning and majesty to the simple, familiar words.

To study Byron and Keats and Shelley and Tennyson and Swinburne and Shakespeare and other great English poets and dramatists under a man who, by his reading alone, could infuse so much meaning and exaltation into words would be like breaking across new frontiers of the mind and the imagination.

No, I wouldn't miss any of Craw's courses, though I should have to wait until my junior year to qualify for his classes.

The freshman year was drawing to a close. It had been an exciting and adventurous time. I asked my friends what they were planning to do during the summer vacation. Clausen was setting off for the Adirondacks to work as bellhop in a resort hotel. Edie was going home to help his father gather the hay crop, hoe corn, and milk cows. Gates, too, was going back to the family farm. A rich brewer's son, he was striking out for the West to work in the harvest fields. Another classmate was taking off for a coal barge on the Erie Canal.

Work! No task was too menial or too arduous. I shouldn't have been surprised, not after my years on the farm, or after observing students mow lawns, chop wood, shovel coal, wash dishes for a living. Yet somehow I didn't expect so personable and brilliant a student as Clausen to turn bellhop or that such accomplished students as Edie and Gates would sweat out their summer on the land. Least of all did I expect the son of the rich brewer to wander off West, perhaps to stand behind the blower of a threshing machine. But they didn't think of themselves as too good for menial work. Work was work, a dollar was a dollar, however it was earned. Overalls and a bellhop's uniform were as respectable as the swallowtails they wore in debating and oratorical contests. To slip from the one into the other was no disgrace.

So it was in the American college: a student today, a worker tomorrow. Yet in one student on the campus who could never help comparing the Old World to the New, it aroused a fresh sense of wonder. He would remember it vividly in the years to come, in all his travels in Europe, Asia, and Africa, in all his discussions with students in Egypt, Iran, Iraq, Poland, Czechoslovakia, and other countries, particularly in Russia. How incredulous Soviet students would be when they heard him say that a rich capitalist's son, a classmate of his, had toiled in the harvest fields like an ordinary muzhik or *kolhoznik* or that the most brilliant student in his class, son of a physician, a *bourzhui* of *bourzhuis*, carried suitcases and fetched pitchers of ice water in a hotel like an ordinary house servant!

I too went off to spend the summer on a farm, this time in the rich dairy country of Jefferson County. Wages there for an experienced farm hand were the highest in the state, fifty dollars a month and board and room.

Chapter 11

A Girl and Football

◄►

In Jefferson County I hired out to a farmer called George Smith, an unsmiling, unsociable man in his late thirties who lived some three miles away from the town of Antwerp, then famed for the soft cheeses manufactured at the huge Baumert factory to which farmers sold their milk.

The land here was more level than in the Brookfield country, the soil was richer, the crops more specialized: far less corn and more grasses, including alfalfa and clover. Cows were more productive and farmers more prosperous. There were about half a dozen families in the neighborhood of the farm where I worked, all living in spacious, fresh-painted two-story houses, all cultivating big gardens and fine orchards.

The man who hired me didn't own his farm, but worked it on shares. Here the farmers, unlike those in North Brookfield, ate more beef than pork, a measure of their greater prosperity and higher spending power. On the eve of the Fourth of July, when the haying season began, George Smith put a barrel of beer into the ice house. Haying, he had told me, would last at least a month, so during the days of toil and sweat, we could refresh ourselves, not with cold well water or homemade cider as farmers in North Brookfield did, but with cold beer fresh from the barrel. This too signified a higher spending power than among the farmers I had known. Remembering Elder Mattison and his hellfire sermons against beer drinking, I was curious whether the minister of Smith's church also anathematized beer. Not at all, Smith replied. In rich haying country, men working in the fields sweated all the time and only beer could slake their thirst. Besides, it was not a minister's business what they drank. Elder Mattison's strictures had not penetrated here.

I grew even more aware of this at the party given by a neighboring farmer's son, Gordon Kellogg, on the evening of Independence Day. A pink-cheeked, jolly youth of about my own age, Gordon introduced me to his sister and the dozen or so young people gathered in the parlor by first names only. Gordon's informality at once put me at ease with the others. We played games and then, to my astonishment, there was dancing, which never happened in North Brookfield.

But, alas, I could not dance American dances. The only dance I knew was a polka, which in my native Russian village children learned almost as soon as they learned to walk. But a girl named Lucy, a high school graduate already enrolled in the Potsdam Normal School (a New York State University teachers' college now), was determined to make me dance. An attractive girl with thick dark hair and big brown eyes, she teased and importuned me until tremblingly I paired off with her. I have forgotten what dance she tried to teach me, but I recall that all I could do was to hop around as in a polka. This amused Lucy and the others so that they too started hopping about in polka fashion. The dance ended in an uproar of merriment and I felt flattered that the muzhik dance I had learned as a child had struck the fancy of the young farm people.

I joined in the cheerful chatter that followed and after refreshments had been handed around—sandwiches, cake, and lemonade—we paired off and went walking in the orchard behind the house. I chose Lucy, and much to my surprise and delight the cat had not got my tongue this time. Maybe my year in college had shaken me out of the numbness that had previously kept me baffled and tongue-tied whenever I found myself alone with an American girl. Or maybe there was something in Lucy's personality—her lightness of spirit, her eagerness to please and be pleased—that had liberated me from my usual shyness. Anyway, we became so happily engrossed in each other that we were the last couple to return to the house. The suspicious glances we drew disconcerted me, but Lucy remained completely composed. Yet for me the long walk was an experience to be remembered and cherished. At last I had found my tongue or my "line," as students called it in those days, with an American girl.

Next to apple picking, I liked haying the best of any work on the farm. We might be working in a broiling sun, but it was clean work, and I know of no sweeter or more bracing fragrance than that of drying hay, a fragrance that lasts throughout the haying season and that sweetens every breath of air one inhales, even up in one's bedroom if the window is open. We and our neighbors had so much hay to cut that we often worked after supper and even on Sundays. Though I did not mind the work, I did not feel happy in the Smith home. I had no complaint against the way I was treated. I had a large room to myself and the food was excellent. But George and his wife were dull unsociable people and even during meals we did not talk much. They never visited back and forth with their neighbors and we were so busy haying that I had little time to call on the eminently sociable Kelloggs or to see Lucy again. She lived in Philadelphia, New York, only a short distance from Antwerp. But there was no time to go there, even on Saturday evenings.

Then one day toward the end of haying, Gordon Kellogg came to invite me to another party at his home in celebration of the end of haying. Yes, Lucy, who was his sister's friend, would be there. The prospect thrilled me and I promised Gordon I would come, whether our haying was finished or not. I might come late, but I would come.

Gordon, who knew that I had hired out to Smith for the haying season only, informed me that if I wished to stay in the neighborhood, the Conklins, a short distance away, would hire me. Mr. Conklin, it seemed, didn't care for farming; he was in the insurance business. But Mrs. Conklin, who managed the farm, was a wonderful woman.

I went to the party at the Kelloggs and it was exciting to see Lucy again. A brunette of eighteen, she wore a red dress that was very becoming, and to me she stood out as the most captivating girl at the party. Impatiently I waited for the time when we would pair off and go strolling in the orchard. The trepidation I had experienced during my years in North Brookfield at the prospect of facing a girl alone now yielded to exhilaration. The three years difference in our age and my much greater maturity were of no consequence, and so when we found ourselves again in the orchard conversation did not flag though I don't remember what we talked about. All I do remember is that we petted and kissed, and I am sure that the other couples in the dark orchard were doing the same. That was why years later when I read in Scott Fitzgerald's *This Side of Paradise* that the "petting party" was a "current American phenomenon," I could only be amused. Among farm boys and girls the "petting party" was as established an institution as the horse and buggy and church socials.

Except for the Smiths, who bored me and with whom I failed to establish any relationship however formal, I had been lucky in the farm families I had worked for. I loved the feeling of home these families provided, doubtless because I had had such a wretched home life during my years in New York. But I was exceptionally lucky when, after leaving the Smiths, I went to work for the Conklins. Mr. Conklin, as Gordon had told me, did not bother with farming. A pale, slender man of medium height, he never stayed out in the sun long enough to brown his face. Mrs. Conklin was one of the most remarkable farm women I had known. A handsome woman of forty, neither plump nor slender, she was a university graduate and mother of five children, the youngest a squalling baby, the oldest a boy about eight or nine; the others were girls a year or two apart. There was another hired man there, Bill Brown, a man in the fifties whose wife and daughter, a high school girl, lived in Antwerp. Bill like myself had the highest admiration for the efficiency with which this educated woman managed the farm and for the gentleness with which she managed her family. I never heard her scold any of her children, yet they were remarkably well-behaved, and Bill and I enjoyed enormously the gay patter at mealtime. Dinner, especially on Sundays, a leisurely and elaborate affair in those days, was something to look forward to. Mr. Conklin whose business was in Antwerp, was always home for Sunday dinner. Yet it was not he, but the children—dressed in their best, always easy to talk to, to entertain, and to be entertained by—and their warm-hearted mother who made the event the gracious experience it was for the stranger in their midst. I came to love these people more than any other farm family I lived with; but at last my time ran out and I returned to college for my sophomore year.

On arriving in Hamilton I was conscious that my small adven-

tures in rural Jefferson County, notably my acquaintance with
Lucy and my stay with the Conklins, had livened and mellowed
me. I was a year older and perhaps somewhat more sophisticated
and more ready for the lighter side of student life than I had been
as a freshman.

Amory Blaine, hero of Scott Fitzgerald's *This Side of Paradise*,
on the conclusion of his sophomore year, exclaims to a classmate,
"Hasn't this year been slick?" Fitzgerald's college generation cor-
responds roughly to my own. And as I look back on my sophomore year I can truly say it was not only "slick" but the liveliest
and most adventurous in the life of the student in those faraway
and untroubled times. Years ago, in an unpublished manuscript,
I wrote:

"As a sophomore you rejoiced that you were no longer a freshman, no longer anybody's underdog. You felt emancipated, and
the world was your oyster. You were as much on your own as the
junior and the senior, though you weren't as settled as the junior
nor as concerned or beguiled by thoughts of life after college as
was the senior. The stretch of three years ahead was an age and
you allowed no thought of the problems and responsibilities of the
future to intrude on the pleasures and the adventures of the
moment.

"You were the wise fool and you gloried in it. You felt a glow
you never felt as a freshman and would never feel as an upperclassman. If you couldn't quite make up your mind that you didn't
run the college, you were beyond persuasion that the college
could run itself without your unsolicited and always secret assistance, first and foremost in your self-assumed lordship over 'the
peevie freshman' as a college song dubbed the first year man. You
cherished the ceremonials and juvenilities of the campus tribalism as you never could while a freshman and never would as an
upperclassman. Yet you became critical of many a situation you
had unquestioningly accepted as a freshman—uplift talks in
chapel, courses of study, the personalities of the professors, the
vagaries of the big shots on the campus, if they strutted their
bigness as some of them did. I am not speaking of the varsity
athletes or the varsity debaters. Their deeds spoke for them to
impress others, especially girls. I am speaking of the chore boys—
the scrubs and flunkies who craved the limelight as the limelight

never craved them and whose sacrifices for the glory of the fraternity or the college didn't always earn them even a numeral for their sweaters.

"As a sophomore you were more mature than the freshman, but you refused to admit it even to yourself. You were more hell-bent on mischief than you were likely ever again to be. At Colgate if you won grace with the outgoing TNEs, they honored you secretly and solemnly by entrusting to you the sacred rite of wielding a paddle over the behind of the self-willed and disagreeable freshman. It was your day of folly and fun, even if deep inside yourself you knew that your primary purpose in college was your studies."

I was amazed to find that on my return to college as a sophomore I had shaken off my old diffidence and become positively genial. A classmate who had reason to believe that I was above such campus frivolities as the annual "salt rush," when freshmen and sophomores, armed with handfuls of salt rushed at one another for a wrestling match, cautiously inquired whether I would lend my work-hardened muscles to licking the frosh. Rather to my own surprise I consented and thoroughly enjoyed my part in the shindy.

Shortly afterwards, during chapel hour a classmate whispered that the freshmen were set to sneak off for their annual banquet and would I cut the next class and help round them up and bind them to trees or chuck them into some cellar. Freshmen mustn't be permitted to outsmart sophomores. Several parties of us searched for freshmen all over the campus and down in the village, everywhere, it seemed, except in the private quarters of professors. We found no freshmen and rumor had it that some cunning first-year man had deliberately spread a false report to make apes of sophomores. But who was the knave? Even I wanted to know and for a perverse reason. I should have shaken the man's hand for his triumphant deception. But the secret was never uncovered, and when finally the freshmen class slipped out of town for their banquet, the sophomores despite all their vigilance were still wondering when the freshmen would hold their traditional feast. Apes again!

Yet my heretic side still survived, just as theirs did in Tom

Healy and the other non-conformists who still found intellectual comradeship in discussions with kindred spirits, often in the back of Carl Baum's tailor shop in the village.

Once I read in the *Madisonensis,* the college weekly, that freshmen who balked at wearing the babyish beanie were disloyal to the college. My sympathies were all with the non-conformists, even though I myself had lacked their courage. Nevertheless, I did go to the editor and told him what I thought of his puerile editorial.

Intrigued by my brashness, he drew me into a discussion in which I mentioned that I had seen several books in the college library that students in Russia were forbidden to read, but which few of our students had bothered to look into. To my astonishment he asked me to write a piece on the subject. Let students, he said, know something about college men in your native land; give them something new to think about and get excited over. Write anything you please and let the chips fall where they may.

I wrote the piece and the editor spread it over a whole page in the tabloid-sized journal. I carefully refrained from drawing direct comparisons between Russian and American college men. Brash as I was, I wasn't brash enough to aim any direct charges of anti-intellectualism at my fellow students. But the implied reproach for their not stretching their minds beyond classroom requirements didn't escape attention. Discussions ensued during walks on the campus and at bull sessions. Varied, profuse, and contradictory were the comments. I was wrong. I was right. I exaggerated. I didn't understand American college men—they did more thinking than I imagined, only they didn't talk about their ideas: they might brag about wowing a girl, but would keep mum about being a shark in mathematics or Greek. I didn't hear a word of resentment nor a single charge that I was an intellectual show-off. The unmistakable implication in my article that unlike Russian students they had no passion for ideas was received with perfect good humor.

As a consequence of my unexpected debut in college journalism, I drew the attention of the more intellectually minded upperclassmen. They invited me around and engaged me in discussions on subjects other than football and girls. One of these upperclassmen pointed out to me an aspect of the American mind the full significance of which I did not grasp until years later when I returned to Russia and began writing on the Bolshevik Revolution.

Duck Conrad was his name. He was a senior studying for the Baptist ministry. Outwardly he appeared more like the humorless bookworm students derided than the man of winning personality they admired. He was slight of build and round-shouldered. He wore large horn-rimmed glasses and was careless of dress. But he was the most brilliant debater in college and his string of victories in intercollegiate contests won him high acclaim on the campus. He was credited with such fabulous powers of persuasion that legend had it he had once gone to the Madison County fair and sold to farmers tracts of land—on the moon. He was one of those campus characters who become myths that survive their college years.

Duck invited me to his fraternity house and together with Carl Miller, a fraternity brother, we sat down to a discussion on the subject of the American college man's unresponsiveness to the challenge of ideas. Duck admitted that with some exceptions this indifference was the rule; that few students cared much for books and seldom read any but those assigned. Reading they more often regarded as a chore than a pleasure. But when these students left college, they left their mental laziness behind them. They *did* things: went into law, medicine, engineering, business, other professions. They built factories, railroads, bridges, power plants. They did a lot of strenuous thinking because they had to, only they related their thinking to practical accomplishments. To them ideas weren't ends in themselves, but means to an end. Ideas were ideas, whether of the man who wrote a novel or of the man who invented a machine. They didn't come out of a void. They came out of a creative mind; and the American mind, rooted in a pioneering tradition, dedicated itself to practical achievement and material reward, which made the mind no less creative than the mind of the man who dealt in ideas for their own sake, for the pure intellectual pleasure they gave.

In 1957, the year of the Sputnik, a distinguished American scientist—Dr. William Barkerhead of the Bell Telephone Research Laboratories—said much the same thing. Americans, he declared, had profound respect "for what's really the end point of brainpower: the automobile, the electric light, television, etc. But they have disdain and even distrust for the actual origin of these things, every one of which came out of some individual brainpower." He ascribed it all to "a fundamental anti-intellectualism."

However, American genius for practical achievement was no new story to me. I had heard of it in my Russian school days. I had marveled at it during my years on the farm. The Yankee farmer's "hang of things" had been an exciting discovery, even in such a simple chore as milking cows, where the easy process of hand pumping was used instead of the arduous Russian method of finger stripping, which is still in vogue on Soviet farms not yet equipped with milking machines.

But from college men I expected more than dedication to the gospel of go-getting, of action and material achievement. I could not rid myself of my Old World heritage of valuing the cultivation of the mind for its own sake, rather than as an instrument of material advancement. Actually, my interlocutors didn't attempt to disabuse me of my exaggerated notion of the intellectual function of the American college. But they did sharpen my understanding of the American college as it was. The new country had evolved its own philosophy of life in which mind and matter, ideas and results were inextricably interwoven. Not meditation and doubt, but action and optimism were in the blood of the American people. Why then expect college men to rise above this level?

In those times it couldn't have occurred to anybody in the world that it would be the Russia out of which I had come, spectacularly changed by the Bolshevik Revolution, that would proclaim this very gospel for the skills and achievements that came out of it more enthusiastically than any nation on earth. European intellectuals might mock (and still do) American dedication to technology and material achievement as the destroyer of cherished civilized values, threatening the dehumanization of man. But the Russian Bolsheviks seized on this gospel of material progress. Despite their hatred of capitalism, Lenin, Trotsky, Stalin, Zhdanov, Bukharin, and other giants of the Revolution perceived in it, and in the spirit of enterprise that it fostered, an indispensable weapon in their crusade for the rebuilding of Russia and converting it into the industrial giant it has since become.

In 1924, before he became the all-powerful Kremlin dictator, Stalin bluntly told the Bolsheviks that their revolutionary ardor "has all the chances of degenerating into empty revolutionary phrase-mongering if it isn't fused with American efficiency of work, with that indomitable spirit that neither knows nor is deterred by obstacles, that pushes on with businesslike perseverance until every barrier is overcome, that must under all circumstances go through a task once it was started."

For over fifty years the Soviets have struggled to "catch up with and surpass" American industrial and agricultural achievement, first and foremost in the productivity of labor without which, according to Kremlin doctrine, Communism can never be achieved. On the third of July, 1968, Mr. Brezhnev, the Party overlord in the Kremlin, in a burst of fury, denounced the United States as "a rotten, degrading, decomposing society." Nevertheless, the gap between American and Soviet labor productivity still remains. In the June 1968 issue of *Molodoy Komunist* (Young Communist), a Professor L. Blyakhman, informs his readers that labor productivity in American industry is two and a half times higher than in the Soviet Union; in agriculture, it is three times higher.

I would not seriously disagree with the professor on his figure for Soviet industry, but for Soviet agriculture, which for over forty years I have observed more intimately than perhaps any other foreigner, the professor is hopelessly wrong. The American farm worker is at least *six* times as productive as the Soviet farm worker. This is not the place to analyze the conditions that make it impossible for the Soviet Union under their present type of leadership to catch up with America in productivity of labor. To me the indisputable fact is that only under a radical shift of leadership and policy can the Kremlin hope, and no more than hope, to come close to American labor productivity in industry or agriculture.

Meanwhile, J. J. Servan-Schreiber, in *The American Challenge*, which has been a sensation in Western Europe and would be in Russia were it ever translated, warns European capitalists that unless they get together and imbue themselves with the spirit of American enterprise, American technology and American business management, they run the risk of losing control of their enterprises to the more farseeing and more enterprising American business circles.

I bring up the subjects of productivity of labor in Russia and of Servan-Schreiber's warning to European businessmen for the purpose of emphasizing the interpretation of the American mind as presented to me long ago by a student named Duck Conrad. From personal experience I had learned that it applied to American farmers, but that it also applied to American college students had to be pointed out to me.

Conditions being what they were, only a small minority of Colgate students rose above the prevailing apathy toward things of the mind and imagination. These few were unimpressed by the image of the successful man—the man who by his polish (a favorite word), his skills, his wits, his energies carved himself a comfortable niche in the world. But it was the minority which gave intellectual luster to the campus and it was wonderful to be with them, whether in Carl Baum's tailor shop or in some student's room where we talked endlessly of books, ideas, movements, purposes in life, the strivings of man to attain his highest potentialities. There may not have been much realism in these discussions, but there was no end of stimulation and exhilaration. We may have been only dreamers, but it was beautiful to dream in those prosaic and tranquil times.

In my freshman year I responded to visiting chapel orators who exhorted us to prepare ourselves for "service to mankind," "leadership in democracy," "dedication to Christian ideals." At best these exhortations were inspirational with little or no intellectual content, and at the time they seemed uplifting, so strong was their emotional appeal. But by my sophomore year they sounded repetitiously trite, hollow, and dull. It was always a relief to hear a missionary from some faraway land tell of his adventures among a strange and primitive people. I was not the only one in my class who preferred missionaries to ministers or to devout-minded businessmen as chapel speakers. Nor was I the only one who grew increasingly critical of the frequent laments of chapel orators, more frequent for some reason than in my freshman year, over the sins of the "young generation."

We didn't think we were as bad a lot as the visiting sermonizers, especially ministers, imagined. We weren't deliberately racing to damnation, even if some of us imbibed on occasion more firewater than was good for us or sneaked off during a weekend to Albany or Utica in search of "carnal pleasure." The most profane four-letter words in our vocabulary were "hell" and "damn," though ministerial students never ventured more than "darn" and "doggone." The obscenities I had heard among farmers I never heard on the campus. If a divinity student was shocked by the mild profanity then in vogue, there was nothing he could do about it. One freshman, a brilliant student preparing for the Baptist ministry, was so grieved to hear a sophomore fraternity brother sprinkle his conversation with "damns" that one evening he called the sinning brother aside and admonished him for his bad language. The sophomore, instead of telling the freshman to "go climb a tree," delivered a little sermon of his own. "You pray a lot," he said, "and I swear a lot. But if the truth were known, neither means much."

A story went around the campus about the idolized Dr. Crawshaw that gave comfort to the profane-mouthed students. The professor had received a book titled *Come to Jesus* by a theologian with literary aspirations who asked for the professor's frank opinion of the work. Unimpressed by either its literary quality or its religious profundity, the professor wrote back he couldn't in all conscience say that he liked the book. The enraged theologian responded to this with notable lack of Christian humility in a curt note that read: "You can go to hell!" Dr. Crawshaw went around the campus saying that the author of *Come to Jesus* seemed of two minds as to where he wanted his critic to go.

There was another professor who grew as weary of the laments of visiting chapel orators over the wicked ways of the young generation as did the students. His name was Dr. Andrews, but we called him "Kai Gar." He taught Greek language and literature and gave courses in art. The oldest man on the faculty, he was also the most distinguished-looking. He was the only professor who always wore a frock coat; he cultivated impressive muttonchop whiskers; he walked with a slow, measured tread, his hands cupped together over his breast as though absorbed in deep meditation, though he never failed to greet any passing students.

Other professors might address them as "boys," but Kai Gar always addressed them as "young gentlemen." He was the aristocrat who was the true democrat, with a vein of rich irony in his mental make-up. A story circulated on the campus that once as he was preparing to leave for Paris, a colleague asked him whether his wife was going with him. His reply was "D'you take a sandwich to a banquet?"

One morning several days after a visiting sermonizer attempted, vainly I thought, to chill our spines with tales of the sins of the younger generation, especially of those who consorted with "fallen women," Kai Gar addressed us in chapel. His opening remarks I remember almost word for word. "Young gentlemen," he began, "you often hear wise men tell you from this rostrum how wicked your generation is. Be of good cheer. When I was a student wise men said the same thing about my generation, and rest assured that when your sons are in college wise men will tell them how wicked *their* generation is. The younger generation is always wicked to people who forget how young they once were themselves."

We applauded enthusiastically. Here was a prof after our own heart, speaking our language, poking fun at visiting uplifters who eloquently, almost tearfully, despaired of our salvation, here and in the hereafter, unless we stopped saying "hell" and "damn," drawing on a tobacco-filled pipe, sipping a glass of beer, tossing down a tumblerful of whiskey, or—horror of horrors—visiting "a fallen woman," which very few of us did anyway. I never heard these uplifters use the word "whore" or "prostitute"; it was always "the fallen woman"—which, when reported to the tailors in Carl Baum's shop, evoked a derisive guffaw.

Football, football—how I detested the game in my freshman year! I had allowed myself to be persuaded by a junior to attend when Colgate met Hobart. I did not understand the plays, but was repelled by the violence of the playing. A Hobart player got knocked out and for some time he lay on the ground seemingly unconscious. When he recovered he limped off the field on the arms and shoulders of two Hobart attendants. I at once decided that football was stupid and brutal. Colgate defeated Hobart and I was loyal enough to the college to cheer the winners—but this didn't mean that I approved of the game. I was like the tailors in Carl Baum's shop, glad when Colgate won, unmoved when it was trounced; and I firmly resolved never to go near a football field again.

In my sophomore year Colgate resumed "diplomatic relations" with Syracuse University, its bitterest athletic rival. The climax of the football season was the encounter between the two colleges, and day by day the student body was working up a head of steam. Yet I remained indifferent to the speeches, the yells, and the songs calculated to whip up "the fighting spirit" of both team and student body.

Oddly enough, or perhaps only logically, two Irishmen, a classmate named Jimmy Duffy from Detroit and a farmer named Terry Murphy, born in Ireland, though strangers to one another, broke down my resistance to football. Duffy was a devout Catholic who often dropped in on me to discuss religion with a non-Catholic. But as the date of the Colgate-Syracuse game was approaching, he centered his attention on my hostility to football. With pencil and paper he sketched over and over again the mathematical intricacies of the game, explaining that it called not only for hard muscle, but agility of movement, ingenuity of strategy, split-second decisions, brilliance in confusing the enemy and in anticipating his strategy and subterfuges. How could I resist so beautiful and exciting a game, the only student on campus with no college spirit? Shame, shame!

Terry Murphy, a short, stocky, bony-faced Irishman with a hearty laugh, a glib tongue, and a delightful brogue, whose farm was close to the campus, frequently hired me to help with the field work. He was a football fan, and had he been a student he could not have been more excited about the forthcoming Colgate-Syracuse battle. He was shocked when I told him I had no intention of seeing the game. Even farmers like himself, he argued, would no more miss the most exciting event of the year in central New York than leave their corn uncut or their cows unmilked. He scolded me even more eloquently than Jimmy Duffy had, and I finally promised both of them that on the great day I would board the special train for Syracuse.

To prepare me for the event Jimmy insisted that I also attend the pep rally on the eve of the game. The rally was held in the

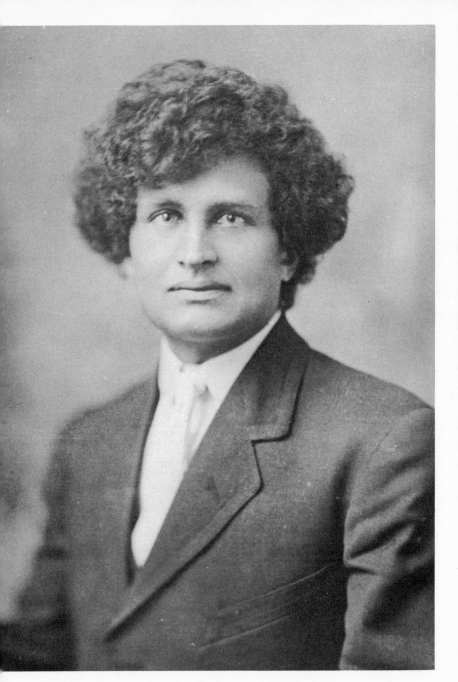

1. Maurice Hindus, the high school student. (*J. B. Wells & Son Co.*)

2. North Brookfield, Madison County, New York, and the Baptist church in Maurice Hindus' time.

3. Jim Moore, the Democrat. (*Hotchkiss*)

4. The campus lake.

Colgate University in Maurice Hindus' time.
(*Colgate University Archives*)

5. A classroom building.

6. Dormitories.

7. Maurice Hindus at Colgate, October 1913. (*Colgate University Archives*)

8. Dr. Russell Conwell, author "Acres of Diamonds" speech. (*Temple University*)

9. Chautauqua tent, local sponsors, and speaker William Jennings Bryan, fourth from left. (Des Moines *Register and Tribune*)

10. Maurice Hindus, the lecturer.

gymnasium and it was packed almost to the roof with students and professors. To my astonishment Dr. Crawshaw, our intellectual idol, was also there. I had not imagined that a scholar of his stature would permit himself to be inveigled into an evening of student frivolities. But here he was, smiling and chatting with the chairman of the rally. He made a few witty remarks on the fun of football and on the glory of victory and got an ovation. Then Bob Cotter, a student from Brooklyn, the head cheerleader, a youth with a puckish face and a booming voice, delivered a memorable oration. The Syracusans, he declared with fervor, were only "bums," and "the gentlemen warriors" from the Chenango Valley (Colgate players) would mop the field with them. Wasn't the color of the Syracuse banner orange, suggestive of yellow, and wasn't the color of the Colgate banner maroon, suggestive of red fighting blood? Of course, of course. By the time the game was over, predicted the fiery cheerleader, the Archbold Stadium (in Syracuse), would turn into a lake of orange juice and would drown the Syracuse "bums." (How the Colgate "gentlemen warriors" would escape the drowning, the redoubtable Brooklynite didn't say.)

I can still see Dr. Crawshaw, whose very name brings to mind a noble period in English literature, lean back in his chair and shake with mirth as though he was hugely amused by the comedy of the rally, perhaps by the comedy of all human life. Nor was my own aplomb left unshaken by the emotion generated by the gathering. The presence of Dr. Crawshaw, whom I had not yet met, snuffed out the last flicker of guilt in me for surrendering to the mass frenzy. I joined in the yelling and the singing, much to the delight of Jimmy Duffy.

Meanwhile the editor of the college paper, who had learned that I was going to Syracuse, asked me to write a piece on the big game. The unexpected request pleased and elated me, but what could I say about a feature of college life that I had openly been deriding and denouncing and had vowed never to be a part of? Wouldn't I make myself the laughing stock of the college? But the editor had ideas of his own. Precisely because I had felt so strongly against the game, I might have something new and interesting to say. As for making a laughing stock of myself, I could laugh back and enjoy the fun as much as others. I must write the piece. I promised that I would.

At the Archbold Stadium, wedged in between fellow students on a tier of cement, I was suddenly overwhelmed by the spectacle that confronted me. Never had I seen so vast an assemblage of people in one place and so rich a display of color. Opposite us were the Syracuse students, the coeds ablaze with orange chrysanthemums, their hats, scarves, blankets, lap robes matching and heightening the color of the Syracuse banner. On our side the girls—alas, how few compared to the feminine throng on the Syracuse benches—had decked themselves with maroon chrysanthemums; their hats, scarves, blankets, lap robes matching and heightening the somber glow of our college banner. No autumn woodland in Madison County could vie with the brilliant pageantry of the scene around me. I was so enraptured that for a few moments I was lost to the sacred duty of joining in the college yell when the maroon-jerseyed players trotted out to the field. Then came the orange-jerseyed players, and cheer followed cheer, now from one side, now from the other, each side striving to outdo the other in lung power.

Legend had it that our college—a little David of some 500 students compared to the Goliath of Syracuse with its 5000 students—always brought a hoodoo with it to the Archbold Stadium that conjured bad luck for the enemy team. Now I saw the man who controlled the hoodoo. He was the tall and dangling Doc Huntington, physical education director of Colgate. On this day of days he had arrayed himself in an ancient yellowed frock coat and a battered bowler hat. He never wore this outfit at any other game or on any other occasion. Doc cherished unshakable faith in its magic power to unleash bad luck on the enemy team.

I had sat in Doc's class in freshman hygiene, compulsory for first-year men, where Doc enlightened us frankly, sensibly, and scientifically on the problems of sex. The sin of sex he left to the sermonizers, who seemed so overpowered by the idea of sexual sin that they couldn't articulate the word "sex." But Doc was a scientist who also taught physiology to pre-med students. He did not mince words, not even when he talked of gonorrhea or syphilis, which in those days were tabooed terms. Doc's language was so harshly realistic that jestingly we spoke of his lectures as "smut"

and even ventured to conclude that he didn't disapprove of sex
affairs, but rather thought them healthy though he strongly cautioned us against venereal infection. But on the day of the big
game Doc transformed himself into a medicine man with as
much faith in the magic of his outlandish regalia as a muzhik
sorcerer in the power of his incantations. Watching Doc stroll
past the players' benches gave me a delightfully eerie and reassuring feeling, and not only me but the throngs all around me including the Madison County farmers who, freshly shaved and
dressed in their Sunday best, shiny with celluloid collar and all,
came to whoop it up for their favorite team.

The teams were so evenly matched that by the end of the first
half, neither had scored. Doc might have left his frock coat and
bowler in the mothballs for all the good they had done. The gen-
eralship of his light-haired, blue-eyed, fleet-footed, keen-minded
son, Ellery, whom a year later Walter Camp would select as
quarterback for his first All-America team and who was to graduate with a Phi Beta Kappa key, failed to shatter the stout-
hearted defenses of the enemy. In muscle, in will, in ingenuity,
in fighting spirit "the bums" refused to be outmatched by "the
gentlemen warriors" from Chenango Valley.

Yet throughout the game it was the ever-changing mood and
movements of the spectators that captured my attention more
than the helmeted men on the muddy turf. The spectators made
exciting theater, enacting the suspense, the anxiety, the disen-
chantment, the triumph that go with drama. They lived their
part with a spontaneity and an ardor that revealed something
new in the temper and personality of Yankees. Now solemn, now
spirited, now groaning with disappointment, now exploding with
joy, now half-hysterical with frustration, they were as unasham-
edly demonstrative as muzhiks at a wedding feast.

It was not until the last few minutes of play in the second half
that Doc's trust in the magic power of his frock coat and crum-
pled bowler was vindicated. In the midst of a play, a Colgate end
discovered that one of his shoelaces had come untied. The player's name was Laje McLaughlin, a short-legged, big-eyed, high-
cheeked, easy-mannered, and jolly Irish lad. Maybe he was acting
on the inspiration of the moment, or maybe the untied shoe was
a prearranged ruse. However it was, Laje, completely ignored

by the Syracuse players, went on fumbling with his shoelace, when suddenly the pigskin flew into the air and soared like a wingless bird in the direction of the deserted end. Forgetting the shoelace, Laje snapped up the ball, wet and muddy as it was, crooked it in his arm and tore off on his short legs into the end zone. The game ended with a Colgate victory, 7–0.

Pandemonium broke loose on our side of the bleachers. Like a roaring Niagara the Colgate rooters, students and farmers, hurled themselves down the tiers of cement. Once on the field, they leaped and danced and yelled and sang at the top of their voices. The delirium of victory turned them into a mass of screaming, whirling dervishes, all but the immigrant sophomore among them, who remembered the editor's assignment. Shoving his way through the milling, rapturous mass, he surveyed the camp of the enemy: dense gloom, impenetrable silence, not a banner fluttering; cheerleaders, players and coaches gone from the field. The golden chrysanthemums faded into the gathering twilight; coeds and their companions, heads bowed, walked slowly, like mourners at a funeral, to the nearest exit.

The thrill of victory died in the observer's heart; the girls and boys of Syracuse University were no longer foes to scorn, but fellow mortals to pity. Fate had struck them a violent blow. So in his piece for the college paper, he commiserated with them and solaced them with the lofty thought that the football game they had lost was like the game of life, victory for one side spelling defeat for the other, the joy of the one paid for by the humiliation of the other.

Corny as these sentiments were, the editor did not delete them.

Chapter 12

The Tailor Shop

◄►

It was inevitable that I should gravitate toward Carl Baum's tailor shop, where a small group of self-taught philosophers gathered to discuss and wrangle over ideas that lay beyond the scope of the Yankee practicality and optimism of those days.

The front of the shop was a quiet, orderly place sparkling with mirrors, where men's clothes and furnishings were sold. Elegant enough to attract the student trade, it was unostentatious enough not to scare off farmers, to whom a shop's "putting on dog" roused suspicions of overcharge.

A high partition separated the salesroom from the workshop; behind the partition tailors and students foregathered to discuss any subject under the sun, particularly how best to deliver mankind from its woes. Young and middle-aged, their intellectual restlessness drew them together to wrestle with old philosophies and new ideologies. A humanitarian elite, they reminded me of the study circles of the Russian intelligentsia.

No rival to the tailor shop existed, not even at intellectually enterprising Hamilton College in the beautiful village of Clinton some seventeen miles away from the village of Hamilton, seat of Colgate. By the accident of nomenclature Hamilton College was in those days, Colgate's—no, not rival, Hamilton would have scoffed at the suggestion—but neighbor, a discomforting neighbor, and most discomforting to the late Alexander Woollcott, one of Hamilton's most celebrated and most dedicated alumni.

I never understood why the two old colleges—Hamilton having been founded in 1812 and Colgate in 1819—were at odds with one another until a classmate informed me that Hamilton professors carried canes, which Colgate professors disdained to do. From this I concluded that Hamilton was a college of blue bloods while Colgate was for commoners and that was why no love was lost between them; nor did long, long acquaintance with the acid-tongued and sentimental Alec Woollcott disabuse me of my original judgment, however unfair in the light of prevailing actualities. No man to keep his pet aversions to himself, Woollcott delighted in throwing it up to me that my college was "a football factory," while his was dedicated to scholarship. In turn, I reminded him that for three successive years during my stay at Colgate, the debating team of "the football factory" had triumphed over his Hamilton intellectuals. Woollcott so genuinely hated Colgate that he never forgave it for excelling in anything, whether football or forensics or for planting itself in the shadow of his beloved college and in a village that bore its name. I pointed out that his college had no business taking the name of the village of my college. But nobody, least of all myself, ever won an argument against the furiously genial Alec; nobody that I knew could parry his verbal rapier thrusts or tire him into silence. He always had the last word.

Yet there was some justification for Woollcott's resentment. Confusing Hamilton College with the village of Hamilton had embarrassed many a pilgrim to his *alma mater*. Having started on a train for Hamilton College, they frequently found themselves stranded in the village of Hamilton, which to Woollcott was enemy territory. It is on record that a student bound for Hamilton College strayed into the wrong Hamilton. On discovering that there was a college right there, he stayed where he was. Four years later he was honored (Woollcott would have said "disgraced") with a Colgate sheepskin and never seemed to have regretted it.

Frequently girls on their way to a prom or a weekend party at Hamilton College, got off the train in Hamilton village; others who arrived safely at Clinton, discovered to their dismay that their trunks were dropped off at the seat of Colgate. By an irony of fate that would have outraged Woollcott, the urn containing his ashes wound up in the place he most detested and where he would have hated to have his remains rest until the end of time. Speedily and respectfully the urn was forwarded to its intended destination, the extra transportation charge of sixty-seven cents duly passed on to Hamilton College. I can think of nothing that would have tormented him more than the knowledge that Colgate had paid for reshipping of his urn to its final resting place on the hilly and beautiful campus of Hamilton College.

Yet in the autumn of 1932, when day after day I piloted the redoubtable Alec through the streets and squares, schools and theaters, houses and clubhouses of Moscow, even prevailing on a gifted and beautiful actress in the Art Theater to allow me to bring him during an intermission to her dressing room, he admitted that Hamilton had never had a meeting place comparable to Carl Baum's tailor shop to foster the intellectual growth of a small body of students. Samuel Hopkins Adams, an alumnus of Hamilton, in his biography of Woollcott writes that in the class of 1909, Woollcott's class, "a group of four . . . whose tastes were intellectual as opposed to—or negligent of—athletics . . . was derisively known as the sorority."

It was Colgate and not Hamilton that was destined to benefit from the intellectual stimulation of the tailor shop when shortly after their arrival in America in 1870 from Heidelberg, Germany, the Baum family, bringing with them an abiding loyalty to the doctrines of August Bebel, the German Socialist leader, bypassed upland Clinton and chose bottomland Hamilton for their home.

Necessarily the charter members of the celebrated tailor shop club were the men who wielded shears, plied needles, pedaled sewing machines, pushed flatirons. Except for Carl, who was born in America, they were all immigrants—Germans, Hungarians, Poles, Austrians, Bohemians (Czechs). Even Carl, though born in America, spoke of himself as "German made," though not of the Germany of the Kaiser and the generals, but the Germany of Bebel and the Socialists.

There were never more than seven tailors, not counting Carl, in the shop at any one time. But they were as restless, inquisitive, idea-hungry, free-minded, and articulate men as I had known. One needed only to cast an idea or opinion before them and they pounced on it with the zest of hungry birds on a handful of crumbs. No wonder we spoke of the shop as Colgate's postgraduate school. If it awarded no credits, issued no diplomas, it stirred the students associated with it into an awareness of ideas and social movements of which they might otherwise barely have heard.

The iconoclastic Tom Healy took me there soon after I had moved from Bronson's farm to the village. But it was not until my sophomore year, when Healy was already a senior, that I began to feel at home in the remarkable tailor shop. Carl was thirty-six years old and looked more like a professor than a tailor. Unlike the other tailors, he was so faultlessly groomed that I assumed he shaved every day. But after reading the first draft of this chapter he inserted a hand-written correction reading, "not true—shaved twice a week, sometimes three times a week—never more." He was an immaculate dresser; Sundays and weekdays he wore collar and tie, even while cutting a suit or ironing pants. Of medium height, with a long sharp-featured face, lighted by brooding gray eyes, he spoke in a deep voice that carried an air of authority. Though he had only a grammar school education he spoke faultless English, another reason I might have assumed he was a professor had it not been for his habit of always chewing on a cigar, lighted or not, something a professor in those days would do only behind drawn curtains.

Carl's father was tall and gaunt, with dark-gray eyes, an unsmiling face, a furrowed brow. Even while sewing buttons, which he usually did standing, he seemed to be ruminating on the teachings of August Bebel whose photograph graced the rear wall of the shop. A weekly shave was good enough for him, and his thick iron-gray hair, beyond control of comb and brush, blew with the wind whenever he ventured outdoors. He was the most intense listener in the shop. But when a debater impugned the logic or challenged the prophecies of August Bebel, he grew unexpectedly loquacious, German words spicing his English, sharp and metallic, like hammer blows. His devotion to Bebel was so intense that he couldn't tolerate even the mention of the Kaiser, Bebel's implacable enemy, for whom he reserved his harshest diatribes.

The liveliest hand in the shop was Gus. Born in Poland of a German father and an English mother, he simplified matters by calling himself a Pole. He was a tall, burly man, red-haired, with a moonlike face and big blue eyes that sparkled like a baby's when he was in good humor and that glowered like an owl's when he wasn't. He was the most accomplished linguist in the community, as fluent in English, German, Russian, and Ukrainian, as in Polish. No professor on the hill conversed in so many languages as Gus. But when the tenets of his socialism were assailed, he grew so vehement that his voice squeaked like the wheel on the ungreased axle of a Polish peasant cart. But there was always somebody ready with a quip or an epigram to cool an inflamed temper. If Gus happened to be the target of the quip, he would pause abruptly without finishing his thought, blink his eyes as though coming out of a trance, then roll back his head and break into a hearty laugh. I never knew a Pole who responded so generously to a witticism at his own expense. If laughing at a joke on oneself is a distinctive American attribute, then Gus was thoroughly Americanized.

It had always seemed to me that Carl hired his tailors not only for their skill with needle and shears, but also for their gift of eloquence and their dedication to some non-existent and ideal social order, not barring the anarchism of Johann Most. It was the paunchy and even-tempered Bohemian tailor, always too serious to laugh, who recounted to me with a preacher's solemnity the story of Most, the amazing German bookbinder who was determined to save the world by abolishing all governments. Obliged to flee from Germany, Most migrated to France. Expelled from France, he found refuge in England, which proved equally inhospitable to his anarchism. Ousted from England, he fled to America, where he freely thundered denunciations of government until the assassination of President McKinley. Even then there was no stopping Most. Put behind bars, he continued to damn all governments and to curse Karl Marx for inventing the monstrosity of the "dictatorship of the proletariat," which to Most meant government gone mad with power.

Though divided as philosophers usually are on many an issue, the tailors were in full accord on one matter: the ideal society that would someday transform all men into brotherly citizens would have to have beer; without beer no society would be worth a tinker's damn. Gus vowed that he would rather live under capitalism with beer than under socialism without beer, to which Carl's father rejoined that if there was no beer there could be no socialism.

Dr. Elmer Burritt Bryan, president of Colgate, a Hoosier from Kokomo, Indiana, though a teetotaler, was charitable toward people who occasionally indulged in light liquors. But he grew uneasy when he learned that some students, despite regulations, were drinking more whiskey than they could carry. Though there were only a few such students, the president threw the support of the college behind the temperance campaign for "local option." The tailors were outraged. They admired the president for his jovial manner and for his democratic spirit. But rights were rights, and the right to refresh themselves with a glass of beer around the corner they would under no circumstances relinquish. No local option for them. The fight was on, president or no president.

To me the battle between the college and the tailors was more a battle of cultures than of persons. The puritanical culture of the president clashed with the Old World culture of the tailors, who were unaccustomed to legal interference with their choice of refreshment. Though born in America, Carl sided with the tailors, and when the president, one of his best customers, sought to solicit his support for local option, he replied politely but firmly, "Dr. Bryan, I like a cool glass of beer once in awhile, and I like it right here in my home town." Gus, who drank less beer than the other tailors but hated the thought of "drying up" the village, warmly applauded Carl's brave words to the leading social figure in the community.

The election came and beer won the day. The tailors rejoiced: the assault on their cherished freedom failed.

What was true of beer was true of smoking. The tailors couldn't understand why professors who smoked—Dr. Crawshaw was one of them—never dared to do so in public. There was something wrong with America when a college professor could smoke only behind drawn curtains.

Once a cadaverous-looking anti-tobacco crusader walked into the shop and presented Gus with a richly illustrated pamphlet depicting the horrors nicotine wrought in body and mind. It was a blood-curdling pamphlet. But observing the visitor's corpselike appearance, Gus asked "D'you smoke?" "No, sir," the crusader triumphantly replied. "You look it," Gus rejoined and handed the pamphlet back to him.

Then somebody broke the news in the tailor shop that on a Saturday evening the formidable DKEs, smoking pipes, would

march in a body to the hotel for a beer. Gus didn't believe it and
rushed to see the procession with his own eyes. He guffawed with
joy and so did the other tailors. There was hope for America, for
the college, for the village when members of the toniest fraternity
marched in a body to assert their right to smoke and to drink
beer.

The moving spirit of the tailor shop was of course young Carl.
One of the most well-informed men in the community, I always
marveled at his expressive English and his flawless enunciation.
"Precisely," the professor of public speaking, couldn't have im-
proved it. Largely self-educated, he was a man of irrepressible
intellectual curiosity and one of the best-read men in the village,
professors included. One only had to mention an interesting book
and he hastened to read it. How so busy a man found time to
read so much was always a mystery to me. When he finished
reading a book, he could summarize it with a perception and clar-
ity that would have won him an A from the exacting Dr.
Crawshaw.

A glutton for ideas, he welcomed every new one that came his
way, whatever its source. One Sunday evening a red-faced, white-
haired phrenologist slipped into a college dormitory and went
from room to room soliciting clients. For twenty-five cents he
gave character readings, probing with long bony fingers the secrets of a student's skull, diagnosing his gifts and failings from
the knobs and hollows. Students were amused and intrigued and
the man did a flourishing business. When Carl heard of it he
sent for books on phrenology, a growing fad of the times. We all
read the books and one evening we engaged in a lively discussion
on the subject, Carl doing most of the talking. He was so carried
away by his argument that he didn't hear a customer walk into
the salesroom. But Tom Healy heard it and, interrupting Carl,
muttered, "A customer up in front, Carl." But Carl was in no mood
to leave off. Spreading out his hands he whispered, "Sh-sh-sh—
keep quiet and he'll go away." The customer did leave and presently the discussion resumed. In the end we unanimously agreed
that we could put a quarter to better use than for having our
skulls probed.

West of Hamilton in East Aurora, New York, Elbert Hubbard
("Fra Elbertus") preached the gospel of self-advancement

through self-mastery. Carl subscribed to *The Fra* and *The Philistine,* Hubbard's popular magazines. He laid them beside the New York *World,* the *Socialist Daily Call,* the *Appeal to Reason,* and the other publications to which he subscribed, all of which we read and discussed. It was in the tailor shop that I first heard of Henry George and the single tax, that I first read serious literature on the I.W.W. (Industrial Workers of the World), never imagining that someday I would see William Haywood, one of its leaders, walk the streets of Moscow, a lonely and disappointed man, with no place for himself or his cause in Lenin's revolution. It was in the tailor shop that I heard exciting discussions of woman's suffrage, of which the tailors though not all the students ardently approved. It was also there that I first read the *Communist Manifesto,* with no thought then that the time would come when I should spend many an evening in the dormitory of some Soviet university, wrangling heatedly with Russian students over its meaning and its predictions. However radical the subject, and however violently it might be mocked and denounced by the popular press, the tailors studied and discussed it. Capitalism, socialism, populism, trade unionism, strikes, lockouts, deism, agnosticism, atheism, anarchism—more isms than I had ever heard of—were analyzed and argued over. No subject was taboo, not even free love which Emma Goldman, the anarchist, was at the time vociferously advocating. Married men with families, the tailors didn't warm to Emma's gospel. There would have to be a limit to certain freedoms under socialism, they insisted, and even under anarchism, despite Emma Goldman and Johann Most.

But the tailors wondered why Emma Goldman should perceive in free love the deliverance of her sex from the physical and spiritual degradation into which, she argued, the manmade institution of marriage had trapped them. Honestly and earnestly they set argument against argument and still kept wondering. Then one day the New York *World* prominently displayed the woman's photograph. The tailors and the students scanned it over and over. There was nothing in the lady's face to kindle a man's blood—she was no Lily Langtry. "No wonder she is for free love," Gus laughingly said, "it's the only kind she'd ever get." But Carl wouldn't tolerate the raw jest at the expense of Emma, whose theories he rejected but whose intellect and sense of justice he respected. Anyway, that was the end of Emma Goldman's gospel of free love as a subject for debate in the tailor shop.

The sessions there were a stimulating experience for an immigrant student. Listening to the earnest exchange of ideas, the good-humored clash of opinion, I became aware that humanity was faced with more problems than I had ever dreamed of, but none, the tailors insisted, that man's intelligence could not eventually and happily solve. They firmly believed that human beings with all their knowledge and science, so highly advanced in America, could now bring about the millennium. The time was ripe for it, the tools were at hand, the blueprints drawn up.

After all, America itself was a miracle. Of course, there were men of great power and great wealth in America who were acting like lords of the earth. They cheated and they robbed. They sweated immigrants and others in shops and mines. They fought strikers with clubs and guns. Even Teddy Roosevelt hated these ruthless moneybags, called them "plutocrats," "hucksters," "glorified pawnbrokers," "tyrants," other names. Had not the robust and fearless Teddy mocked Socialists as "tomfools" and "mollycoddles," the tailors would have acclaimed him as a hero if not a prophet.

Even so, America, the tailors agreed, was a shining example to the old Europe from which we had fled. Here was a vast, rich, and beautiful land where you could wander anywhere you pleased without benefit of police permit, without any plutocrat's interference. Even if you were only a tailor, you wore a hat and collar and tie, at least on Sundays, and if you lived in Hamilton you had a house all to yourself, with plenty of space and sun and air and trees shadowing your porch; and your children went to the same school as the sons and daughters of the banker, the professor, the president of the college. And the new land was free of hereditary monarchs, of lords and barons, of princes and counts ("discounts," Gus called them), of a class that in Europe arrogated to itself privileges, power, property at the expense of the man with the needle and shears, the plow and the hoe. Here were no gaudy uniforms, no epaulets or swords, which authority in the Old Country still displayed. America was the place where the poor and the disinherited, the misfits and the outcasts of Europe could walk like men, subservient to none. America then was the only land in which the millennium could be attained: such was the opinion of the tailors and of the students who hob-nobbed with them.

Nor were they alone in their search for the millennium. The college faculty and administration, the visiting speakers in chapel were equally zealous in its pursuit. They too were mindful of the infirmities of human nature, of the failings of human society. They were as eloquently certain of the millennium as were the tailors. However, they differed with the tailors on the speediest way to reach it. They placed their faith in the moral regeneration of men through Christian principles.

But the tailors despaired of man's capacity to regenerate him-self by any religious faith or creed: after nineteen centuries of exhortation to mercy and love for his neighbors man was still obdurate. Something was wrong, not with the message of mercy and love, but with man. The tailors too respected the message, even the agnostics among them. But something else was needed to bring man to his senses—a society that would make it impos-sible and unprofitable for him to yield to his baser nature. If man could not remold society, society must remold man, and of course only a Socialist society could achieve the great transformation. It was as simple as that, as simple, beautiful, and inevitable. The one remaining task was to persuade the mass of citizenry, so the tailors insisted, to vote the Socialist ticket and to elect Eugene V. Debs, the only true prophet of the day, to the White House. Then and only then would there be abundance and happiness for everybody, for immigrant and Yankee and even for the Republi-cans and the Democrats who jeered at the Socialists. Carl, it must be said, finally became disenchanted with Debs and cast his vote for Woodrow Wilson and his New Freedom.

It was an age of innocence and faith, of exalted moralizing and glowing idealism. We were, as I look back to those years, in-toxicated with good will, enraptured with panaceas, Christian, Socialist, and other. America was so tranquil and trustful, so secure and self-assured; it had neither the time nor the disposi-tion for self-doubt, knew no fear of anything or anybody, not even of the Socialists—not yet—nor even or very little of Emma

Goldman. Nobody thought of a "lost generation," least of all the students in college, though in less than a decade it would storm onto the American scene and decry the gods of its elders. Nobody envisioned an "age of anxiety," though in time, after war and depression, that too would darken the American horizon. Until the Bolshevik Revolution broke out, not even the valiant Eugene Debs could have foreseen what Lenin, Trotsky, and Stalin would make of Marxism; not even Teddy Roosevelt or William Jennings Bryan could have forecast the rise of a Mussolini and a Hitler. No popularizations of the new psychology had yet bewildered us with the news that we were as infested with inferiorities, frustrations, alienations, complexes, inhibitions as a dog is with fleas. We still thought of our stomachs too much to bother about our psyches; we were happy to leave well enough alone. And not least, America was so dedicated to the cause of world peace that the Carnegie Foundation zealously promoted intercollegiate oratorical contests, in which peace was extolled and pacifism pledged by swallow-tailed college orators.

Not even the European-born tailors were aware of the storm that was secretly brewing on the continent they had fled and that would explode into two World Wars whose flames would burn to ashes the illusions they with their Socialist gospel and the college with its Christian gospel, America with its utopian dream, so lovingly cherished. Europe was so far away that to the average student it was more a name than a reality. Even to those of us who had come from there, and remembered the contumely we had suffered because of our lowly origin, the continent seemed too remote, too backward, and too militaristic to be able to affect the destiny of our new homeland, to suck any of us into its fierce jealousies and its flaming feuds.

Well might Europe in those days envy us, and well might Europeans crowd the filthy steerages of every ship on the ocean in their flight to the New World, which was still freely welcoming them. Letters from Mother in New York brought me the news that more and more young muzhiks from our old village were joining the flight, and well they might: fleeing from the cruel mud and the savage dogs, from the fleas and the lice, from malign landlords and bribe-hungry officials, from poverty and despair.

They were bringing with them as their sole link to the New World and as a talisman against misfortune a neatly folded piece of paper secreted like a jewel inside a linen pouch next to the skin. The little paper bore my mother's name and address.

Chapter 13

A Man Who Loved Teaching

◆

I did not move in Alec Woollcott's circles in New York. Nor did I count myself a close friend of his. But I was helpful to him during his lively and much publicized trip to Moscow in the autumn of 1932. I was acquainted with many literary and theatrical Muscovites whom he was particularly eager to meet and I introduced him around. Afterwards, whenever I happened to be in New York, he would invite me to an occasional meal in one of his favorite restaurants.

As host he was both charmer and monster, more monster than charmer toward me. He complimented me on my book *Red Bread*, but he took fiendish delight in castigating me whenever I disagreed with him on anything.

One evening in Moscow as I escorted him back to the National Hotel from a dinner party given in his honor by Alexander Afinogenov, the Soviet playwright, I told him that Afinogenov, who knew English, loved to read the Bible, especially the King James version, a copy of which he had borrowed from me and was in no hurry to return. We discussed the Bible and I mentioned that the Book of Job was one of my favorites. Instantly Woollcott snapped that only an ignoramus would be impressed by a silly fable that was without any literary merit. I didn't yet know Woollcott, so I told him that it was nonsense to say that the Book of Job was not a great piece of writing. Thereupon he belabored me with a string of uncomplimentary epithets for daring to contradict him. Then he brought up my college. "Only idiots go to Colgate!" he half screamed at me.

The years have mellowed the ancient and rather petty animosities between the two old colleges—Colgate and Hamilton. Disparagement and invective are no longer hurled back and forth between the campuses. Nowadays the two colleges even cooperate on certain educational projects. But Woollcott always cherished his old animosity.

Once I went to his apartment to pick up some presents he wanted me to deliver in Moscow to Walter Duranty for his infant son Mike. As we were talking, Noël Coward came in. Woollcott greeted him with an elaborate insult and Coward replied in kind. For some minutes the two celebrated wits engaged in a duel of lurid vituperation and invective. They had a beautiful time at it and I envied Coward for being able to pay Woollcott back in his own coin. My lack of this peculiar ability frequently incited Woollcott into taking advantage of my defenselessness, as he did of anyone who could not stand up to his stinging wit.

Once after I had delivered a lecture at Hamilton College, students gathered around for questions. Suddenly as if out of nowhere, Woollcott appeared draped in a black, scarlet-lined cape. "Hello, stupid," he said, "I understand you gave an interesting lecture." The students were somewhat startled at the greeting, but by this time I knew Woollcott too well to be offended. In the supersophisticated literary circle he had gathered about himself, this kind of put-down was considered fashionable and smart, but to me it was silly and repugnant. So instead of replying "Hello, repulsive," I merely said, "Hello, Alec." The dedication in Samuel Hopkins Adams biography of Woollcott reads, "To the thousand friends of Alexander Woollcott, this book is, with *fear* and *trembling* [my italics], dedicated by one of them."

The brilliant and pugnacious Woollcott was a disturbed man. Mrs. Grace Root, daughter-in-law of Elihu Root—except for Ezra Pound perhaps the most famous alumnus of Hamilton College—knew Woollcott well during his undergraduate years and spoke of him as inclined to be "half boy, half girl." He loved to play feminine leads in theatrical productions presented by the college dramatic society. Then after graduation he was stricken with the mumps, which, in the words of Samuel Hopkins Adams, had "permanently depleted him of sexual capacity." This condition had made him obese, and whenever he and I walked the streets of Moscow, his enormous rotundity drew the amused stares of passers-by. Obviously, Woollcott strove to compensate for his physical inadequacies by showing up the intellectual inadequacies of others.

Yet on one subject Woollcott and I never disagreed: a student needs to come under the influence of only one exciting professor to feel the effects of it all his life, even to have the course of his life changed. In the instance of Woollcott, the professor who evoked his highest tributes, at least in conversations with me, was Arthur Saunders, head of the department of chemistry, a subject that held no interest for Woollcott. He never sat in any of the professor's classes. This remarkable man had studied in Germany, which in those days denoted a man of outstanding scholarship and intellectuality. He loved trees and flowers, literature and art, music and astronomy. He loved conversation, and, in the words of Mrs. Root, he was blessed with "a very poetic personality." Because of his great charm and cultural versatility he attracted the more artistic and intellectual students and faculty members, and his home became a salon where Woollcott was privileged to listen to brilliant conversation on a multitude of subjects and where he too could talk himself out. He benefited enormously from these informal and always stimulating gatherings and more particularly from his friendship with Professor Saunders himself. As Mrs. Root explained, "Saunders taught him as he taught all others—just by talking and associating with him." No wonder that Woollcott spoke of Saunders with a tenderness and reverence that made one forget the monster in him.

As for myself, the professor who exercised the most powerful influence on my mind and life was Dr. William Henry Crawshaw, head of the department of English literature. But I had to wait for my junior year before I qualified for any of his courses.

Meanwhile during my sophomore year I was obliged to endure the agony of studying literature, my major, and history, my minor, under so-called "textbook" teachers. Such teachers are in my judgment a blight on the minds of students. "The letter killeth and the spirit giveth life." A teacher like Ralph W. Thomas had the gift of infusing "spirit" into the dull prose of Genung's *Rhetoric* and was immensely popular with students. But in my sophomore year the professor of literature, a genial and kindly man, and the instructor in history, a fast-talking colorless young man, clung to their textbooks like setting hens to their eggs. Neither man was imaginative enough to rise above "the letter" of the printed page. Plainly speaking, they were bores. I concluded that the primary concern of these teachers was not to stimulate our minds, but to stuff them with data so we should not need to think. With sufficient cramming a student could pass his exams. To me the method was practical, dull, and in the end fruitless.

Bernard Clausen, who by this time had become my closest friend, and I abominated the factual dry-as-dust textbook teachers. To escape the boredom of our history course we would select an outstanding figure of the period we were studying and read a book-length biography of the man. This way we learned infinitely more than the textbook told us and when examinations came, we easily answered the questions, enlivening our pages with allusions to ideas and situations on which textbook and teacher had been silent, which, incidentally, impressed the teacher when he marked our papers.

In our literary course we used Dr. Crawshaw's own textbook, which was lucid enough but so condensed that it needed explication and amplification, of which our teacher was incapable. Clausen and I decided to read Matthew Arnold, among other English critics, and also Hippolyte Taine and Georg Brandes, the Danish critic, both of whom I had heard of from Edward King, the scholarly Scotsman on New York's Lower East Side.

I was happy when my sophomore year came to an end. I spent my summer vacation in 1913 working on a dairy farm near Sherburne, in Chenango County, New York, the hometown of a classmate, Clark Trow (subsequently professor of education at Michigan University), whose father was a Congregational minister. A soft-spoken, studious man, I admired the minister for his broad-minded approach to religion. I could not know then that someday he would play an important part in my life.

When I returned for my junior year I was richer by some one hundred dollars and I eagerly looked forward to studying at last under the idolized Dr. Crawshaw.

Yet to me college was more than professors and studies. I was always conscious of being an immigrant plunged into another America, very different from both the America of the Lower East Side and the America of the upstate farms. Not only the college community interested me, but also people outside, like the small clan of Irish immigrants, all peasants, some of whom worked on the campus, and others like Terry Murphy and his two brothers who were settled on farms of their own. There was also a fourth Murphy brother, Pat, working on the campus who was virtually disowned by the others. Pat managed to stay sober on workdays to the satisfaction of his foreman, another Irishman named Gilmartin. But every Saturday evening he would make a beeline for the saloon where he usually got roaring drunk. One Saturday evening as I was on my way to the village I met Pat, happily singing as he staggered home. He clutched me by the arm and stopped me. I was then a freshman as revealed by my beanie. "Ye're a freshman," he said, "and in four years ye'll graduate. But I've been in this university twenty-five years and I ain't graduated yit." He slapped me on the shoulder, gave a hearty laugh, and, resuming the singing, continued his way home. Though Pat in his cups was never mean and was even known as something of a wit, his respectable brothers could never forgive his love of the bottle and never liked to hear his name mentioned.

What amazed me about these Irish immigrants was the ease with which they had fitted themselves into the American community. I knew no immigrants like them—I mean immigrants who had not had to struggle and struggle in their effort to make a place for themselves in the New World. Of course, the Irish had one supreme advantage—they spoke English, however thick their brogue. But more than language facilitated their assimilation. By comparison with Russian muzhiks, Polish, Hungarian, and Ukrainian peasants I had known as hired men on farms, they did not strike me as peasants at all. In personal manners and social habits, they were completely Western. They did not need to unlearn the practices I had brought with me from a Russian village. Their table manners—their very table settings—were no different than those of Yankee farmers.

When I worked for them, I sometimes had meals in the home of one of the Murphy brothers, where even the cooking was purely American. They loved apple pie and shortcake, doughnuts and cookies, gravy on potatoes or on bread as much as any Yankee farmer. During the threshing and silo-filling season, the Murphy wives set before their voraciously hungry extra help as sumptuous a table as I had ever sat at, every dish as American as apple pie or succotash. Except for their brogue and their Roman Catholic faith, they might have been born Yankees. They had fled from a poverty-stricken Ireland of which they told endless stories, and they hated England, nor did they conceal the fact. They were exemplary citizens in every aspect of their lives. I therefore could not understand the ill repute in which they were held in certain circles, especially in Boston, as I learned when I matriculated at Harvard for postgraduate work. The expression "Boston Irish" denoted supposedly inferior people whom you didn't invite to dinner.

However, I made friends with some of the Irish families in Hamilton and often visited them. They were a warmhearted, family-loving people and an evening in their company was always a refreshing experience.

But what most interested me was the human scene at college, however different it had turned out to be from what I had imagined. My junior classmates were perceptibly changing and maturing, and to observe this process was as interesting a part of my education as any course under the best of teachers.

A junior, having reached the mid-point of his college years, looked back on the rivalries and skirmishes between freshmen and sophomores as kid stuff, which he wouldn't have missed but which he didn't regret leaving behind. Now an older brother to the freshman as the senior was to the sophomore, he no longer had to connive against or bully anyone. Though he might still swell a commotion in the village movie house or abet a prank on the chesty village cop or the witless mayor, he walked the campus in peace.

He felt under compulsion to take fresh stock of himself and he knew what the score was: he had survived scholastically as an underclassman and he was determined to survive to the end. He meant to study harder and he did, for the world beyond the campus was no longer as nebulously distant as when he first came to college or when aglow with a youthful self-conceit he had swaggered across the campus a sophomore. If mathematics or science was his major, he was burdened with assignments and laboratory work that crowded his hours more than in any previous year. He knew that the professors of these subjects were tough and the nature of these subjects too demanding to permit half-hearted attention in class or lackadaisical preparation of assignments. When examinations came he had better be certain of his answers or he would be mercilessly flunked and all his plans for the future shattered.

With greater maturity his habits of thought had become more fixed than he imagined. If he hadn't yet cultivated the habit of browsing in the library stacks, the chances were that he never would, and he would grow up to distrust those who lived by ideas that he and his social group didn't share and hardly cared to explore. Meanwhile his application to the humanities had most likely become a routine performance, especially if he sat in classes presided over by textbook teachers. He didn't grumble about it as much as he used to; he had been in college long enough to know better. But he would be glad when the ordeal ended. He'd welcome the morning when he would awaken with no burden of reading assignments or reports to be written hanging over him.

But should he have the good fortune to fall under the influence of the right teacher, he could be stirred to an awareness of intellectual and creative resources within himself that he had never suspected were there. This one professor (and has there ever been a college however remote and provincial that has not been brightened by his presence?) might well change the course of the student's life. But whether this happened or not, the student would always remember him, whether with affectionate gratitude for having shown him his proper path in the world or, if he had taken a less strenuous way, with fading regrets. In this case he might sometimes ask himself how and why he had let the excitement and sense of wonder, the determination to achieve great things die in him. How had it happened? He knew and he didn't. Now he was comfortable, mediocre, and successful. Old dreams could not be revived, and why should they be? But he, no less than those who had persisted, whether to success or failure, would treasure the memory of the one man who had given him a new insight into himself and had opened up perspectives into the world of intellect and imagination he might otherwise never have even glimpsed.

In his third year in college the student became more keenly aware of the importance of good manners, which he might have lacked or even derided (I did) during his underclassmen years. Even though no fraternity embraced him, he somehow acquired a little social polish. He mastered the intricacies of getting into and out of tails; he didn't feel lost when a professor invited him to tea, which he discovered meant a full-course meal, where he found himself confronted with a perplexing array of silverware. There was always somebody (Clausen, in my case) to tell him that the soup spoon should be dipped away from and not toward himself; that he disgraced himself if he dunked a doughnut in his coffee, spread gravy on bread, ate peas with a knife, all of which he might have done at home, certainly if he came from a farm.

The third-year man was all the more concerned about the social graces because he couldn't help thinking of the junior prom, the swankiest social event in his college years, when he must dress up in tails and pass muster before a bevy of resplendently arrayed girls. It was his first bow in society, and he spared no effort to appear at his most gallant and sophisticated self.

But some of us were actually too poor to think of attending the famous prom. Nevertheless, even though we could not afford the admission fee we were not exempted from the five-dollar levy that would contribute to the festivities for the more fortunate. On hearing this I complained bitterly that such a levy was unjust: hadn't I been taught that there should be no taxation without representation? Derisive laughter drowned my protests and I was accused of showing a reprehensible lack of college spirit. Suppose others took this stand? Suppose it got around at Vassar, Smith, and Mount Holyoke that the Colgate juniors were pikers and that their prom wasn't a patch on the Ivy League proms—not to mention Hamilton's. The levy paid for the decorations, buffet, and orchestra, and they must all be the best. As for the admission fee, if I couldn't pay that, at least I could slip into the gallery where formal dress was not required and regale myself with the festive splendor below and take pride in the social triumph of the Colgate juniors to which my five dollars had contributed. Now would I please fork up?

As a junior, with half my college years behind me, I, too, took stock of myself, and it dawned on me that I was wasting precious time stoking furnaces, planting vegetable gardens, and helping farmers thresh grain and fill silos. I wearied of being half student and half worker. I wanted to make the most of my time, and I felt I was getting more out of discussions with the tailors and the more intellectual-minded students and from books than out of most of my classes. Many books that I still wanted to read I knew I would never find time for because of the burden of earning a living. I decided to throw off this burden. The respect which Americans have always felt for a student who worked his way through college failed to compensate for the sacrifices I was making.

But I had to think of finances. My savings from a summer's work on a farm, augmented by the special scholarship the president had awarded me from which tuition was deducted, protected me against immediate want. Yet unless I could tap a fresh source of income without grubbing for it with my hands, I should find myself penniless by midwinter. Why then not try to make some money from writing? Excited by the idea, I stayed up nights grinding out stories and articles. Confidently I mailed manuscripts to various magazines. Regularly the manuscripts were returned with printed rejection slips. All hope of obtaining income from writing blew away like the smoke from farmhouse chimneys. But I was not discouraged. More scholastic prizes were available for juniors than for any other classmen and I competed for every prize open to me. I won about one hundred dollars and a set of Browning exquisitely bound. As I lived frugally the additional funds sufficed to carry me through the year without worry and without hardship.

In her illuminating autobiography—*My Several Worlds*—Pearl Buck relates that when she found herself hard-pressed for money in her senior year at Randolph-Macon Woman's College in Lynchburg, Virginia, she decided to compete for prizes offered for the best short story and the best poem submitted. She won both and was glad of the cash, but "what astonished and wounded me was that in the congratulations of my fellows I discerned a slight hostility, a hint of complaint that one person had been given the two best prizes." Nothing of the kind had happened to me. In the congratulations of my fellows I perceived no hint of jealousy or complaint. If anything, my friends were overly generous, as was demonstrated by an incident in my senior year.

The Baptist Education Society offered a prize of one hundred dollars to students in Baptist colleges, regardless of their religion, for the best essay on the prohibition movement in Europe. World War I was raging and in Russia the Czar had proclaimed prohibition. Having known first-hand of Russian addiction to vodka and having sensed the dramatic implications of the Czar's decree, I submitted an essay. I won the prize and some of my fellows approached me with the suggestion that the student body take up a collection to send me to the Baptist Conference in Los Angeles to receive the award in person. I vetoed the suggestion, but the thoughtfulness of my fellow students speaks for itself.

After reading Pearl Buck's account of her experience I wondered why college girls resented and college men didn't the special awards earned by one of their fellows. Was it because girls are more money-minded and more jealous of one another than men? Perhaps there was another explanation but I could not think of it.

The high points of my junior year were the two courses I took under Dr. Crawshaw. One was called "The Age of Wordsworth," the other "The Age of Tennyson." Now that I was attending his classes regularly, I understood more fully why he was so idolized by generations of students, even by football players. As I was leaving a lecture on Wordsworth, a classmate remarked, "I never knew poetry could be so interesting."

Crawshaw's manner of conducting a class was unique at Colgate. He never sat at his desk. He always stood up as though he found a chair too confining. He never invited discussion from the students, and this was not only because of his faulty hearing. He preferred to talk with students in the privacy of his home or office where it was easier for him to hear the voice of the caller. Like a concert artist or an actor, he evoked a mood in the classroom that general discussion would have disrupted.

Not famed like Irving Babbitt under whom I studied briefly as a graduate student at Harvard, Crawshaw crusaded for no particular school, theory, movement, or tendency in literature. He had his preferences, but he was never dogmatic about them. I never heard him disparage any author as caustically as I heard Babbitt disparage Dreiser and Dostoyevsky whose form, style and spirit did not accord with his own classicism. Craw had set for himself the task of transmitting to students his own great love of literature, which to him, in the words of Matthew Arnold whom he had met and often quoted, was a mirror of "the best which has been said and thought in the world." It was his aim to give students a vision of this best and to make them conscious of values other than those of the business and professional world they were about to enter.

He drew students with the magnetism of a Broadway star drawing audiences, and he had the signal gift of holding their undivided attention. I never knew his students to fidget, yawn, or whisper as they did in other classes.

His principal accomplishment as a teacher was his masterful reading, a lost art in an age of Ph.D. researchers. On meeting us for the first time, he told us that nobody could teach us anything and that the most he could do was to point the way to learning; we would have to do the rest ourselves. Even so, his way of guiding us to an understanding of the power and the beauty of great books by his inspired reading was unfailingly stimulating. He did not elocute, did not overdo or "ham" his recitations. Whether he was reading Wordsworth or Coleridge, Keats or Shelley, Tennyson or Browning, his natural tone of voice was never lost and he used it like a musical instrument that brought out the rhythm, the power, the beauty, the exultation, the poignancy of Wordsworth's *Prelude* or Coleridge's *Kubla Khan*. A consummate artist, he was intensely alive with the intelligence and the imaginative power that can impart the higher truth of a poem. I shall always remember his rendition of Coleridge's *The Rime of the Ancient Mariner*, which I had read and been enchanted by in high school. But Crawshaw made me feel that I was hearing it for the first time.

In whatever disapproval he may have held a writer's moral character—and Craw was a deeply religious man—he judged his works by literary standards alone. Shelley's atheism and sexual irregularities never counted against him as a poet; and though he had no great regard for Byron's work, he derided the pious Victorian reviewers who had applied a moral yardstick to the poems. When he read us the *Ode on a Grecian Urn* or *Kubla Khan* his brown eyes would kindle with rapture over the lines. Or, if he had chosen to read some inferior work to illustrate how poetry should not be written, they would narrow in distaste. At these times the unassuming old man with the slight narrow-shouldered frame was transformed into a giant of wisdom and authority.

Now that I no longer had to work for a living I had more leisure to visit the tailor shop, where discussion of current events in America and in the world outside was always exciting. Now I had more time to read. Not since I had left the Old Country had I read Russian fiction. In those days there were no novels in the Russian language in the college library (there are plenty of them now) and very few in translation. I found a copy of Turgenev's *A Nest of Gentlefolk* and recommended it to Clausen who had not yet read anything by the gentle-natured, melancholy Russian author. The novel moved him as profoundly as it did me. Its religious overtones as reflected in Liza, the heroine who withdraws for life to a nunnery to escape the torment of an unrealizable love, held special meaning for the divinity student.

Then I came across a translation of Dostoyevsky's *Crime and Punishment*, which I had never read before. In the Russian school I had only read *Poor Folk*, so Dostoyevsky was almost as new to me as to Clausen. He read it first; and when I finished it late one evening I was so overpowered by the novel that instead of waiting for our Saturday afternoon walk when we usually discussed books, I knocked on his door. He was as eager to talk about it as I was. There was always a tin box full of white sugar cookies in his room which we munched as we talked over the haunting scenes and characters in the story. Clausen read aloud Marmeladov's words in the tavern on forgiveness and pity. He was an excellent reader, and as I listened in the quiet dormitory the words became more moving than when I had read them by myself. Nothing in the world seemed so sacred and so beautiful as forgiveness and pity, the essence of the faith to which the gifted Clausen had dedicated himself. Although I did not share his faith, I was touched by his belief, naïve even in those innocent times, that someday mankind would accept Dostoyevsky's message and the world would be gloriously changed.

Anyway, we had discovered a new and exciting writer and we pressed the college library to obtain more of his works. But at the time only one other of Dostoyevsky's novels—*The Idiot*—was available in English translation. When Clausen and I read it, it occurred to us to prevail on Dr. Crawshaw to give a seminar course on the nineteenth-century novel that, of course, would include Dostoyevsky. At first the professor was reluctant to assume responsibility for a new seminar, but Clausen and I persisted until he finally agreed to hold the seminar the following year, which was our graduation year.

Only about half a dozen students enrolled for the course. We met once a week in a small room where we crowded around a little table so Crawshaw could hear us without difficulty. We read one novel a week. Being neither pundit nor pedant the professor never attempted to steer us into scholarly dissections of them. We read for plot, character, atmosphere, historical setting, psychological insight.

I was disappointed by Crawshaw's lack of enthusiasm for Russian fiction. His taste was plainly Victorian, though of Victorian morals he often spoke with light-hearted derogation. He delighted in Thackeray's asides in *Vanity Fair,* but Tolstoy's asides in *War and Peace* left him unimpressed. He reveled in Dickens but Dostoyevsky bewildered him. The Russian's thieves, harlots, drunks, murderers, dilettantes, peasants, aristocrats, each devoured by his own passions and appetites, spoke a language that did not move him. Not even Dostoyevsky's compassion for the injured and the insulted moved him. The women were too demoniac, the men too monstrous or too saintly, the stories of their lives too fierce for his comfort. Only the disciplined and melancholy Turgenev aroused his admiration.

Yet one day as we drifted into a discussion of European character traits as reflected in fiction, the professor casually came out with a statement that at the time struck me as fanciful, but in the years to come would gain startling validity. "The Latin race," he told us, "is the race of the past, the Anglo-Saxon race the race of the present, and the Slav race the race of the future."

In explanation, he said that while Russian fictional portrayal of life neither pleased nor moved him, he was nevertheless impressed by the extraordinary imaginative power and the torrential vitality of Russians as mirrored in their fiction, especially in Dostoyevsky, to him the least tolerable of them all. The trouble with the Russians was, he went on, that they poured their vitality and imagination into the most uninhibited talk he had read. But once they stopped talking so much and directed their mental, physical and imaginative energies into action, there was no telling what they might do. For good or ill, there would be no holding back these strange and powerful people.

What a prediction to have made in the year 1915!

Chapter 14

Age of Illusion

◀▶

Nowadays with the arrival of spring, even before campus lawns and trees turn green, a host of conservatively dressed and persuasively tongued scouts from big corporations beset the more promising seniors with offers of jobs that often pay salaries that may well rouse the envy of newly appointed Ph.D. instructors.

But in my day, by early spring the campus was overrun with loudly dressed, glib-tongued salesmen who came to recruit students for peddling jobs during the summer vacation. A student could peddle sets of books, food extracts, cosmetics, aluminum kitchenware, Fuller brushes, rich-colored lithographs, stereopticon outfits, and other articles of appeal to farm and small-town families—except silks and rugs, which were still the monopoly of itinerant Syrian and Armenian vendors. The summer student-peddler wandering afoot or in horse and buggy over country roads was no unfamiliar sight during my years as a hired man.

The man who came in my junior year to recruit agents (he never used the term "peddler") for his stereopticon outfits mesmerized me with his smooth patter. He assured me that I could earn twice or three times as much selling his product than I could working on a farm. The fact that he was the only salesman who wore a frock coat and a black bow tie and spoke excellent English lent his assurances the persuasiveness of a gentlemen of parts. So I signed his contract. After college closed I was to go to Carthage, New York, and make my pile in the town and the surrounding countryside.

Cautious as I was, I decided to get some practice before the summer vacation started. On Saturday morning I hired a horse and buggy from the local livery man and drove hopefully to the village of Morrisville for my first encounter with the American housewife. I conscientiously followed the studiously memorized instructions of my frock-coated mentor. I knocked on doors and when the housewife appeared I put on my best smile, introduced myself as a student working his way through college, and asked for the privilege of showing her sights of the Holy Land at no cost to herself. The guileful introduction was supposed to rouse a motherly sentiment for me so that housewives wouldn't slam the door in my face as on an ordinary peddler.

The trouble was that while out of respect for my status as a student in the near-by college, housewives didn't shut their doors on me, they invariably managed to contrive some excuse for declining my offer. But one lady, wife of a teacher in the local agricultural school, must have been so touched by my downcast expression, which my best smile couldn't conceal, that she invited me into the kitchen for coffee and doughnuts. Still, I made no sale. Another woman, quite elderly, whom I must have wakened from her after-dinner nap, for she was slow in answering my knock, cut short my introduction and growled that a strong young fellow like me working his way through college should find himself an honest job and stop pestering folks who wanted to be left alone.

Whether peddling was an "honest job" or not, I couldn't imagine one more disheartening. I soon realized that selling stereopticon sets demanded gifts of character which I hopelessly lacked. I quit knocking on doors and drove back to Hamilton. Without any loss of time I wrote the frock-coated gentleman in New York that I was utterly unsuited for the job. A correspondence followed, which jolted me into the fearful awareness of the trouble a man courts when he defaults on his signature, however justified by circumstances beyond his control. I had complacently assumed that by putting my name on the document the frock-coated salesman had slid before me I was merely indulging in an expression of good will toward him. But he was determined to hold me to my written commitment, come what might. He argued and cajoled. He scolded and raged. He mocked and shamed me. I thought I had learned all there was to know about character from farmers in North Brookfield: I couldn't have been more wrong. I was made to feel like a defaulter and a scoundrel in whom no spark of honor survived. It was a painful, expensive experience, and since then I have been almost as wary of a man who holds out a paper for me to sign as a dog is of a threatening stick.

Sobered, I turned again to farming. This time I inserted a want ad in the Syracuse *Post-Standard* offering my services, the quality of which I didn't underestimate, to a farmer prepared to pay the highest wages, a sum not specified. I was surprised at the number of replies I received, among them one from a Mr. Lacey, a banker in Syracuse.

The banker was a distinguished-looking gentleman, smooth-shaven, white-haired. He wore a gray frock coat, a gray felt hat, a white bow tie. As we sat on the tree-shaded porch of his large frame house he asked me about myself, and when he learned that I was Jewish, his big brown eyes lighted up with incredulity. He had never known any Jewish farmers and asked how it was that I had taken up farming. The question amused me as it always did, as though nature herself had decreed farming out-of-bounds for a Jew or endowed Jews with an instinctive abhorrence of work on the land.

I explained to the wondering banker that my paternal forebears, as far back as I could trace them, which in the absence of written records did not go beyond my great-grandfather, had always earned their living by working land. Other Jews in the same part of the country I came from had also grubbed in the earth for a living, at times mixing farming with trading. This was all new to the gentleman-farmer. He was silent for a few moments, then he paid me the compliment which is always good for a few extra dollars a month to a hired hand. "I am sure," he said, "that being Jewish you won't get drunk on Saturday night."

He asked what my wages had been last year. "Fifty dollars a month," I replied. "Supposing," he proposed, "I pay you fifty-five a month, will that be satisfactory?" I assured him it would. He told me to go by train to Baldwinsville, a town near Syracuse, and ask for the team from the Lacey farm that would take me to the home of his caretaker.

The caretaker was a German-American by the name of Weber. He cultivated the flower and vegetable gardens and mowed the lawns around the banker's summer home, high on a knoll overlooking the farm. A childless couple, Mr. Weber and his wife, though born in this country, had never lost their taste for old-fashioned German peasant cooking which in many ways reminded me of Russian peasant food. Like my mother in the old village, Mrs. Weber filled tin pans with milk and set them away until the cream, thick and rich, rose to the top. The cream was churned into butter, leaving the buttermilk which Yankee farmers usually fed to pigs and chickens. She fixed *Salzkartoffeln*—unpared potatoes boiled in salted water—and dished them up with the clabber left in the milk pans after the cream had been skimmed off, and I delighted in the familiar peasant repast of fragrant, hot potatoes smothered in cold clabber.

Though Mrs. Weber could turn out delicious American farm pastries, she still baked her own German-style rye bread; her soups were real soups, the *Kartoffelsuppe* thick with potatoes, onions, and herbs. Best of all, there were always cucumbers on the table to eat with meat, to slice into her homemade cottage cheese or into a bowl of clabber, the clabber and the cucumbers Yankee farmers despised. Many years had passed since I had had my fill of old-country dishes, nor had the lapse of time dulled my peasant appetite.

The Lacey farm was the only "gentleman's farm" I had worked on, and I soon saw that such a farm was a luxury that only a man of wealth could afford. The land was rich and the owner had spared no money on the latest agricultural machinery and on choicest cows and horses. He also paid high wages. The foreman, a tall, big-boned, muscular man of cheerful disposition, was an able and hard-working manager. But the farm was too big for him to supervise alone. The three permanent workers, all married and living in large houses on the farm, were fairly honest men. But in haying and harvesting season from three to ten extra hands were taken on, few of whom ever performed their tasks with any degree of diligence.

One afternoon when four of us were cultivating a big cornfield, I reached the end of a row and was about to turn my horse into the next row when one of the other men came over and ridiculed me for working so hard. Lacey, he argued, was a rich man and it was not up to any hired man to make him richer. He and the other hands in the cornfield took their time, knocked off for a chat now and then or even a game of cards, and I should do the same. In the tall corn nobody would see anything.

The longer I stayed on the farm the more waste I observed, waste of grain, waste of hay, above all waste of labor, especially by the extra hands who loitered along their way to and from the fields, at loading and unloading hay, and lounged around the barns. A farm not managed by its owner, especially a big farm, was never as efficiently run as a dirt farmer's, whether he worked his land with or without hired labor.

I have never taken as pessimistic a view of Soviet state and collective farms as have many observers of the Soviet Union. Yet absentee ownership, whether on state or collective farms, is the chief curse of Soviet agriculture. Neither the Communist Party nor the Soviets have succeeded or ever will succeed in giving farm workers the incentive to hard work and efficient performance that individual ownership provides for the American farmer.

One sunny day a Danish hired man and I went to rebuild a barbed wire fence over an inflow from the river in the cow pasture. We worked stripped to the skin, and, waist-high in the water, set up the poles, stretched wire, and stapled it to them. We were in good spirits and laughed heartily when one of us slid on a hidden rock or lost his balance and splashed into the water. Finally the dinner bell rang. Down went our tools and we plunged into the river for a swim. Amidst hoots and yells we splashed and ducked one another and raced each other across the deep swift-flowing stream. Alone by ourselves, out of sight of people, we were as boisterously playful as small boys, and only the pangs of hunger made us come out of the river, dress hurriedly, and race home for the savory dinner that awaited us.

But the moment I walked into the Weber house my gay mood was shattered. As solemn as at a funeral the tall, bald-headed, long-faced Mr. Weber brandished before me the newly arrived Syracuse *Post-Standard*. Staring at me from the front page were big black headlines announcing the outbreak of war between Germany and Russia. I stood transfixed, too confused to say a word, only faintly hearing Mr. Weber's moan, "How terrible, how terrible!"

After I finished reading every word on the war, my first thought was that had I remained in Russia, I would, because of my age, have been forced into uniform and under compulsion to fight for the pogrom-making Czar. Here, thank heaven, I was beyond his reach. Then I thought of the muzhik women in my old village and their hysterical wails on the autumn day in peace time when the *novobrantsui*—the new conscripts—crowded into straw-filled carts and rolled away to serve in the Czar's army in some distant region. Conscription in those days was a fate as unavoidable as death and no less bitterly lamented, and I thought of the wild despair of the women now that their men were being sent to kill and be killed for the Czar. Mr. Weber kept muttering "How terrible, how terrible," grief-stricken at the ordeal ahead for the people from whom he had stemmed.

When Mrs. Weber announced dinner, we washed and sat down to eat, talking of the war which I denounced as another periodic explosion of European wickedness, to which as if by the will of God or some immutable law of nature, non-military America was as happily immune as to the plagues that periodically ravaged the Russian countryside. The Webers shared my views. The terrible war would never touch us, never! In the peace and tranquillity of the banker's farm, with birds chirping and flowers blooming, with broad cornfields gleaming in the hot sun, we felt fortified in our mutual assurances.

And so our tranquil summer passed. On Saturday evenings I dressed up in my Sunday suit and with other hired men walked or drove into Baldwinsville for an evening of sociability. The streets were lined with horses and buggies. Shops were jammed with customers. Saloons were crowded with hired men, farmers, townspeople drinking beer and whiskey, telling jokes, joshing one another, laughing, and as unconcerned with the European blood-bath as with last year's snows. From their pulpits preachers thundered threats of hellfire on young people who went dancing, but still the dance hall in Baldwinsville was crowded with farm and town boys and girls, dressed in their best, stepping and shuffling to the small orchestra. The town too was untroubled by Europe's tragedy.

When I returned to college for my senior year I found the campus as unperturbed by the war as the banker's farm and the town of Baldwinsville had been. The war was a madness from which fortunate America was protected by the Atlantic Ocean. Our history professor assured us that we would never become involved in any European conflict. Most students were more excited by the forthcoming World Series and the prospects of our football team than by the titanic struggle on the other side of the Atlantic.

But the tailor shop stormed with debate, speculation, and prophecy, and a visit there shook me out of my complacency. Our native lands seemed less distant, and the terrible bloodletting loomed up as shattering reality. We cursed kings and emperors more roundly than ever and lamented the lot of their subjects. We compensated for our helplessness with romantic visions of that millennium of peace and brotherhood that would come some-day, if only the world would follow our advice. We were all agreed that the three archfiends leading mankind to destruction were the Russian Czar, the German Kaiser, and the Austrian Emperor. If war should topple their thrones, then the chains that had fettered their subjects would snap asunder and a golden dawn would rise over Europe. The proud and volatile Hungarian envisioned a gloriously reborn Hungary; the portly and stolid Bohemian, a happily resurrected Bohemia (Czechoslovakia) after three centuries of subjugation to Austria; the effervescent Gus, a thrillingly independent Poland; and I envisioned a Russia with-out landlords, the big estates parceled out among the muzhiks; Carl's taciturn and husky-voiced father, still mourning the recent death of his revered August Bebel envisioned the fulfillment of Bebel's prophecy for the *Vaterland*—a Germany flowering into Socialism. Enraptured by his vision, the aging German tailor pre-dicted that Bebel's Socialism would sweep all Europe, even to the steppes and forests of dark Russia.

But none of us had heard of the chunky little man with the lofty forehead, the slanting eyes, the high cheekbones from the mud-drenched tree-shaded Volga town of Simbirsk, who as an exile in Geneva, nurtured visions of his own of a world to come out of the flames of war. Lenin didn't exist for us. Neither did Trotsky, with his own vision of Russia's and mankind's des-tiny. Unknown, too, was the mustached, pock-marked son of a Georgian shoemaker Joseph Stalin, then serving a sentence in the bleak wastes of Northern Siberia.

Carl's solemn father would have roared derisive laughter had anyone, even of the ghost of Bebel, told him that an obscure, impoverished Austrian painter, then a volunteer in the Bavarian army, would soon proclaim his own vision of a Reich rising to a thousand-year glory over millions and millions of corpses. Mesmerized by our own utopianism, we couldn't imagine any designs for the future less noble than ours.

Meanwhile the American college community was raising its voice in the growing peace movement. That year Colgate was host to the annual intercollegiate oratorical contest, whose contenders spoke on peace. Smartly dressed society women up from New York added glamour to the assemblage of academicians, students, and townspeople in the Hamilton Baptist Church whose auditorium was the only one in the village large enough to accommodate the crowds.

Clausen was chosen to represent the college. A dedicated pacifist, the war haunted him more than anybody I knew on the campus; and while other contestants, immaculately attired in tails and white ties thundered against militarism and bloody slaughter, my closest chum struck a discordant note. I can still hear his memorable words, "Search Europe for peace, you will find it only in the faces of the dead." Despite the brilliance of his style and the excellence of his delivery, he didn't win the prize. Perhaps the judges found him too realistic or too foreboding, not optimistic enough. I still marvel at the naïve credulities of that now vanished age, when the college, the tailor shop, America at large stirred with visions of the inevitable day that would see peace eternally enthroned on earth once the European holocaust was over. Doomed though it was from the beginning as an act of quixotic folly, Henry Ford's Peace Ship, *Oscar II*, sailing for Norway "to get the boys out of the trenches by Christmas" 1915, was no doubt the most sensational expression of those innocent times.

With not a speck of a war cloud hovering over our skies, life on the campus flowed on in its customary way, which, by the time one was a senior, was more amusing than exciting, except of course for football, of which I had become a dedicated enthusiast. I could yell "Beat Syracuse!" as loudly as any of them.

As seniors my classmates felt themselves quite grown-up and mature. With rare exceptions they knew now what they were going to do and what they wanted out of life. They had confidence in themselves and in the world about them. It was their world and there was nothing much wrong with it, not in 1915.

Largely of farmer and middle-class origin, no doubts beset them; they were unconscious of any inner darkness to explore, of secrets to probe and uncover, not even the secret of sex, if it was still a secret. Long ago the tall, gangling Doc Huntington in his "smut" lectures to freshmen—how long ago it seemed now—had stripped the subject of its mystery and bafflement, never damning it as a defilement of body and soul as the preachers did. There was talk that Doc didn't believe in "original sin." He certainly didn't fulminate against it, which prompted some wag to declare, "Doc thinks it's healthy." For a professor in those times in a college bound to a strong religious tradition, Doc Huntington was an exceptional man.

Scholastically speaking, the fourth year was the most rewarding of all for both Clausen and myself, principally because we had drawn close to that prince of teachers, Dr. William Henry Crawshaw. We were taking his course in Shakespeare and the Elizabethan drama, the most popular course in the curriculum, and attended the new seminar on the nineteenth-century novel. It was always a delight and inspiration to sit at the same table with him, agree with him or contradict him, and always to be stimulated by his great love of England, his reminiscences of his literary pilgrimages there, and his profound knowledge of its history. In his autobiography, in speaking of Clausen and myself, he records, "We seldom agreed on anything, but that made it all the more fun. When they got through with me they probably already had me headed toward the road which I was to travel with increasing delight throughout the rest of my teaching days."

We were amazed how lively and sociable the professor was when we were alone with him, which in my instance happened more often than with Clausen. Actually, Clausen and I had completed our undergraduate work in three years, but for sentimental reasons we wanted to graduate with our class and stayed on for an extra year. Our studies during the fourth year were credited toward a master's degree, which necessitated the writing of a thesis. For my theme I chose Thomas Hardy, and Clausen, a Greek scholar, selected, if memory serves me, Greek tragedy. Hardy was no particular favorite of the professor, which did not prevent him from helping me with suggestions about books to

read and with the outline of my thesis. He did more—he oblig-
ingly read my pages as soon as I wrote them, as he did for Clausen. He also read papers that were not required in the course,
but that we did for our own edification. He praised and encouraged us to go on with a view to eventually becoming professional
writers. The encouragement was cheering, though Clausen who
was to study at Union Theological Seminary, had decided to
dedicate his writing exclusively to religious subjects. As for myself, I early decided that newspaper work was not for me. But I
kept on turning out essays, stories, plays. I even won the dramatic
club award for a three-act play, which fortunately was never
produced. Words flowed freely and easily from my typewriter,
though editors continued to return my manuscripts. I finally
ceased to bother them. I didn't care to collect any more rejection
slips, tacit hints to a student with literary ambitions that he had
better check his eagerness until some editor confirmed the judgment of his English teachers, even the best of them, that he had
the making of a professional writer.

Then from an alumnus associated with the editorship of *Youth's
Companion,* I heard of Dean Le Baron Russell Briggs at Harvard
and his writing class for graduate students of literary promise.
Here, I thought, was the very man to guide me. If the dean accepted me into his class of select students, I should know that
Professor Thomas's counsel in my freshman year and Dr. Crawshaw's encouragement should be acted upon. If the dean rejected
my application, it would mean that I was deluding myself.
For me the issue was as simple, as clear-cut as that. In any
case, a year of postgraduate study at Harvard would be of value.
I was set for Harvard.

But where was I to get the money? I could always earn high
wages on a farm, but it would not be enough for a year's stay in
Cambridge. I could teach and, with a master's degree coming,
I could be certain of a respectable salary in some high school. But
I did not relish teaching. I thought it a boring profession and
regarded myself as unfit for it.

Then the unexpected occurred. The Reverend Mr. Trow, the
Congregational minister at Sherburne, wrote inviting me to address a regional convention of young people at his church on the
subject of Russia, which because of the war and the desperate

plight of the Czar's armies, had roused nationwide interest. I accepted the invitation gladly, and several days after my talk at the convention, I received a letter from a lecture manager in Syracuse asking whether I would consider lyceum lecturing under his management. I had been recommended to him by Mr. Trow and he was ready to give me a contract. Correspondence followed, resulting in a guarantee of fifteen hundred dollars and all expenses for one hundred and fifty lectures during a period of seven months. The thought of repeating the same words evening after evening appalled me, but it was the only way open to me to earn the necessary funds for a year at Harvard.

Then shortly before commencement I received another inquiry from the manager of the bureau asking whether I would care to lecture on a Chautauqua circuit in the Middle West. Of course I would.

So once again a Protestant clergyman had played a decisive role in my life. Had it not been for the Baptist elder in North Brookfield, I should never had thought of applying for admission to Colgate, and now a Congregational clergyman had opened up for me the profession of lecturing which otherwise I would never have thought of entering.

Chapter 15

A Diploma and a Job

◆

Just before commencement I hiked over to North Brookfield to spend a weekend with old friends. I had become strongly attached to the community where I had discovered a new life in a new world. During my four college years I frequently went back there for Christmas and other vacations or for weekends.

This time I stayed with the Ramsdell family in the village. Johnny Ramsdell (everybody, even children, addressed him as "Johnny" though he was fifty or older) was a short, stocky man, with a thick muscular neck, a broad back, and big protruding eyes. One of the first farmers in the countryside to foresee a big future in pure-bred Holsteins, however high-priced, he began to stock his barn with them. "A bear for work," people called him, he never bragged of his successes with the new breed of cattle, but he was reputed to be the richest farmer in and around the village. He lived in a big two-story house, painted red and white, beside a gurgling, never-drying creek. Not a highly educated man, he had an inquisitive mind and never tired of questioning me about life in my native village. It was hard for him to imagine people like our muzhik neighbors who were so poor they lighted their houses with long birch-wood faggots and were so primitive they fed their pigs, summer and winter, in the family's single room.

His wife, Eve, a handsome woman with thick dark hair and dark eyes, a pillar of the Baptist church, which Johnny never attended, had taken a maternal interest in me from our first meeting, when as a boy of seventeen I had come to work for Jim Moore. During my college years whenever I stayed with her family, she never failed to bake a chocolate layer cake for me to take back to my room. As two of the Ramsdell children, Bert and Georgiana, had been my classmates in the local union school, staying with the Ramsdells was like staying with close relations.

As I wandered around the village, I observed that outwardly it had barely changed in the four years I had been away. Not a single new house had been built, though the old ones had been freshly painted. But the lawns were still nowhere as well tended as in other villages. Only the magnificent shade trees in full foliage saved the village from complete drabness.

The party-line telephone was of course in common use, but electric lights in barns and homes were as yet unknown. In "the backwoods," as city salesmen called North Brookfield, it was still the age of the kerosene lamp and the lantern. The tractor had not yet roared into the fields and the horse remained the universal source of draft power for all field work. The hired man was usually a young peasant from Eastern Europe. Though roads, especially through the lowlands, were still bad, the Model-T Ford was beginning to appear on them, often to get stuck in a mudhole requiring a team of horses to pull it out. But in those days farmers rarely traveled and when they did, it was by train. Nobody had yet foreseen the invention of radio, still less of television, and farmers spent their evenings visiting one another, gathering in the post office, in the general store, or in the saloon— there were still three of them in the village. Old Ely Hibbard's bologna basement was as popular as ever, especially with the boys who had attended the local school around my time.

One could still see spittoons in the houses of tobacco chewers and in public places—the station, the post office, the general store, the bologna basement. Yet the new generation of boys was breaking away from the habit of their fathers.

Viewed in retrospect, the general store was an amazing institution. There had been nothing like it in the villages in the Old Country. It sold groceries of all kinds, including heavy sacks of white flour, for farm women were still baking their own bread, their own pies, their own cookies and doughnuts. It also sold salt pork and ciscoes, both in wide demand, shoes and work clothes from overalls to shirts, horse collars and harnesses, saws and axes, nails and hammers, rakes and hoes, milk pails and crowbars—in fact, any hand tool a farmer might need. People came to the store not only to shop, but also to while away their spare time: to catch the latest gossip or to expatiate on the news in the local paper. The store dispensed a wider variety of merchandise than I had imagined a store in a village of some three hundred would carry. Farmers made themselves comfortable around the potbellied stove, the inevitable spittoon handy, for a chaw and a talk.

On this visit I stayed away from the saloons. I was no longer interested in the bawdy stories that the purely masculine atmosphere released. Though I never regarded myself a puritan, the influence of college and especially of the divinity student who was my closest friend had made me intolerant of barroom obscenities. But I happily returned to the general store, the post office, and the bologna basement. I still loved the talk of villagers and farmers. Non-intellectuals, these hardheaded people were concerned only with practical matters, not with the mind. I didn't care; whatever the subject of conversation, even if only petty gossip, it held my attention. I felt at home with them—and with insatiable curiosity I listened to everything they said about themselves, their neighbors, the world outside, about new crops and new methods of farming. One farmer, an old friend, on shaking hands with me, ran his palm over mine and remarked with a laugh, "As soft as a girl's, no dirt farmer's hand any more." I told him that I might yet go back to dirt farming, if my aim to make a living as a writer should fail.

I have just finished reading *Making It* by Norman Podhoretz. Despite the vulgarity of the title, I found the book of absorbing interest, principally because the author, though much younger than I am and born in America, had come out of much the same background as I had, only he had lived in Brooklyn and I in the squalor of an East Side slum. "When I was in college [Columbia]," writes Podhoretz, "the term WASP had not yet come into currency—which is to say the realization had not yet become widespread that white Americans of Anglo-Saxon Protestant background are an ethnic group like any other, that their characteristic qualities are by no means self-evidently superior to those of other groups and that neither their earlier arrival nor their majority status entitles them to the exclusive possession of the national identity."

The people in North Brookfield who gathered in the general

store, the post office, the bologna basement, or even the saloon, with the exception of the very few second- or third-generation Irish among them, were of as "white American of Anglo-Saxon Protestant background" as any that had presided over the destinies of Columbia University. But I had never known them to show any sense of racial superiority or to look down on their hired men, illiterate or semiliterate peasants from Hungary, Poland, the Ukraine, Russia. Descendants of pioneers who with their sweat and blood had conquered a forested wilderness and converted it into a blooming countryside, they were too keenly aware of the meaning and value of physical labor not to respect those who did an honest day's labor for them. I could only feel grateful for the instinct that had prompted me at a very young age to flee to the upstate countryside, where I would never hear of nor suffer from the snubs and social humiliations of which Podhoretz writes. Nor had I encountered them at white Anglo-Saxon Protestant Colgate. Maybe it was because at the time I was a senior there were only four students of immigrant origin there—a Persian, a Lebanese, a German, and myself. There may have been students who thought themselves superior to these foreigners but if so, they kept their sentiments to themselves.

The one change in North Brookfield that saddened me was the departure of Elder Mattison, whose warm-heartedness in my moments of loneliness and discouragement had so often comforted and encouraged me. But the three hundred dollars a year he earned, though supplemented by an occasional honorarium from weddings, funerals, or other functions, were not enough to get along on, even though he lived rent-free in the parsonage, one of the largest and most comfortable houses in the village behind which stretched some ten acres of level land. The elder could have kept a cow, but didn't. He could have raised his own pork, but didn't. But with the help of his wife and children he cultivated a fine garden. He suffered from a weak heart and couldn't stand hot sun and prolonged physical effort, so except for the garden he made no use of his land. Once he tried to earn extra money by painting Johnny Ramsdell's barn. But he never finished the job; the work proved too strenuous. When a larger community offered him a higher salary he left North Brookfield.

A new minister, the Reverend George Linderman, came to officiate in the Baptist church. An elderly man of medium height with a closely trimmed dark-brown beard, he was not a "powerful" preacher like Elder Mattison. He spoke in a flat, raspy voice and he lacked his predecessor's gift of enlivening his sermons with stories and anecdotes or quaint figures of speech. He too was a fundamentalist and didn't believe in dancing, card playing, smoking, drinking—but no sin, however heinous, could arouse him to the elder's heights of thunderous denunciation. A phlegmatic man, nothing really excited him, least of all young people. So the old Sunday school class for young people with its biweekly socials and literary evenings, which were Elder Mattison's achievement, was falling to pieces. The church was still the center of all social "doings" in the community—Ladies' Aid suppers, oyster stew dinners, Sunday school picnics—but the new minister lacked the gift of his predecessor of investing social activity with a spirit of jollity and camaraderie. Even Johnny Ramsdell, no churchgoer, lamented Elder Mattison's departure.

The Reverend Mr. Linderman was a healthy man and loved work. He specialized in raising onions, a profitable cash crop. One could always see him in overalls, hoe in hand, working in the onion field in back of the parsonage. When he broke off the tops, the onion smell in the neighborhood was as overpowering as a skunk's, and hardly less unpleasant. Neighbors grumbled at it, but nowadays old-timers who remember the industrious minister never fail to bring it up with amusement.

Before returning to Hamilton for commencement I went walking in the countryside, dropping in on farmers I knew and finally calling on Jim Moore. I found him in the hophouse sitting on a crate and examining with his still sharp blue eyes the new apiary fixtures he had just received from a manufacturer in Ohio. He was over seventy now. The shiny patch on his skull had broadened and the upstanding fringe of hair had turned completely white. But he appeared as "spry," one of his favorite words, as when I had first come to work on his farm. He paused in his work, emptied his mouth of tobacco juice, and we started to talk. He asked what I was going to do when I got out of college and I told him of my lecture contracts on the Chautauqua and lyceum circuits.

"You come a long way," he said, "since you left that goddamn stinkin' village of yourn in Rooshia."

We continued talking of old days on his farm and, of course, of politics. "Them Republicans in yer college," he asked, "hain't made a Republican out of ye?" I replied that I was not yet a citizen, but that I was planning to go to Wampsville, seat of Madison County, to get my citizenship certificate. He abjured me never, never to vote the Republican ticket and to please the old man, I promised. When I was ready to leave he stood up, gave me a piercing look, and said, "Now that ye've got yer college edication and be goin' to earn big wages lecturin', don't ye never get stuck on yerself. It's the worst thing a man can do and don't ye never forget it. Folks around here hain't never give a damn for the man who got stuck on himself."

The old farmer wasn't telling me anything new. In the lore and culture of the pioneering countryside, the show-off, the man who was "stuck on himself," betrayed a lack of faith in his inner self and invited ridicule. For the young immigrant this was a lesson he would always remember. Whatever social snobbism (which Jim Moore called being "stuck on oneself") he would encounter in subsequent years, he would shrug off as easily and as contemptuously as Jim himself had done.

That was why I was amused when I read in Podhoretz's *Making It* of "the stock market report" on the reputations of the superintellectuals in "the family" of which the author is supposedly an honored member. He says that "every morning a stock market report on reputations came out in New York. It is invisible but those who have eyes to see can read it. Did so-and-so have dinner at Jacqueline Kennedy's apartment last night? Up five points. Was so-and-so *not* invited by the Lowells to meet the latest visiting Russian poet? Down one-eighth. Did so-and-so get nominated for the National Book Award? Up two and five-eighths. Did *Partisan Review* neglect to ask so-and-so to participate in a symposium? Down two!"

For one who in his younger years had absorbed and been molded by the culture of such sturdy sons of pioneers as Jim Moore, Johnny Ramsdell, and men like them, nothing could be more foolishly pretentious than "the stock market report" which Podhoretz presents so solemnly. To boost one's ego in the reflected glory of others, however exalted their position in society or the literary world, is a form of obsequiousness which the upstate Jims and Johnnys would only guffaw at.

Late the next Sunday afternoon I left for Hamilton. This time, instead of a chocolate layer cake that she was too busy to bake, Mrs. Ramsdell packed for me a box full of homemade cookies and doughnuts. She and Johnny came out on the porch to see me off. "Come and see us," she said, "whenever you can. Our home will always be open to you." Johnny repeated the invitation.

I have been back many times since then, though not always to stop with the Ramsdells, even when Eve and Johnny were still alive. I can no more keep away from that remote countryside that had opened a new life and a new world to me, than I can keep away from food when I am hungry.

Commencement came. At last it was good-by to the sun-streaked willow path, the shimmering lake, the pair of proud white swans gliding imperiously over the water; good-by to the gray stone buildings on the hilltop, the rolling emerald lawn, the round-towered library rising like a European castle above the grassy hillside; good-by to the panorama of hills and fields, of wood lots and meadows sweeping into a distant blue haze—a countryside that was an extension of the pioneer farm that had been the original campus.

Though it was the most idyllic place I was ever to live in, I was leaving it without regret. I was in fact longing for an escape from an environment so removed from all outside turmoil; its very beauty soothed unrest of mind and fret of soul. Yet a twinge of melancholy came over me as I thought of breaking away from the little tribal world, so different from the other worlds I had lived in or was ever to live in again and in which I had spent four rewarding years. When I first came, it had been so bewildering and disturbing that I felt lost and alone, and I had cherished my aloneness so proudly that I was glad to sequester myself on Bronson's farm. Now that I was leaving, everything was familiar, nothing was disturbing, and I had lost my loneliness.

When I first came to college I was too stiff with purpose for my own good. In the grim scheme of things of Russian village life, I had matured beyond my years. I had in fact barely known the age of adolescence, in which American boys and girls, as I discovered in college, lingered on for an incredibly long time, longer than in any country in the world, carrying over into college years. The spirit of Huck Finn was incarnated on the campus in youths whom Huck would have called old men.

It had taken me a long time to become attuned to the carefree spirit of my fellows, to their bright inconsequential chatter, the irreverent spoofs at their professors who to me were to be revered as great scholars and great spirits. It had shocked me to hear them mocked, even though in good humor and without a touch of malice. But the ease and warmth with which I was accepted finally broke down my reserve; and though I could never completely enter into the lively game of make-believe that ignored so much of their inner natures, I learned to respond to it and at times even to enter into it for purposes of my own. I had a past and my classmates didn't; their life was all of a piece, with no sharp divisions in it, no change of worlds like mine, and they would go on being what they were born to be. Knowing them had been as much of an education as all the courses I had taken, all the books I had read.

The Ivy League fashion in those days was a blue serge jacket, white flannel trousers, and low white shoes, and those of us who could afford the outfit and some who couldn't appeared in this admired regalia at our last sing together on the smooth lawn at the edge of the lake. Sitting on the grass, surrounded by faculty and townspeople, we exuberantly sang one song after another, with no quaver of solemnity in our voices. It was only a few weeks after the sinking of the *Lusitania* by a German submarine with the loss of more than a thousand lives, many of them American. Led by Theodore Roosevelt a clamor for war against the Kaiser's Germany reverberated over the land. Echoes reached the tranquil campus and though we could not escape an undercurrent of anxiety, we couldn't imagine ourselves slipping into soldier's uniforms and going off to war. How absurd to think of killing or getting killed in faraway Europe at one of the most triumphant moments in our lives!

The next day was the march of the faculty, guests, and seniors from the campus to the Baptist church where the commencement exercises were held. It was a gala day for the faculty. Like spring flowers, our soberly dressed professors blossomed out in a pageantry of color, the gold tassels on black caps, the white and orange, blue and scarlet of hoods sparkling in the brilliant sun. Like priests in resplendent vestments leading a feast-day procession, they headed the march to the church to the beat of the stirring music of the village band between rows of admiring farmers and villagers. The ceremony revealed a talent for mounting spectacles exceeding anything I had ever seen in the old country.

The crowded church was aglow with flowers and bright summer dresses, but the center pews were dark with the massed seniors in tasseled mortarboards and black gowns. The organ pealed the opening bars of a hymn and we stood still and solemn as at Sunday service. Then came the baccalaureate address, not a particularly exciting one, as I distinctly remember seeing many a suppressed yawn at the interminable homilies and precepts offered to young men who had already heard enough homilies and precepts to last them a lifetime.

At last, one by one, we were called to the platform. Pausing before the brightly hooded president, we received the rolled parchments, which we acknowledged with a smile and amidst the applause of the audience, and walked back to our seats. The ceremony ended with the singing of the melancholy "Alma Mater," and I could sense a stir of emotion among my classmates, though whether sorrow or relief I couldn't tell.

Then came the inevitable good-bys. For four years at college we had been a closely knit community, but now that it was breaking up nobody seemed at all regretful. There were ninety of us in the class and for one more brief moment we surged with warm sentiment for one another. We joshed and we bantered. We might only have been leaving a jolly bull session.

One good-by I remember with particular vividness. Bob Markwick from Jefferson County, who in my freshman year had told me of the high wages farmers were paying experienced hired men, called me "old geezer" and wished me to remember that if ever again I wanted a farm job Jefferson County was the one and only place to look for it.

That was the last time I saw Bob. He went to France and never returned. Buried with him in the soil of France is the age of illusion and innocence whose slogan was "Make the world safe for democracy." Even the Carl Baum tailor shop was never the same again.

Chapter 16

Again Another America

◆

Living in upstate New York I could not help hearing of Chautauqua County, Chautauqua Lake, the Chautauqua summer institute where Dr. Elmer Burritt Bryan, president of Colgate, was a distinguished lecturer. But of "Chautauqua" as a cultural movement, popular in the Middle West, I knew nothing until I signed a contract to lecture on Russia for the Midland Chautauqua Bureau with offices in Des Moines, Iowa.

The terms of the contract called for me to be a "filler-in" to appear in towns where an extra program number was demanded or to substitute for a lecturer or performer who was unable to appear on the program of either the five- or seven-day circuit. It was not until the following year, the summer of 1916, that I became a regular "attraction" on the seven-day circuit, one of the most select in the Middle West, lecturing seven afternoons a week.

While the financial returns for part-time lecturing were not particularly rewarding, the prospect of traveling in the Middle West excited me. Here was an opportunity to become acquainted with the heartland of America and to see with my own eyes the fabulous farms in Iowa and Nebraska I had read about in agricultural journals during my years in North Brookfield. I knew that these were among the so-called "homestead states," and the term "homestead" with all that it signified of free or cheap land, of which no muzhik in Russia could even have dreamed, held a special significance for the young immigrant from a muzhik village.

Arriving in Des Moines several days before the opening of the Chautauqua season, I checked in at a small but comfortable hotel and went to the bureau office to become acquainted with the people there. They loaded me up with literature on the cultural aims of the Chautauqua movement and with colorfully printed programs of the two circuits they managed. Back in the hotel I studied the literature, and the more I studied it the more fascinated I became by the nature of the culture disseminated from one community to another under brown-canvased tents. Chautauqua offered both enlightenment and entertainment: lectures and concerts, poetry recitals and travelogues, theatrical performances and play readings, magicians and animal acts. There were also "junior girls," college students or graduates who in the mornings told stories and played games with the children.

The programs were attuned to the diverse tastes of the community, and, it was emphasized, not a number but was "morally clean and uplifting," which I interpreted to mean free from any hint of profanity, any allusion to sex, any tinge of racial or religious bias. Considering the temper of the times, the programs were ingeniously put together—no offense to anybody, culture and pleasure for young and old.

I did not know any of the men and women whose faces beamed at me out of the lavishly illustrated programs, smiling faces, happy faces as of people enraptured at the prospect of performing for an audience inside the big brown tents. The list of lecturers who were the "heavies" on the programs intrigued me. Principally they were preachers, educators, politicians, congressmen, and senators. Their lectures, to judge by the titles, were largely of an inspirational nature, a type I had often heard during chapel exercises in college and which had always left me apathetic. The permanent star on the seven-day circuit was the minister of a Baptist church in Philadelphia, Russell Conwell, of whom I had never heard but whose biography in the bureau's circular sounded extraordinarily impressive. The lecture he was booked to deliver was called "Acres of Diamonds," a lecture he had delivered over five thousand times, which I thought a momentous achievement, indicative of some inner hope or yearning of the lecture-going public. Yet to me, in search of fresh meanings in the New World, the most striking feature of Conwell's lecture career was not the enormous popularity of his one lecture, but what he did with his fees from it. The circular said that he donated them all to Temple University in Philadelphia, which he had founded (1884) and of which he was president, for the education of boys and girls of the poorer classes. Though over seventy years of age, he did not seem to mind the arduous travel of those times for the sake of the cause to which he had dedicated himself. A truly great and noble man, I concluded, to whom the gospel of the brotherhood of man was no mere rhetorical phrase but a consuming passion. I hoped to be able to hear the lecture and to become acquainted with the lecturer somewhere along the far-stretching circuit.

Helen Keller, the blind, deaf woman who had learned to speak and had graduated from Radcliffe College, was to make guest appearances in several towns. William Jennings Bryan was also billed. At that time Bryan was an idol of mine, not only because of Jim Moore's eulogies of him, but also because his address "The Cross of Gold" which had electrified the Democratic convention in 1896 into nominating him for the Presidency when he was only thirty-six years old, was to my high school and college generation a favorite oration in declamation contests. I had read and heard it on several occasions and was captivated by its eloquence. I had also read of Bryan's journey to Russia (1906) to meet Tolstoy in his rural retreat at Yasnaya Polyana. The pilgrimage to the distinguished author marked Bryan for me as a man of exceptional intellectual distinction; I knew nothing of his religious fundamentalism, nor would it have mattered to me, any more than it would have to Jim Moore who though religious was no fundamentalist, not even a churchgoer. I viewed Bryan's politics through Jim's eyes and saw him as a powerful defender of the underprivileged. So I had high hopes of hearing both of these great figures and of possibly meeting them too. I was now glad that I was only a part-time lecturer and would have days off to travel to the near-by towns where they and Conwell were scheduled to appear.

Meanwhile, I proceeded to explore Des Moines, then a city of about 100,000 population. I know of no better way of learning about the life and the spirit of a community than by wandering from street to street, square to square. Nowhere in my wanderings in Des Moines did I come on slum neighborhoods like those I had seen in Utica, the only other small city I had known, much older than Des Moines. The capital of Iowa was so orderly, so clean, and so modern that it was hard to believe that it was a new city, chartered only a little over half a century before. Of course, as a state capital it had grown rapidly, but the people who settled there had not permitted slovenliness to accompany fast development. Cresting a hill gleamed the gilded dome of the capitol building, the most impressive structure in the city which, like a lighthouse, enabled me to find my bearings whenever I lost myself in my rambles.

Des Moines was a friendly city. In restaurants, in shops, in hotel lobbies where I loved to loiter people were as informal and sociable as in North Brookfield. They easily engaged in conversation, and some of my encounters in the Hawkeye capital have remained vivid in my mind to the present day. Once while sauntering about the immaculately kept capitol grounds, I struck up an acquaintance with two young men, one like myself just out of college, the other still a student at Drake University in Des Moines. When they learned I was Russian-born and had come to lecture on Russia for the Midland Chautauqua Bureau, they questioned me about Russia and the war which was going miserably for the Russian armies. Time passed quickly and as the dinner hour approached one of them invited me to his home for the meal. His father, he informed me, was German, son of an early settler in Iowa. He was deeply interested in the war and would be pleased to talk with me. I gladly accepted the invitation.

The father, a big-boned man with whitish hair and a sunscorched face and the mother, a short portly woman, who it turned out was the daughter of a Swedish settler, welcomed me with warm handshakes. Through dinner and afterwards we talked of subjects other than the war and of course of the pioneering years in Iowa. The old man said that he had been a boy of ten when his parents migrated from Germany to become homesteaders in Iowa. Many, very many Germans and Scandinavians, all of peasant stock, had been lured there by the promise of large allotments of virtually free or low-priced land. The father remembered well the ordeals of pioneering even in Iowa where, unlike New York State, there had been no forest to clear, no stumps to uproot, no steep hills for man or horse to climb. Life was tough in those days, but his father never grew discouraged because after all the land was his, lots of land, a quarter section of 160 acres, as good land as there was anywhere on earth. After his father died he took over the farm and added to it another quarter section which he bought from a neighbor. He would still have been on the land but rheumatism had got him down, and his son (my new acquaintance) would rather teach school in town than work the farm. So he had sold his half section and moved to Des Moines, built himself a frame house, planted a lawn in front and a vegetable garden in back. He still loved to grub in the earth even if only in a garden. Iowa had been good to its German and Scandinavian peasant pioneers.

At the very time these peasants from Northern Europe were emigrating to America to take advantage of the Homestead Act of 1862, the Russian muzhiks, though liberated from serfdom in 1861, were still very much at the mercy of their former masters, the big landholders. More and more I had come to realize the basic importance of landownership to any country, a fact that burned itself into my mind and was to become decisive in my interpretations and judgments of the Russian Revolution which Lenin was soon to hail as the torch that would set the world aflame with more proletarian revolutions. But Lenin failed to recognize the historical significance of the Homestead Act or the importance of the individual farm, and had the Czars been farsighted enough to break up the enormous badly managed holdings of the landed nobility and introduce a policy of land distribution, the world would never have heard of Lenin and Russia would never have been shaken by Bolshevism.

On another occasion in Des Moines some young people with whom I became acquainted in a park invited me to a party. It was a lively affair, principally of college students and graduates of both sexes, though most of the evening was spent in my answering questions on Russia and the war. It was obvious that my Russian origin served me well in those days in the cultivation of new acquaintances, even in the isolationist Middle West. None of the young people at this party, like young people in the East, harbored the least premonition that eventually America too would be drawn into the struggle. But they were intensely in-

terested in the possible outcome of the war and whatever light I
as an American of Russian origin could throw on the matter.

Then one afternoon, as I was reading a magazine in the lobby
of my hotel, a middle-aged man with pink cheeks and a neat
mustache sat down beside me and opened a conversation about
Russia and the war. He had learned about me, he said, at the
office of the Midland Chautauqua Bureau for which he too was
scheduled to lecture. He identified himself only by name, Lafayette Young. We talked a while and when he left the hotel
clerk called me over and asked whether I knew that I had been
talking to a United States senator who was also the editor-owner
of the Des Moines *Capital*, the daily newspaper. No, I replied,
the man never mentioned his high office or journalistic attain-
ments. So modest a behavior in a person of such distinction
strengthened my impression that there was nothing "uppity"—to
use a farmer's expression—about the people in Des Moines. The
social cleavages and class barriers that made Czarist Russia a
house divided against itself, symbolized by the uniforms of military and civilian officials, were as alien here as in the little village
of North Brookfield. Only the police wore uniforms in Des
Moines.

From the window of the daycoach taking me to my first
lecture in Iowa in the Chautauqua town of West Branch, I
looked out upon a new and different land. Here were no swamps
or forests as in Byelorussia, no wooded hillsides as in upstate
New York, but a wide, gently rolling, unbroken stretch of prairie
reaching to the clearest and bluest horizon I had ever seen. The
train rattled through mile after mile of cornfields, green-gold in
the sun, hooted now and then for a grade crossing where a dirt
road cut through the section lines. Red barns with huge silos,
frame houses half hidden in shady groves, cattle grazing on the
knolls—all this swung past my fascinated eyes. I even noted that
here the horses were predominantly white, not bay as around
North Brookfield. I was traveling through the land of the homesteaders, the choicest farming land in the world, a landless
peasant's dream come true.

West Branch was the birthplace of Herbert Hoover, but at
the time I came there (1915) for my first Chautauqua appear-

ance Hoover was no public figure. I had never heard of the man who was to become President. A small town of some six or seven hundred population, West Branch was too small to bear the financial burden of a Chautauqua circuit. But like other towns in the state, it was situated in the midst of prosperous farming country and farm people were as eager as town people to break the monotony of their isolated lives with the cultural offerings of Chautauqua performers. They therefore helped to finance the imported enterprise and dressed in their Sunday best they came with their families, mothers often carrying babies in their arms, to the programs inside the big brown tents.

On my arrival in West Branch, as I walked the streets, I had the impression that the town was made up overwhelmingly of children and old men with beards. Children, crowds of them, were everywhere, in the streets and on the Chautauqua grounds, as playful and as noisy as children anywhere. One could only conclude that the people here were extraordinarily fecund. Old men too seemed to be everywhere and of a somewhat original presence. Tall, lean, upright, with weather-beaten bearded faces, they carried themselves with remarkable dignity and spoke in slow and subdued voices as though the raised voice was a profanation of good taste or good morals. Their form of address was "thee" and "thou," which sounded as quaintly archaic as the "ye" and "yourn" of North Brookfield. I had never before encountered this form of address in America.

However, the out-of-town superintendent of the Chautauqua circuit explained that West Branch was a Quaker community and "thee" and "thou" were common usage here. The old men that I saw around were retired farmers, taking life easy while the younger men were at work in the fields and the women, of course, busy in the houses. Like all Quakers, the superintendent continued, these people knew their Bible thoroughly and were rigidly puritanical. That was why he felt it necessary to caution the "crew boys" (college students who took care of the tent) and the younger people on the programs against any show of levity in public and against the use of unseemly language. He also cautioned me against "talking down" to the audience. Quakers didn't expect a lecturer to crack jokes or make witticisms from the platform. They were serious-minded people, quite well educated, and I could talk to them as to intellectual equals. Of course, he added, if I were to interpolate a biblical verse or use some incident in the Old or New Testament to illustrate my point, it would win special appreciation. Anyway, Quakers loved lectures and no speaker could wish for a more courteous or attentive audience.

I did not tell jokes for the simple reason that I never cultivated the knack of telling them. Nor did I allude to the Bible, not fancying myself as a preacher. Instead I concentrated on presenting the one subject I knew best, that had once been part of my life—the story of the Russian villages where over four-fifths of the country's population lived. I described the daily life of muzhiks, the houses they lived in, the food they ate, the clothes they made for themselves out of their own wool, flax, and hemp; their mode of farming and the ancient implements they used; their dark superstitions and their high illiteracy; their love of song and story, of secular ceremony and religious ritual; their rich social life; their religiosity with its roots deep in ancient paganism; their hatred of landlords and their helplessness before the uniformed and corrupt officials. I related in intimate detail the life of the muzhik as I knew it, with all its adversities and torments, its diversions and merriments. I did not sermonize, delivered no message, moral, political or other. Of course, I did not fail to contrast the distribution of land in Iowa in pioneering times, when anybody who wished could acquire a farm of his own, free or cheap, with the mode of acquisition in Russia where Catherine the Great alone gave away as gifts to favorite lovers countless acres of the choicest land in the country, along with the serfs who worked it and who were as tightly bound to the land and as subservient to the landlord as the Negro slaves had been to the plantation owner in the South. I did not discuss the political issues involved in the war: I knew little about them. But I did express the hope that when the war ended there would be no Czar and no Kaiser. Like the tailors in Carl Baum's shop, I was naïve enough to believe that once the Russian and German thrones were toppled, an age of justice and redemption would dawn for both Russia and Germany and that universal peace would reign at last.

I had no difficulty in holding the attention of the audience that packed the big, dimly lit tent, an audience mostly of farm folk. While listening to me they could and doubtless did draw contrast after contrast between their own condition and that of the muzhiks.

From the response of my audience that day, I concluded that a lecture built around the living conditions and daily routines of far-off people held a special appeal. In subsequent lectures I followed this pattern and it never failed to interest the most diverse audiences—businessmen, school teachers, and even Harvard professors. The lot of the muzhik as I depicted it from my own memories was a disturbing revelation of a virtually unknown aspect of Russian life.

After West Branch I spoke on an evening program in another Iowa town. When the lecture was over a man came to the back of the tent and greeted me with a Russian "*zdravstvuite*" (How do you do). I replied and asked whether he was Russian. He smiled and shook his head—he knew no more of the language than the greeting; he was a Bohemian. Presently his wife and teenage daughter came over and he introduced us. The wife invited me to their house for a cup of coffee and homemade Bohemian cake. I gladly accepted.

They lived a short distance from the Chautauqua grounds in a two-story frame house with a big open porch set back on a shady lawn. There was nothing foreign about this house and obviously this was not a poor family. We sat out on the porch and talked. At the time Bohemians were not yet known as Czechs; I knew only that they were Slavs like Russians, though their language was quite dissimilar. So we conversed in English.

Several of their neighbors, also Bohemians, joined us on the porch, and as we sat around and talked I learned that, like the Germans and Scandinavians, many Bohemians, mostly peasants and a few artisans, had migrated to the Middle West in response to the Homestead Act. It was the same story over again: cheap land and hard labor had made for one of America's greatest achievements.

Someone asked whether I had been in Nebraska. Not yet, I replied, but I was going there. Well, then, did I know that there were so many Bohemians in Nebraska that among themselves Bohemians spoke of it as "Bohemian country"? It was land of course that had lured their people to the neighboring state. To a Bohemian, land was gold.

My new friends were sons and daughters of pioneers, though some of the younger ones, like my host and hostess, were born in America. The others had come over with their parents when they were children. Yet they all spoke fluent English with hardly a trace of an accent or none at all. Their children were attending American schools and colleges—yes, colleges—because Bohemians were great believers in education. Not one of them who had come from the Old Country but had had a common school education. I asked the golden-haired daughter of my host whether she spoke Bohemian. Instantly the mother turned to the girl and chided her for being too lazy to study it and said to me that she was trying to make her learn it. The girl herself laughed and said something in Bohemian. Then in English she confessed that the old-country language didn't interest her—it was of no use in America. But the older people present assured me that they didn't permit their sons and daughters to forget it. So among the Bohemians in Nebraska, as among immigrant groups in the East, keeping the language of their origin alive was a problem and a struggle.

As we continued our conversation on the brightly lighted porch, I was surprised to learn that despite Czarism and feudal landholding Bohemians venerated Russia. They had fled from the hated Austrians, who centuries earlier had destroyed their independence and butchered their educated classes—a historic crime that was kept alive in every Bohemian home from generation to generation. They looked to Russia as their big Slav brother and as the only power in Europe that might someday liberate their people from Austrian subjugation. And Russian music, how they loved it! Of course, Bohemians had a natural passion for music, but Russian music found special favor with them: it was so Slavic, so soul-stirring. Still, they were astonished at the miserable condition of the Russian peasantry I had depicted in my lecture.

In subsequent Chautauqua appearances in Iowa towns I met other Bohemians. In fact, wherever there were Bohemians they invariably came over to introduce themselves and invited me to their homes.

Then I came to lecture in Crete, Nebraska. I discovered that I was in a virtually Bohemian town, though outwardly, save for names over shops, there was nothing foreign about it, either in the architecture or in the appearance of the people. Here the Bohemians seemed fully assimilated into American civilization. Yet because I had come from Russia and was lecturing on Russia, I was, figuratively speaking, embraced by the Bohemian community. I was wined and dined and drawn into lengthy conversations with my hosts and their friends who, like the Bohemians in Iowa, venerated Russia as the big and powerful brother of all subjugated Slav peoples whom only Russia could liberate. This feeling for Russia, I was assured, was universal among Bohemians in the Middle West. We talked of Pan-Slavism, with Russia as the natural and inevitable leader of the movement. Bohemians, I remembered, had been welcomed by the Czarist government, not only as teachers of gymnastics but also—what was even more significant—as teachers of Greek and Latin in gymnasiums and other educational institutions all over the country. In those days I knew little of Pan-Slavism and I could only think of the Bohemian glorification of Russia as Russophilism.

I had several days free and was so captivated by Crete that I stayed there until it was time to leave for my next Chautauqua engagement. While visiting around with Bohemians, I heard story after story of the hard pioneering days when their fathers and grandfathers first came to Nebraska. Yes, life for the original settlers had been very hard, but it had also been replete with adventure and with the promise of a better future.

The stories fascinated me as pioneering stories always did. Several years later when Willa Cather's *My Antonia* was published, I read and reread it with ever-growing admiration for the author, a non-Bohemian, who wrote so warmly and so movingly of pioneering Bohemians in Nebraska. The novel and my own experiences among them had convinced me that Bohemians were culturally the most advanced Slav peasants in the world. They readily assimilated into American life, though they clung to some old-country usages such as the *Sokol* (falcon) gymnastic societies, martial bands, songs and dances, Bohemian dishes, and a sentimental esteem for Russia.

Over fifty years have passed since then, and in Nebraska, where they came in much larger numbers than to Iowa, Bohemians have done remarkably well, not only in agriculture but in business, the professions, and even in politics. Republican Senator Roman Lee Hruska is of Bohemian descent. By and large, Americans of Bohemian extraction in the corn-husking states have been conservative. Though far away from their homeland, they have not lost interest in it. But if through the years they had retained their old-time Russophilism, it was shattered by the Moscow-engineered Communist coup in February 1948, which with one blow converted their homeland into a servile satellite. The Moscow-led military invasion of the country in August 1968, in the dead of night when the people were asleep, has replaced the century-old Russophilism with a fierce Russophobia.

Still, to this day I treasure my encounters with Bohemians many years ago in Iowa and Nebraska. Even in those far-off times, they were unlike the Slavic peasants I had known. In the sixties of the nineteenth century, when they first began migrating to the Middle West, they were almost universally literate, a condition the muzhik was to attain only about a century later. From them I first learned of the spiritual heritage bequeathed to them by John Huss (1369–1415), the Bohemian priest-reformer who was one of the great humanists of all time and who was tried as a heretic and burned at the stake. From them I also learned of John Comenius (1592–1670), the other great Czech humanist who revolutionized the educational system of his day. These Nebraska Bohemians were a revelation to me—Slav peasants who prized learning as no other Slav peasants I knew; and they were so warmly hospitable that I soon came to feel a close kinship with them.

I remembered them and spoke of them over and over and with fervor many years later when I traveled in Czechoslovakia to gather material for the three books I have written about that eminently civilized and tragic country.

Chapter 17

Troupers to Remember

◆

One morning while studying the Chautauqua schedules I found that Dr. Conwell, whose famous lecture "Acres of Diamonds" I very much wanted to hear, would be speaking in a town only fifty miles away. I had long been curious as to why this particular lecture had become so popular and through just what particular magic it moved its vast audiences so that many who heard it came back a second, third, and even fourth time.

There was no train connection between the town in which I appeared and the one in which Dr. Conwell was scheduled to speak. Luckily, my own lecture on that day came in the afternoon and Dr. Conwell's in the evening when men who worked during the day could hear him.

I hired an automobile and drove to the town. It was evening when I arrived at the Chautauqua grounds. I could hear the musical prelude which always preceded a lecture, so I knew that the minister-educator had not yet begun to speak. In the back of the tent, which was curtained off from the platform and served as waiting and dressing room, I found Senator Lafayette Young and Dr. Conwell. As they spoke on the same days, the senator in the afternoon and Dr. Conwell in the evening, they traveled together. The senator recognized me and introduced me to Dr. Conwell. We shook hands and talked until the platform superintendent signaled Dr. Conwell to be ready to mount the stage for the introduction.

He rose from the folding bench and I was at once impressed with his striking appearance. He was tall, powerfully built, with broad shoulders and a deep chest. He had a thick black mustache and warm smiling eyes. He wore a dark-gray business suit and a small black bow tie and looked more like a successful insurance executive than a minister-educator. Obviously, formality meant nothing to him or he would have worn a black frock coat like other ministers.

The tent was packed to overflowing and I joined the standees who were several rows deep. Still I could hear every word. Dr. Conwell had a clear pleasant voice with plenty of carrying power. He was no orator and did not embellish his speech with fanciful language, poetic images, rhetorical perorations. He depended for appeal not on flights of eloquence, but on the ideas he presented, ideas that at first shocked and then dismayed me. The burden of his thinking was that acres of diamonds—actual riches—lay within a man's reach. Anyone who searched diligently enough would find wealth in his own backyard. There was no need for anyone to be poor when he could as well be rich. He cited examples of poor boys becoming rich in the manner of Horatio Alger's heroes and of men who needlessly left hearth and home in search of fortune, never suspecting that what they yearned for was hidden in their own backyard waiting for somebody else to discover and profit by.

His most vivid example of such shortsightedness was that of a Pennsylvania farmer who sold his farm for a pittance and moved to Canada to join a cousin in the oil business. But it was the farm that proved rich in oil from which the new owner made his fortune. With enthusiasm Dr. Conwell related that this farm was now the site of the town of Titusville, famed for its oil wells.

Dr. Conwell denied that money of itself was "the root of all evil," and when a young student of theology challenged him on this point, he replied that he had never found it so stated in his own Bible, which, he declared, said simply that "*the love* of money was the root of all evil." He scoffed at surviving religious prejudices against money-making, as though poverty in itself was pleasing to God. Not at all. But, he insisted, wealth should be amassed by honorable Christian methods and should be dedicated to the welfare of one's fellow man. Money, he kept repeating, meant power, and power should be used for the good of others: for building better homes, better schools, better churches, and bringing greater happiness to people.

Manifestly he practiced what he preached. From his lectures he made plenty of money and he gave it all to the university that he had founded and to other causes that he sought to promote. In his day he was called "the penniless millionaire"—the rich man who never put money into any bank account for himself. Born on a poor rocky farm in New England, he was reared in poverty and had never acquired a taste for luxurious living; traveling on the Chautauqua circuits in those days, he was lucky if he got to a hotel that offered a room with private bath. But he never complained. Chautauqua managers spoke of him as a "cheerful trouper." He was too dedicated a Christian to care for worldly pleasures other than those that came his way accidentally, as when he was entertained by some millionaire or traveled abroad on some cultural or social mission.

The catalogue of Temple University for the college year of 1967–68 is a thick book of 359 pages. The university, I learned, is now one of the largest in the country, with an enrollment of 38,000 students. It has seven professional schools offering degrees in, among other fields, medicine, pharmacy, law, dentistry, and includes six baccalaureate colleges. The graduate departments offer courses for master's and doctor's degrees, and the library contains more than half a million volumes and subscribes to over 2000 journals in numerous fields of knowledge. Since 1965 the university has been linked to the state of Pennsylvania and holds down tuition fees pursuant to its founder's wishes.

The university is a monument to the self-sacrifice and dedication of its founder. The Samaritan Hospital (now Temple University Hospital) is another public creation of the author of "Acres of Diamonds," who cultivated his own fruitful acres with the sole purpose of serving his fellow man, regardless of race, creed, social origin. Religious prejudice, notably the sweeping anti-Catholic crusade of his times, he had always denounced with all the vigor of his strong mind. And the Grace Baptist Church of Philadelphia which he built up from a small congregation into one of the largest and most socially concerned Protestant churches in the country, with a membership of over 3000, was another of his achievements.

Yet on the memorable evening so long ago when I heard him deliver his famous lecture, I was somewhat disturbed by his confident conviction that riches, actual money, were within the reach of anybody who set his heart and mind on gaining them and that nobody had a right to be poor. In the light of my farm experience, the good man's exhortation made no sense at all. Jim Moore had loved his hilly and bottomland acres and worked hard all his life; but he was always cash-poor and could never save enough to pay off the mortgage. But I never questioned, nor did any farmers I knew, that the moneyed people in the city, by which they meant Wall Street, controlled the price of farm produce. There may have been some exaggeration in this widespread belief, yet in the main it was the truth. Unorganized as they were in those days, farmers were helpless before the powers that controlled the markets.

I knew successful farmers in and around North Brookfield who lived comfortably and never had to worry about a rainy day, none of whom was rich by Dr. Conwell's standards. Though they sweated over their acres—their "backyards"—they never found a single diamond. In the cities and in the business world the situation was different, and Dr. Conwell held the rich in such regard that he had only praise for John D. Rockefeller, Sr., and for Andrew Carnegie—men whose unconscionable skulduggery I had read about in college and whom the tailors in Carl Baum's shop always execrated. Indeed, the tailors would have had a derisive laugh over Dr. Conwell's lecture.

Yet on the conclusion of the address that evening the audience burst into thunderous applause. They were obviously heartened to hear that they too might someday find the "acres of diamonds" in their own cornfields. I joined in the applause if only in admiration for the undramatic, unoratorical minister who had been able to hold a packed tent of hardheaded farmers enthralled for nearly two hours. I went back stage, shook his hand, and congratulated him on his ability to hold a large audience spellbound. But I did not mention my doubts about the diamonds.

Chautauqua publicity styled Helen Keller "the blind, deaf and dumb wonder of the world," and for days before her arrival in a town the platform superintendent would call on audiences to spread the word far and wide of this lifetime opportunity for young and old to hear, yes actually *hear*, "the blind, deaf and dumb wonder." Such an announcement preceded my afternoon lecture in one of the larger Iowa towns. It sounded more like ballyhoo for a circus and I boldly told the man who made it, a small-town Protestant minister, that Helen Keller deserved a more dignified introduction. The remonstrance was futile; in the evening he waxed even more florid.

Helen Keller was to appear the next afternoon, a Sunday. I had time to stay over and hear her. Though her book *The Story of My Life* had already been published, I had not heard of it. For some reason it had escaped the attention even of that omnivorous reader Carl Baum. Of course I had heard of the famous woman herself, and what had especially impressed me was that she had graduated *cum laude* from Radcliffe. I knew that a student, once having met the basic requirements, could select "snap" courses and "sail through" to a diploma with little exertion. But Helen Keller had not chosen the easy way. I was eager to hear her message of "cheer and happiness" that the platform superintendent had announced. That a woman so greatly handicapped should become an exponent of "joy in living" was a wonder to me.

I went to the tent early that afternoon to make certain of a seat and found one about midway from the platform. The tent was filling rapidly. I had never seen so many children come to a program. They sat, as usual, crowded together on the grassy ground in front of the platform, with a watchful junior girl in a chair facing them. Nor had I ever seen so many mothers with babies there—an augury of possible outbreaks of disquiet, which would not of course disturb Helen Keller but would be a nuisance to those who had come to hear her.

During the musical prologue the platform superintendent searched me out and whispered in my ear that Helen Keller had heard of "the young Russian who was lecturing on Russia" and wanted to meet me, and I promised to come back stage after the lecture.

I am rather hazy as to whether it was Anne Sullivan Macy, the blind woman's celebrated teacher, or Polly Thompson, her secretary, or somebody else who opened the lecture with a brief history of Miss Keller's life and struggles to overcome her terrible disability, but whichever it was, she remained on the platform to interpret for the blind woman.

Then Helen Keller came on the stage smiling and bowing to the applause. (I later learned that she could feel the vibrations of the applause through her feet.) She was tall, strongly built, with a radiant expression on her exceptionally handsome face. No audience could help responding to such grace and vivacity. Yet when she began speaking one felt painfully uneasy. Her voice was guttural and forced and difficult to understand. The interpreter repeated her words almost sentence by sentence. I remember distinctly that she began by lamenting the war raging in Europe. She expressed the hope that America would never join in the fighting, which won her fervent applause. Then she began speaking of herself, and by this time one began to make out her words and to forget the unnatural quality of her voice. One was only aware of her dignity, charm, and intelligence. It did not really matter any more what she was saying; merely looking at her, watching the mobility of her handsome face, the warm smile, the uplifted arm held the audience enraptured. Even the children sitting on the grass at her feet were still, as carried away by the magic of her presence as were their fathers and mothers.

I was told later that she did not much like lecturing before Chautauqua audiences. But I could not imagine an audience more appreciative of any speaker than the one in that Iowa town that afternoon.

When it was over I went back stage and was introduced to her. Now I could easily understand every word she spoke, and she listened to me with her fingers on my lips. She told me that she was a great admirer of Tolstoy and that she was heartsick over the war and over the sufferings of the people in the war-stricken countries. But I was so enraptured with just being in her presence that I could hardly discuss the war, though I did manage to tell her that I too lamented it. But I only wanted to tell her of my great admiration for her unmatched achievement and so stammered out one compliment after another.

Later I reproached myself for not having been alert enough to pay her the one compliment that might particularly have pleased her. As I have mentioned, since my school days in Russia I had been an avid reader of Turgenev and an ardent admirer of his heroines, who to me represented the highest qualities of Russian womanhood—splendid femininity, will to action, social purposefulness—in short, all the qualities exemplified by Helen Keller. So

I regretted that I had not told her that Turgenev would have adored her and that she was in truth a Turgenev heroine.

In 1942 I went to Moscow as a war correspondent and one day I visited a school for blind, deaf, and mute children. All the teachers were middle-aged women, the younger ones and the men having gone off to war or to work in defense industries. When I told the teachers that I had met Helen Keller whom they revered, they were delighted and asked endless questions about her. Among other things, I said that it had been my everlasting regret not to have told her that she was a perfect embodiment of the most endearing traits of Turgenev's heroines. Thereupon one of the teachers, a stubby woman with thick dark hair cut short, flung her arms around me, kissed me on the cheek, and said, "Nobody could have paid her a greater compliment!"

In one and only one respect, William Jennings Bryan was like Dr. Conwell. His "Prince of Peace," a lecture on Jesus Christ, was in as great demand as "Acres of Diamonds." In all other respects the two most popular Chautauqua lecturers were utterly unlike. Bryan was the supreme orator as Conwell was not. Bryan, the layman, made a fortune which he kept for himself from a lecture that was in truth a sermon. Conwell, the minister, made a fortune which he gave away from a lecture on a subject that was more secular than religious. Bryan's appeal was principally to the emotions and to the common man's search not only for an understanding of the riddle of the universe, but also for a source of solace and uplift outside himself. Conwell's appeal was principally to the ambition of man. I have always remembered the gist of Conwell's lecture, but my mind grows hazy when I try to recollect the substance of Bryan's oratory; it gets mixed up with sermons I had heard over and over in Protestant churches.

I do not recollect whether it was in Nebraska or Iowa that I heard Bryan deliver his "Prince of Peace" to an evening audience. He was still one of my idols, the Great Commoner, champion of the underdog, as farmer Jim Moore had called him. The fact that he resigned from the office of Secretary of State under Woodrow Wilson rather than sign the stiff note of protest the President had drawn up on the sinking of the *Lusitania* (May 7, 1915) by a German submarine demonstrated to me that the Commoner would rather abide by the dictates of his conscience than go along with the President's *Realpolitik*. Cartoonists might mock him for his advocacy of prohibition and for serving grape juice instead of wine at the official dinners he gave for foreign diplomats and for planning a Chautauqua lecture tour while he was still Secretary of State. But like tailor Carl Baum, who was contemptuous of Bryan's prohibition (as I too was), I respected the man's spirit of independence and his refusal to compromise his pacifist beliefs. Naturally I was beside myself with anticipation and excitement when I walked into the big brown tent where he was to appear. I had arranged with the platform superintendent for an introduction and if possible for an interview with him.

The tent was of course crowded, indeed overcrowded, as it always was on "Bryan day." He was the biggest drawing card on any Chautauqua circuit. Small as a town might be, people flocked from all over the countryside to hear him. In the cities of the East, especially among intellectuals, he might be derided as a fanatic and even a clown, but in the countryside of the prairie states, he was the trusted and beloved Tribune of the People.

Like Conwell he was a big man, tall, strongly built, but paunchy. He perspired profusely as he spoke, his bald head shiny with sweat. He kept fanning himself with a five-cent palm-leaf fan and cooled himself with drafts of ice water that he poured into a glass from the pitcher on the table beside him.

To me the most impressive feature of his performance was not his ideas but his voice. Never in my life had I heard a voice like it, truly golden, with a smooth lyrical resonance that enchanted the ear. It was pure delight to hear him even if one was not carried away by his "message." I had already heard it propounded over and over, though not in such an oratorical style by the fundamentalist Elder Mattison in North Brookfield. To Bryan, as to Mattison, the Book of Genesis was the sole authoritative record of creation. To Bryan, as to the rural minister, it was a sin to doubt the miracles recorded in Holy Scripture. The one thing I clearly remember was the comparison Bryan made between these miracles and the miracle of the tiny watermelon seed which when planted grew into a forty-pound melon. The comparison evoked loud applause. Bryan was a matchless artist on the platform and it was thrilling to observe his complete mastery over the audience.

On the conclusion of the lecture he was besieged by men and women who rushed to thank him for his "message" and to shake his hand. Flushed and sweating, he smiled and smiled as he shook one hand after another, hundreds of hands. He responded warmly to the admiration, or rather adoration, of his hearers. He really loved to be lionized. At last, when the crowd had melted away, the platform superintendent introduced me to him as a lecturer on Russia. We shook hands and he asked whether I had ever met Tolstoy. No, I replied, and hastened to add that I had read of his trip to Tolstoy's home. "A great Christian, one of the greatest in the world," Bryan intoned in his golden voice. Thereupon the superintendent suggested that we all have breakfast together the next morning so he could tell us more about his trip to Tolstoy. Bryan agreed, and the next morning when we met in the hotel dining room, he again extolled the Russian novelist as one of the world's greatest Christians. That was why, he explained, he had made the long journey to visit him. Bryan's beautiful voice throbbed with fervor as he spoke of Tolstoy's warm hospitality. He had intended only a brief visit, but the bearded old man in a peasant smock had kept him for hours and hours, from morning until late in the evening. They went walking and horseback riding together and of course talked of America and Russia, of Christian morality and of the doctrine of non-resistance so dear to both of them.

Bryan described the room he stayed in in Tolstoy's house, where there was a ring in the ceiling from which, Tolstoy told him, he had at one time contemplated hanging himself. Proudly Bryan informed us that after this meeting Tolstoy and he corresponded with one another.

Many years later I myself was to visit Tolstoy's home in Yasnaya Polyana. The time was September 1942, shortly after the Red Army had driven the Germans out of Tolstoy's estate. Russian-born Alexander Werth, a British fellow correspondent in Moscow, made the trip with me. Sofya Andreyevna, Tolstoy's granddaughter, a stately and handsome woman of forty-two, with a lofty forehead and heavy brows like her grandfather's, received us and showed us around the place. She led us to the room where

Tolstoy had written *Anna Karenina* and the adjoining guest room where he had entertained Bryan. It was a small room, simply furnished with a plain iron bed, a square table, a stand with bowl and pitcher, and a few pictures on the wall.

Her grandfather, Sofya Andreyevna told us, had at one time been on the point of hanging himself, and she pointed to the wooden beam over the door where he had intended to tie the rope. Yes, he had told Bryan all about it, but Bryan's memory was at fault about the ring: a wooden crosspiece over the door was to have served the purpose. But Sofya Andreyevna confirmed all the rest of Bryan's story that morning at the breakfast table in a small Middle Western hotel. The old man had admired Bryan for his defense of working people, his Christian morality, his faith in non-resistance as the sole way of drawing individuals, states, and nations into peaceful relations with one another. Obviously Bryan's fundamentalism as expounded in "The Prince of Peace," never came up for discussion.

She remembered too that Bryan and her grandfather had corresponded. But I find only one letter, from Tolstoy to Bryan, which the Great Commoner included in his *Memoirs* and written in English:

Dear Mr. Bryan,—

The receipt of your letter gave me great pleasure as well as reminiscence of your visit.

I had in the Russian papers news about you. I wish with all my heart success in your endeavor to destroy the trusts and to help the working people to enjoy the whole fruits of their toil, but I think this is not the most important thing of our life. The most important thing is to know the will of God concerning one's life, i.e., to know what he wishes us to do and fulfill it. I think that you are doing it and that is the thing in which I wish you the greatest success.

Yours truly
Leo Tolstoy

2 February, 1907

The breakfast with Bryan was a memorable occasion not only because just listening to him was a privilege, but also because he revealed something about himself that surprised me. He kept ordering one stack of griddlecakes after another. I had never known a hard-working farmer to eat as hearty a breakfast. He was in truth an irrepressible glutton, and gluttony eventually caused his death in July 1925 in Dayton, Tennessee, where he and Clarence Darrow, the noted Chicago lawyer, faced one another as attorneys in the so-called "Monkey Trial." Bryan ate a hearty dinner, lay down for a nap, and never awoke.

Still, meeting him in the prairie country which he loved and where he was loved was an experience I have always cherished. Ever since I can remember, I have felt a close kinship with people of the soil, and it flattered me to learn that Bryan too felt this kinship. He had always fought for the man behind the plow and always would, he assured us, just as that old farmer Jim Moore had said. He was indeed the Great Commoner, a man of incorruptible integrity, far in advance of his age in some of his ideas and lagging behind in others. Like Dr. Conwell he did not mind the discomforts of travel in the Middle Western countryside in those times. He was a seasoned trouper, accepting the discomforts of the road with as little fuss as those of us who were much younger than he. An astonishingly handsome man, he was indifferent about the way he dressed; he came down for breakfast in the same baggy trousers in which he lectured. I remember him as a simple man who gladly agreed to breakfast with a mere Chautauqua platform manager and a twenty-four-year-old Russian immigrant. He was a fascinating conversationalist, and I am certain he never suspected how thrilled and honored the young immigrant lecturer felt to be sitting beside him and listening to his talk.

Chapter 18

The Preacher and
the Lawyer

◀▶

"D'you like poetry?"

The question was put to me by Dr. Frank Wakeley Gunsaulus, minister of the Independent Central Church of Chicago, shortly after we met in the Iowa town where the Midland elite seven-day Chautauqua circuit was starting. In the summer of 1916 the minister and I were booked to lecture on the same day, I in the afternoon, he in the evening.

I replied that though I read a great deal, I had centered more attention on the novel than on poetry. Pleased that I cared for books, he invited me to join the poetry readings he occasionally held with his "family," as he called his traveling companions: his daughter Helen, a dark-haired, dark-eyed, keen-minded young woman of thirty who always traveled with him and the two musicians, a young pianist, Priscilla, and a young tenor, Tom, who performed the preludes to his lectures.

Poetry for him, the minister went on, was more than a pleasure, it was a deep necessity. He always packed several volumes of poetry in his suitcase.

Never before had I heard a Protestant minister or a Chautauqua lecturer speak so fervently of poetry.

From the publicity department of the Chautauqua Bureau, I had already learned of some of the man's remarkable achievements. When he was only thirty-four years old and already a celebrated preacher in Chicago, he once chose for a Sunday morning sermon the secular theme of "what I'd do with a million dollars." He told the huge congregation that he would establish a college of applied science in Chicago, which the growing city badly needed and which would offer special opportunities to disadvantaged youths, regardless of race, religion, or nationality.

The project struck a responsive chord in Philip Armour of the packing family who was in the congregation. After the service Armour went straight to Dr. Gunsaulus' study and told him that he, Armour, was ready to put up the money if the minister would pledge at least five years to the building up of the school. Dr. Gunsaulus gladly accepted the proposal and the Armour Institute of Technology was founded. (In 1940 it was merged with the Lewis Institute and is now known as the Illinois Institute of Technology.)

Dr. Gunsaulus went on the lecture platform and donated his earnings to the new school. Unlike Dr. Conwell he was a man of wide and diverse cultural interests. He was a noted connoisseur of art, an authority on Wedgwood pottery and was closely associated with the Chicago Field Museum of Natural History, one of whose halls bears his name. He lectured to select audiences on celebrated painters and was consultant to the Chicago Art Institute and to private collectors on their prospective purchases. His taste in music was so exacting that he never permitted a Chautauqua management to engage the musicians for his lecture preludes. He selected his own performers and consulted with them on the programs. This time, a Midland executive told me, he was to be accompanied on tour by the tenor of his church choir and the young woman who was both pianist and organist. No other lecturer, I was told, not even Dr. Conwell or William Jennings Bryan, ever demanded such a privilege.

The first time I saw him was in the lobby of the Iowa Country Hotel where the Chautauqua performers stayed, and I was awed by his impressive presence. Tall, broad-shouldered, with a large, finely shaped head and thick grayish hair, his pale handsome face and dark eyes wore an expression of aloofness and reserve.

I felt weak in the knees when the platform superintendent called to me to come over and meet Dr. Gunsaulus. But then his sudden warm smile, firm handshake, and informal manner allayed my anxiety. I observed that he walked with a limp, a painful one, I later learned, especially during spells of raw weather. But he showed no signs of discomfort as he talked of his love of poetry and the joy it gave him.

Dr. Gunsaulus introduced me to his "family" and we all had lunch together. He was a lively talker and, unlike many lecturers on the Chautauqua platform, a good listener as well. He wanted to hear about my background, my education, my plans for the future. He listened intently to what I recounted of my past and of my hopes for the future and warned me not to think of making lecturing my life-work. In time, he said, it would stultify my mind and close it to new ideas. I said that I had no intention of remaining a lecturer to the exclusion of other work; if I failed to establish myself as a writer, I would go back to farming.

The incongruity of my alternatives amused his daughter and the young musical performers at the table. But Dr. Gunsaulus understood and approved of my decision. If farming, he declared, appealed to my taste, then once I became convinced that writing held no future for me, I should turn to farming. He pointed out the importance of taste in his own life—civilized taste he hoped—not only in personal relationships, but in all his activities: in art and literature, in religion and education. Taste, he insisted, was a molder of the human personality; good taste was goodness itself and could only do good in the world. To me this was a new concept, something to reflect on afterwards and never to be forgotten.

He made it clear, though, that self-indulgent enjoyment alone was not his primary guide to action. Being wanted or needed by others, whoever they might be, was the most powerful driving force in his life. No, there was no contradiction between taste and serving others. Often one supplemented the other. He became a minister because he was honestly convinced that he was needed and could be of help to others, to people with baffled minds or sick souls.

The luncheon was the beginning of one of my most stimulating summers. Dr. Gunsaulus was an immensely erudite man who could discourse as freely on Matthew Arnold and Robert Browning as on Plato and Johann Fichte, the German philosopher; on Carlyle and Cardinal Newman as on Gladstone and Disraeli. He had read Darwin and Alfred Russel Wallace and accepted their theories of evolution, which lifted him above crude fundamentalism of clergymen like the Baptist minister at North Brookfield or of such prominent laymen as William Jennings Bryan.

His daughter Helen, a graduate of the University of Chicago, shared her father's interest in poetry and art and we soon became close friends. Because of his crippled leg, Dr. Gunsaulus could not go on long walks, but Helen enjoyed hiking through the countryside as much as I did. On one of our hikes I told her that her father was an enigma to me. Here he was, a man of high literary and artistic tastes, yet instead of an arts college, he founded an institute of science and engineering. How did she explain it?

Other people, she said, asked the same question because they didn't know how varied her father's intellectual and artistic interests were. Actually, science and technology fascinated him almost as much as poetry and art and he followed scientific publications as avidly as literary ones. He felt, as he had explained to his congregation at the time he envisaged the technological school in Chicago, that the moment was ripe for it; and did I know, she asked, that her father was editor-in-chief of a ten-volume encyclopedia of science and engineering? He felt there was an urgent need for it and the subject fascinated him.

She told me something else—that her father was one of the best known bibliophiles in Chicago. An enthusiastic collector of old books and first editions, he often attended gatherings in a certain bookshop where he and other bibliophiles discussed their hobby and bragged about new finds.

Dr. Gunsaulus possessed a keen sense of humor and was an amused observer of the more absurd aspects of the human scene. Once he told of being introduced to a lecture audience in a town in his native Ohio by a man who fancied himself a local Mark Twain. "Ladies and gentlemen," the man began, "we have a great gun aimed at us this evening; a man built like Saul who will fire at us. Ladies and gentlemen, I take pleasure in presenting to you Dr. Gun-Saul-us." He laughed at the sheer inanity of the introduction. At another time we traveled by day coach with a Chautauqua entertainer who was billed as "Professor Pamahasika and his Pets." The professor had his tame birds and animals in cages in the day coach. Suddenly one of the cages sprang open and a duck jumped out and, quacking indignantly, waddled off down the aisle. "There goes our talent," laughed Dr. Gunsaulus.

But it was his poetry readings that made the summer particularly memorable for me. A man of dramatic temperament, with faultless diction and a light baritone voice of wide emotional range, he interpolated his readings with digressions on his philosophy of life and religion, which could be summed up as dedication to the ennoblement of man.

Matthew Arnold, Robert Browning, Alfred Tennyson were his favorite poets; he was also a great admirer of Coleridge and Wordsworth, Keats and Shelley. On several occasions he read to us Coleridge's pronouncement on the Bible as a fount of light and life, of truth and love. Coleridge, he said, spoke not for himself alone, but for every thinking Christian to whom the old credos "God is love," and "The kingdom of heaven is within you" embodied the truth and the nobility of the Christian faith.

For Dr. Gunsaulus, poetry bore an intimate kinship to religion: emotion and imagination had contributed to the rise and flowering of both. That was why, he argued, a truly great poet, even when he proclaimed himself an atheist as Shelley did, was at heart too spiritual to be irreligious. He cited the Psalmist as a supreme example of both poet and believer; he viewed great poets as the true prophets of their time. Once he told us that whenever he lectured to theological students, he urged them to read and study poetry. Poetry would nurture their imagination and emotions and give them a more profound grasp of religion.

Nor were the forms and rituals of religion, the dogmas and sacraments, images and symbols of much consequence to Dr. Gunsaulus, though the artist in him was not oblivious to the aesthetic appeal of certain external features of worship in this or that church. But aside from music, any embellishment of worship only obscured and detracted from the meaning of religion and weakened its power to regenerate and ennoble man.

At the time I was not particularly interested in religion, though to my college generation it was far more compelling an influence than it is today. I had heard endless sermons on the themes of "God is love" and "The kingdom of heaven is within you," but I had never before heard the simple words invested with so much meaning and beauty. Without love "the kingdom of heaven" was beyond attainment. While others proclaimed the Fatherhood of God, to Dr. Gunsaulus acceptance of such Fatherhood entailed the recognition of the brotherhood of man.

Man and his relation to his fellow man was always his principal concern, the quintessence of his religious thinking and preaching.

So once again I was the beneficiary of the warm attention of a Protestant clergyman, the most erudite, most literary, most cosmopolitan, most sophisticated, and least sectarian, I had ever known. I learned to love the man not only for his humanization of religion, but also for his delightful and edifying companionship. He was the teacher, his daughter and I the faithful pupils whom he treated now with solemn earnestness, now with outgoing joviality, and always with a sense of style—taste, he would have called it—that enhanced the pleasure and the illumination of his readings and his disquisitions. Ever afterwards, until his death in 1921, whenever I was in Chicago, I never failed to telephone him and invariably he invited me for dinner to his house on Prairie Avenue.

I could not know at the time that it was to be his influence more than any other teacher's that was to serve me so well in my approach to the anti-religious crusade in Bolshevik Russia. His remembered words were to help me in understanding the reasons for its triumph among the illiterate or semiliterate, superstitious, ikon-worshiping, Orthodox muzhiks and its failure among the literate, Bible-reading, rationalistic, and social-minded Baptists, many of whom were muzhiks. Since the middle of the nineteenth century the Baptists had been a growing force in Russia.

Measured against Dr. Gunsaulus, the professional Chautauqua lecturer—the man who lectured the year round on the circuits—was to my mind a small, dull, inconsequential personage. However polished his platform manner, he could not rise above the sentimental clichés, the banal optimism, the home-mother-and-heaven inspirationalism he spouted so glibly. There was nothing scholarly or intellectually provocative about his lecture. And he gave the same one, his "big hit" lecture, year after year. No wonder Dr. Gunsaulus had warned me of the intellectual stagnation that awaited me if I were to make lecturing my life-work.

Thinking back to those days, I realize that these professional lecturers reflected the social spirit of the small town with its close ties to the farming population, off which it lived and prospered. These descendants of pioneers, the farm people of the Middle West, were even more optimistic and self-assured than the farm folk around North Brookfield. They cultivated larger farms, better land, built bigger barns and owned more cattle than the New Yorkers. In Iowa and Nebraska, hogs were an unfailing cash crop. Bohemian immigrants and their sons rapidly assimilated the spirit of optimism that prevailed all around them. They too might complain of the low prices of dairy products and hogs, but the land they owned and tilled gave them a deep-felt security which immigrants in the city rarely knew. They owned their own homes and had no worry about monthly rent bills. Unemployment was no problem. The education of their children, even of those who went on to college, was no special burden, and they could pay their doctor bills.

When I arrived in Chicago after my summer on the Midland Chautauqua trail, Miss Caroline McCartney, the alert secretary of the International Lyceum Association (ILA), after hearing my opinion of most of the professional lecturers on the circuit, hastened to introduce me to two young men, newcomers like myself to the lecture platform, who were to become my lifelong friends.

One of them was an Australian poet, Tom Skeyhill, a veteran of the disastrous Gallipoli campaign of 1915. Many years later he stumbled on the late Sergeant Alvin York's war diary and was so carried away with it that he decided to write York's biography. By that time I had already broken into print, and Skeyhill asked me to go with him to Jamestown, Tennessee, a few miles from the York farm, to help him write the book for Doubleday. Meeting the sergeant, his family, and his minister was a delightful and exciting experience for both Tom and myself. I shall always remember the dispassionate manner in which the tall, red-haired sergeant described to us how the hunting skills he had acquired in the woods and mountains of his neighborhood had helped him to achieve the most sensational one-man exploit of the First World War: killing thirty-two German soldiers who had set out to kill him and capturing 132 more, all of this singlehanded.

Tom Skeyhill was about my own age, but the other young lecturer, Glenn Frank, to whom Miss McCartney introduced me, was three or four years older. Born in a small town in Missouri, Frank was a graduate of Northwestern University and he brought to the lecture platform a sophisticated discourse that bristled with sharp and witty castigations of the political practices of the day. A handsome, lively, amiable young man, he proved a sensation on the Chautauqua circuit, though toward Skeyhill and myself he behaved with modesty and friendliness. We had dinner together several times and he told us that lecturing was a side line with him. Writing was his real interest; and when in 1921 he became editor-in-chief of the *Century Magazine*, then a monthly of high literary standing, he opened its pages to many newcomers including myself. In fact, it was he who made possible my first return to Russia, in 1923, to gather material for a series of articles for the *Century* on peasant life under the Bolsheviks.

In the autumn of 1916 Frank, Skeyhill and I stayed through the convention of the ILA which was made up of Chautauqua and lyceum, lecturers and entertainers. After the convention I lingered in the city for a few days, principally to see more of Dr. Gunsaulus, to whom I had become closely attached. One day while I was having lunch with her, Miss McCartney asked whether I would like to meet Clarence Darrow, the famed criminal lawyer. Of course I would, I replied. Darrow and his wife Ruby were among her dearest friends. She had once come to Darrow's assistance, she explained, at a moment in his life when he was virtually broke. She had persuaded him to mend his fortunes by lecturing, and to meet in debate with well-known figures among Chicago's intellectual elite on subjects on which he held strong convictions. His lectures and debates were a sensational success and since then she and the Darrows had been the warmest of friends.

On our return to her office at the old Auditorium Hotel, Miss McCartney telephoned Darrow and asked him to meet a friend of hers, a young man of Russian origin who was lecturing on Russia. He told her to send me over at once, and overcome with excitement I went to his office.

Clarence Darrow had been a magic name to me since the time in Boise when he defended William Heywood, secretary of the Western Federation of Miners who, together with two other officers of the federation, George Pettibone and Charles Moyer, was charged with conspiracy to murder Frank Steunenberg, Idaho's governor. In December 1905 Steunenberg was killed by a bomb at the gate of his home and Pinkerton detectives had laid the murder to officers of the Miners' Federation.

At the time of the trial I was still a student at New York's Stuyvesant High School, and every morning I rushed out to buy the New York *Times* to read of the latest developments at the Boise courthouse. Darrow's address to the jury in behalf of Heywood lasted eleven hours, and youthfully impressionable as I was, I read it with a lump in my throat. The jury returned a verdict of "not guilty" and among laboring people on the East Side where my family lived, Darrow became known as a dauntless champion of the weak and defenseless. My fellow playmates on the block, American-born sons of immigrants who idolized Theodore Roosevelt, made Darrow their hero. In a public library I found his book *Farmington*, the fictionalized story of his boyhood in the small town of Kinsman, Ohio, and reading it was a moving experience. I have reread it several times since and I can still be touched by the tale of the hopes and struggles, raptures and disillusionments of the sensitive small-town boy in the Middle West.

Years later I heard more of Darrow in Carl Baum's tailor shop where his reputation as defender of the underdog had made him almost a legendary figure. One of the most brilliant lawyers in the country, he could have become a millionaire had he continued working for the railroads. Instead he chose to dedicate himself to the cause of those whom the big corporations were striving to repress and to victimize. A saintly man, indeed, such was the sentiment of the tailors and of the students who hobnobbed with them.

Full of trepidation at being face to face with the man I had so long revered, I walked into the sunny office and found him in a rumpled shirt and galluses. He rose from his desk and greeted me with a firm handshake. He was tall, sturdily built, with broad shoulders and a massive head. A lock of brown hair fell over his wide brow; his face was lined and strong. With a few words in a deep voice he banished my diffidence and I found myself perfectly at ease in his friendly presence.

Like most great men, Darrow was interested in what other

people had to say, and in the light of later events there is some irony in the fact that one of the first questions he put to me was the very same that William Jennings Bryan had asked at the breakfast table that morning in Iowa: did I know Tolstoy? These two giants of the prairies, the religious fundamentalist and the atheistic humanist, who were to clash in ideological battle at Dayton, Tennessee, both deeply reverenced the Russian novelist as the champion of non-resistance. To Bryan the doctrine of non-resistance was inseparable from the Christian faith, while to Darrow it was the stand of rational men striving to turn the world from self-destructive violence.

As he sat there behind his desk, the thick fingers of both hands hooked into his galluses, he expatiated on the evils that beset mankind, nation rising against nation, class against class, man against man. He believed as strongly as any Christian in the brotherhood of man, in mercy and love. But unfortunately man was incapable of attaining these virtues. How was it possible to believe otherwise, with war drenching Europe in blood and with the spectacle of powerful Germany hurling herself on small and defenseless Belgium? By nature, he went on, he was a pacifist, and if he had his way, he would destroy all armaments the world over. But he could not forgive Germany for her crime against a weak and innocent neighbor! The spectacle of so much human folly, greed, and brutality had made him a pessimist. He couldn't even say, he repeated several times, that life was worth living.

It was startling to hear such despair from the man who had distinguished himself as one of the foremost humanitarians in the country and who had so successfully championed "the insulted and injured" in courthouses all over the country. I did not share his pessimism and told him so. He envied me, he said, he wished he could agree, but history and the facts of every day life were against me. I then ventured to ask whether he thought socialism, like Christianity and all religion, was powerless to discipline and regenerate man?

Instantly he arose, rummaged in a shelf of publications behind his desk, came up with a pamphlet which he presented to me. It was a published copy of his debate with a socialist leader, Arthur M. Lewis, on the subject of Marx and Tolstoy.

Lewis upheld the Marxist doctrine of class struggle and Darrow set against it the Tolstoyan doctrine of non-resistance.

Read nowadays, in the light of the so-called "workers'" state in Russia, Darrow's arguments, even to a man like myself who saw more in the Soviet Revolution than terror and blood, repression and destruction, sound frighteningly prophetic: "I wouldn't be so much opposed to force if I thought it would win. But I have seen the game tried so often I know better. . . . Suppose the working class could turn society over, which they cannot, but suppose they could and that they got the guns and cannons and swords, and they were the state. Then what? D'you think they'd be any better? I know them too well. . . . They would be just like the rest. They have got to learn that punishment is wrong. They have got to learn fundamental things—charity, humanity, brotherly love which is the basis of it all. . . . My friend is wrong when he says that all strife comes from capitalism. It lurks in the human heart. It is part of the savage. It is in the beast from there to man . . . and the savage fights as much as the civilized."

So, long ago Darrow ripped to tatters a basic tenet of Marxism-Leninism, a tenet that is drummed into the mind of every child in the Soviet Union—that the worker is endowed by nature and circumstance with a superior intelligence which makes of him a moral superman, destined to bring about the ultimate classless society and the true brotherhood of man. Darrow's disbelief in the theory that the proletariat was the only class capable of establishing freedom, peace, and brotherhood in the world was fully justified once again by the tragic events of August 1968 when Soviet "brother workers" in tanks bristling with guns led the soldiers of the Bulgarian, Hungarian, Polish, and East German "workers' democracies" into Czechoslovakia.

But at the time I was neither experienced nor learned enough to dispute the gloomy philosophy of one of the most eminent and humane lawyers in the country. I was still under the influence of Carl Baum and his shop workers who firmly believed that Socialism would eventually redeem mankind. Then, too, stripped of its theology, which meant nothing to me, Dr. Gunsaulus' approach to religion seemed to confirm the Socialist theory as I understood it. Gifted with imagination and emotion, man, Dr. Gunsaulus held, could cultivate inside himself "the kingdom of heaven," or love and all that it connoted for his fellow man. After all, I reflected, Dr. Gunsaulus had risen above the petty denominational squabbles of the Protestant churches; he approached religion not in terms of dogma but in terms of man's potentialities.

I couldn't argue with this learned and eloquent pessimist. He was in sympathy, Darrow said, with the aims of Socialism. But he could never accept its methods, because he had no evidence that Socialism in any form could guarantee individual liberty, which he prized above everything else in the world. He had too little faith in human nature to believe that a dictatorship of the proletariat was any guarantee of liberty and justice for all. He couldn't make himself believe that mass rule would respect individual liberty or could usher in utopia. No, he wouldn't want to trust his liberty to the masses. (The last time I saw Darrow was in the winter of 1935 in the Mayflower Hotel in Washington and he pointed to Soviet Russia as proof of his lifelong belief that the masses cared nothing for individual liberty, had allowed it to be suppressed more brutally than in any capitalist country.)

But as I sat across his desk listening to his jeremiads on the nature and fate of man, he appeared relaxed and at ease. Intense as his convictions were, he never raised his voice and, save for snapping his galluses now and then, used no gestures. Nor did he express any rancor toward anyone. Singularly calm and composed, he betrayed no hint of boredom with life (which was not worth living) nor with his work on behalf of the underdogs and the unjustly accused. For all his grim pessimism, I couldn't make myself believe that he wasn't enjoying life to the full.

I thought I was overstaying my time and rose to go. But Darrow motioned me to remain seated. Caroline, he said, had told him that I was of Russian origin and lectured on Russia; could I perhaps explain why the Russian armies were performing so miserably in the battlefield? I said I was hardly qualified to answer the question, but that my experiences in America had made me very aware of how backward a country Russia was. This might be one reason for the sorry performance of the Russian armies.

Darrow wanted to know what I told my audiences about Russia. I replied that the peasants as I knew them were the one subject on which I felt competent to speak and briefly outlined my Chautauqua lecture. Darrow listened intently and asked question after question. He had not believed, he said, that the condition of the peasant was as dismal as I had painted.

When I left he made me promise that if I ever came back to Chicago, I would communicate with him.

But the very next day Caroline McCartney telephoned saying that Darrow wanted her to bring me to a certain German restaurant for a sandwich and a beer that evening. He had invited his friend Professor George Burman Foster, a progressive theologian at the University of Chicago Theological Seminary, and a few others to talk to me about the religion of the Russian peasant. Darrow's request flattered me, though I was puzzled why to an agnostic like him the religion of the Russian muzhik should command any interest at all.

By the time Miss McCartney and I reached the restaurant, Darrow, his wife Ruby, a handsome, soft-voiced, gentle-mannered woman, Professor Foster, a man of about sixty with fine iron-gray hair, a smooth-featured, boyishly animated face, were already there. We sat around a bare, long, wooden table with a heavy top and thick square legs—a truly peasant table. Several other friends of Darrow joined the party.

As we kept on talking, it became obvious that Professor Foster had come under the influence of certain British writers, notably Stephen Graham, who had resurrected what appeared to me the long discarded Slavophile idea of the redeeming Christian goodness of the Russian muzhik, of his innate humility, piety, and love.

The question had come up while I was still in college and I had discussed it with Clausen and several professors. I had scoffed at Graham's assumptions, and once while I was reading one of his brilliantly written eulogies of the muzhik's religion in a magazine (I believe it was *Collier's*), I was so provoked that I scribbled in pencil on the margin "romantic lunatic." The librarian discovered the scribbling and I was roundly scolded for defacing college property.

I proceeded to refute Stephen Graham in my own way. Graham and British writers like him, I explained, had mistaken the muzhik's servility for Christian humility, his material wretchedness for Christian resignation or self-denial, his political helplessness for submission to the will of God. Graham, I contended, didn't know the Russian muzhik, hadn't even bothered to learn about his place in Russian history, his bloody wars against the feudal nobility and his undying hatred of the landed nobles, his readiness when he had the chance to burn their mansions, loot their forests, barns, and warehouses, and swing an ax over their heads. I spoke of the bloody vengeance the peasants had taken on the landlords during the brief revolution of 1905, the very year my family had emigrated, atrocities that Graham so conveniently disregarded. The muzhik, I said, was a warmly sociable fellow and very likable, but he was virtually illiterate and ignorant of the substance of Christian faith. Only two or three of the 150 or so families in my village owned Bibles. Several peasants who could read had bought paper-bound lives of the saints in the near-by market town, and as a boy I was often called upon to read aloud from them at gatherings in some neighbor's house. Though I knew very little about official Orthodoxy, I had lived long enough in a peasant village, I thought, to be certain that the muzkik did not, as Stephen Graham insisted, constitute a living symbol of the Christian faith. The muzhik's religion, as I had known it, was concerned mainly with magic and miracle working, with spells and exorcisms invoked by priest and sorcerer against the age-old calamities of peasant life—sickness, plague, and drought. Its spirit and many of its forms were actually pre-Christian; and this paganism persisting under a superficial Orthodoxy had been mistaken by Stephen Graham for Christian fervor.

Professor Foster seemed loath to be disillusioned, but Darrow accepted my view and a lively discussion went on until past midnight.

My two summers on Chautauqua circuits, spent mostly in Iowa and Nebraska, proved an adventure and an education. I had seen a part of America new to me and that still, even its cities, breathed the spirit of the prairie.

Meeting such personages as Senator Lafayette Young, Dr. Russell Conwell, Helen Keller, William Jennings Bryan, Dr. Gunsaulus, and Clarence Darrow was a privilege I have always cherished. If Conwell's lecture "Acres of Diamonds" baffled and irritated me and Bryan's "Prince of Peace" fascinated me by its oratorical virtuosity, both men moved me by their generous-mindedness and simplicity of manner. Despite the high distinction they had won in their respective careers, there was no hint of pomposity about them. I am certain that meeting them fortified the spirit of independence and self-assurance I had acquired on the farms and at a rural college.

The one dark feature of my Chautauqua experience was the presence in some towns of rock-ribbed fundamentalist ministers. Rigidly puritanical, fanatically intolerant, frenziedly anti-Catholic, they would have poisoned the culture of the country had it been within their power to do so. But the pioneering spirit and the spaciousness of the prairies were against them. Despite their interdictions, boys still played baseball on Sunday, even if it had to be done out of sight of the joy-killers. Ministers warned girls to stay aloof from Chautauqua talent, especially from actors and singers. But the girls went walking with them anyway.

Discussion, I discovered early in my Chautauqua days, with these pious, ignorant, and intolerant sectarians, was unprofitable: God was always on their side of any argument. Dr. Gunsaulus used to advise them to improve themselves as Christians and as community leaders by reading poetry. I doubt that his advice was ever followed.

Life in those times in the Middle West was even more tranquil and more uncomplicated than in the New York State countryside. It was blessedly free from the turmoils, anxieties, irritations, and uncertainties that beset America today. Nobody then would have dreamed of a racial explosion. Few Negroes were migrating to that part of the country; even in 1920 they constituted less than one per cent of the population of Iowa. There was no segregation in the public schools or the colleges. Why on the conclusion of the Civil War they did not rush to take advantage of the Homestead Act as did peasants from Western Europe I do not know.

Life in the colleges and universities in those days was full of youthful boisterousness, but no campus presented scenes of rioting and violence, and no students would ever have dreamed of spitting into the face of a professor or hurling obscenities at a president. Nothing was more remote from the minds of the Middle Westerners, especially farmers, than the fears that beset the nation now—fear of taxes, of inflation, of crime, of atomic war. Family life was closely knit, and among immigrants from Europe, notably Germans and Bohemians whom I knew best, children respected and obeyed their parents. In the presence of company they behaved politely, but with none of the timidity and self-effacement they would have shown in the Old Country. The American school, association with American children, the freedom and spaciousness of the prairies inculcated in them an ease, a geniality, a self-assurance that made them as delightfully companionable at the table and around the house and farm as the children in the much older pioneering country of North Brookfield.

I remember the American-born Bohemian farmer and his wife in Nebraska who one Sunday afternoon after my lecture invited me home for supper. They cultivated a half section of land and ran a big dairy. They had a houseful of children, and at milking time everybody in the family except the younger children went to the barn. I too donned overalls, picked up a stool and a milk pail, and to the amusement of all of them proceeded to help with the milking. It was easy to make myself a part of the large and happy family far out on the prairies of Nebraska.

At suppertime my host's brother and his wife and children who lived on a near-by farm joined us, and we stayed up late, eating, talking, singing Bohemian and Russian peasant songs. The world was a comfortable and cheerful place then and seemed likely to go on being so.

Chapter 19

Harvard and a Guide

◀▶

I had been around Harvard Yard only a day when I learned that applicants to Dean Le Baron Briggs's English 5 were required to submit manuscripts or published works by which the dean could judge their qualifications for admittance to his course. The dean's fame was nationwide, and from all over the country graduate students and teachers of literature who aspired to professional status as writers came seeking admission to his class, limited to some thirty members.

I submitted my thesis on Thomas Hardy, written for a master's degree at Colgate. In his office at University Hall the dean hurriedly ran his bespectacled eyes over several pages of the manuscript and accorded me admission.

The other professor I hoped to study with was the Russian-born Leo Wiener, father of Norbert Wiener, the mathematical genius who created the science of cybernetics. Leo Wiener was one of the most distinguished Slavic scholars of his time and had been teaching Slavic languages and literatures at Harvard for some years. He had translated twenty-four volumes of Tolstoy's writings and compiled a two-volume anthology of Russian literature, which despite its conciseness, remains to my mind an unsurpassed survey of the subject since the beginnings to the early part of our century.

I had seriously begun to think of writing a book on the Russian peasantry, a subject in which, to judge by the response of my lecture audiences, it was easy to arouse interest and of which little was known in America. My childhood and early boyhood years in a Russian village provided an excellent background for the book, but I realized that I would need to know much more than I did about the peasant's place in Russian history and above all about the manner in which he was depicted in Russian literature to make it a full-bodied and authoritative work. A scholar like Professor Wiener would be of enormous help.

I found the professor in his study in the basement of the Widener Library. A short, slender, and wiry man, with big dark eyes that peered sharply through his spectacles, he sat at a desk piled high with books. An informal man and a ready talker with a somewhat shrill voice, he pointed to the books and explained that he was devoting himself to philology. He said that he already knew so many languages that he could easily acquire a new one in a very few weeks. Nor did he impress me as boasting of his achievements.

He led me to the Russian section of the library, guided me through the stacks, and proudly pointed out the more important books and documents on Russian history and literature. Somewhat dazzled by the treasures around me, I reminded myself that I had expected nothing less of Harvard.

Professor Wiener obtained desk space for me in a stall in the Russian section of the library, and on my first day there he appeared with an armful of books and laid them on my desk. He called my attention to the two-volume Russian edition of Paul Milyukov's *Outlines of Russian Culture*, which I had never read. Milyukov, the professor told me, was a close friend of his and was one of the most distinguished Russian historians and political reformers. He urged me to read the work at the earliest opportunity, and on leaving, assured me again that I need never hesitate to come to his study should I wish to discuss any of the books I would be reading. No, he didn't want me to attend his classes. All I needed was an occasional private conference with him.

I had imagined that a Harvard professor as absorbed in research as Wiener was would be too pressed for time to be so concerned even with a graduate student. Now I knew I had been wrong.

I enrolled in two other courses, one under Bliss Perry on Thomas Carlyle, the other on comparative literature under Irving Babbitt. The learned, easy-mannered, witty Professor Perry was a delight to his students, and though he had a very large class he too made himself available for advice and discussion. But after only a few lectures by Irving Babbitt, I realized that I did not belong in his class. I was not scholarly enough to absorb the theories that he so vigorously propounded. Nor was I appreciative enough of his attitude toward literature and art to feel that his course, however challenging, would be of value to me. I should need to divest myself of the thoughts and emotions that certain authors—Dostoyevsky, for example—had roused in me and whom he caustically criticized in order to accept his purely classical approach. My own literary tastes, first shaped by my teachers in Russia, clashed with the tastes and judgment of that great enemy of romanticism, the formidable Professor Babbitt. His preoccupation with style and form, I felt, barred him from appreciating the mind and soul of those writers who had lived like Dostoyevsky, in "the house of the dead" or, like Gorky, in "the lower depths." I did not pretend to be a literary critic and mine was a purely emotional reaction to his theories and judgments.

I quit his class and enrolled in a seminar course on Goethe's *Faust* under Professor Waltz. There were only about ten students in the class, one a young woman. Except myself, they were all teaching or preparing to teach German in colleges. We met once a week for about two or three hours. My highly articulate and highly intellectual classmates and professor made the weekly meetings one of the more memorable and enlightening experiences of my Harvard days.

But Dean Briggs was the professor I idolized from the first day I walked into his classroom. A blue-eyed, gentle-mannered New Englander with a high forehead, sparse hair, a long wrinkled face, he walked with a quick springy step and radiated a boyish enthusiasm. One gained the impression that he was never bored and never unhappy. He met us once a week, and the first time he appeared before us, he made it clear that he could not teach us how to write; he could only teach us how not to write. Obviously he did not want us to harbor illusions about what he could do for aspirants to literary fame.

At every meeting he read aloud one or two of the long themes we had written for him, the ones he liked best, and made a few comments, usually about style. He inveighed against the use of hackneyed words and expressions, strings of adjectives, and all verbal deadwood. Then, as an exercise in extemporaneous writing, he would ask for a one-page comment on the themes he had read. He did not depend on an assistant, but read all our papers himself, occasionally making comments in red ink in the margin. At the next session he began by reading several of the previous week's comments and followed as before with a reading of a theme or two. He never held any discussions in the class, though he occasionally invited us individually for a conference in his office.

Robert Hillyer, a slight retiring youth who wrote melancholy verses that brought to mind Matthew Arnold, was a member of the class and so was the poet Joseph Auslander, a jolly and talkative extrovert.

Perhaps Briggs's most brilliant student was Ralph Boas, older than most of us and a teacher of English literature in some small college in the state of Washington. Another gifted writer was Robert Cutler, a handsome, amiable, athletic Bostonian, who had already written a novel, *Louisburg Square,* that Macmillan had accepted for publication. Boas' essays on matters of current interest were so well written that Dean Briggs read them to us more often than those of any other student. An associate editor of the *Atlantic Monthly* who frequently visited the dean's office in search of new writers selected one of Boas' essays for publication in that highly esteemed periodical.

The dean read only one of my own themes—a description of Russian peasant weddings, which my classmates seemed to find amusing. The dean thought well enough of it to offer it to the *Atlantic Monthly,* but Ellery Sedgwick, the editor-in-chief, rejected it. He did however invite me to come to see him. Nothing happened—neither my style which lacked polish nor the ideas which interested me suited his purpose. Yet the fact that the editor-in-chief of the *Atlantic Monthly* invited me for a talk was a flattering experience.

None of us in those days would have imagined that the talented Robert Cutler would make a career in law and banking instead of becoming a successful author. One of the most active public figures in Boston, he became chairman of the National Security Council Planning Board during the Eisenhower administration. I never heard what happened to Ralph Boas, the star of the class. Nor have I come across the names of many of the others either in the pages of magazines or on the title pages of books. Gallishaw, whose themes were frequently read to the class, wrote several short stories for quality magazines, then started a correspondence school in writing, which appears to have had no outstanding success. Only three of us, as far as I know, Hillyer, Auslander, and myself remained in the field.

One of the more promising of the dean's students wrote to me years later that he had abandoned writing because the girl he wanted to marry hadn't been willing to wait for him to establish himself in a literary career. She had argued that he could write evenings and weekends and finally won him over. But providing for a family left him little time and energy for anything else. Now he was a minor executive in the circulation department of the *Saturday Evening Post* and deeply regretted that he had not stuck to writing as I had done.

Harvard, I was convinced, perhaps wrongly, was the magnet that drew the brainiest and most ambitious college graduates in the country, far more so than any other university. I met these students in class, in the Yard, at study desks in the library, in eating places, at the cooperative bookshop (the "Coop"), and even in my rooming house. I occupied a small apartment on the second floor front, the much larger rear apartment was rented to two Amherst graduates who had been classmates: Joe Snyder, a bony-faced youth with a sober expression and Jack (John J.) McCloy, a handsome, soft-voiced law student. I doubt if these two ever missed a single concert of the Boston Symphony or any play that came to Boston. Intellectually inquisitive and well-read, they studied hard, but there were times when we got together for long discussions which I thoroughly enjoyed. Snyder finally rose to a professorship in the Harvard School of Business Administration and McCloy became Assistant Secretary of War during World War II, president of the World Bank, United States Military Governor and High Commissioner for Germany, and has since remained on call for delicate diplomatic assignments from the White House, whether presided over by a Democrat or Republican.

On the floor below mine lived a research assistant of Professor Albert Bushnell Hart, the noted historian. A man of about thirty or a little older with a broad face and big blue eyes, he frequently came up to my apartment to discuss the war. He was troubled over what seemed to him America's strange position. Woodrow Wilson had been returned to the White House under the slogan "He kept us out of war," the mere mention of which saddened and angered the young historian, whose name escapes me. He was convinced that America could not possibly stay out of the war, and when I asked him what America could gain by joining forces with the Allies, he lectured me in some detail on historical British-American relations and argued that not only for cultural but political, economic, and other reasons America could never permit the defeat of England. Anglophile though I was since high school days, this was a new idea to me. The more I talked with the young historian, the more convinced I became that he was right. In the years ahead his argument became so much a part of my own thinking that I made use of it when Ilya Ehrenburg and I discussed Anglo-American relations.

Several months after Great Britain declared war on Nazi Germany in September, 1939, I brought up my Harvard friend's argument again. Lord Lothian (Philip Kerr), who years earlier had invited me to write for the liberal quarterly *Round Table,* which he had helped to found and to which I had for a long time been a frequent though anonymous contributor, was the new British ambassador in Washington. I called on him there and as he strode up and down his office, he spoke peevishly of America's ingratitude to England in remaining neutral in the war. I replied that a young Harvard historian had convinced me a long time ago that America would never permit a foreign power to subjugate England and that sooner or later America would be in the war. I also said that farmers I knew in upstate New York were denouncing Neville Chamberlain who was still Prime Minister, and who, I said, was the reason for a certain lack of sympathy here for his country. Infuriated, the usually equable diplomat snapped, "Only Communists and Jews talk like that." It was no use telling Lothian who had favored—had in fact helped to fashion the Prime Minister's policy of appeasement—that these farmers were neither Jews nor Communists; with the exception of a few Irish among them, they were Anglo-Saxons and Protestants. This was the last time I ever spoke to him.

Douglas Wendell, a Quaker from Haverford, Pennsylvania, one of the brightest students in Dean Briggs's writing course, became one of my close friends. Fascinated by Russian folklore and folk customs, he and I often sat on the steps of the Widener Library, where, notebook in hand, he would jot down much of what I told him of my boyhood days in a muzhik village. Once he invited me to dinner in a friend's house with some fifteen graduate students from the Philadelphia-Baltimore area, some of them also Quakers. They were a lively and stimulating group and I too started coming for dinner to this house. On weekdays we usually broke up early enough to study an hour or so, but on weekends we might gather in our landlady's big parlor for conversation or we might descend on Boston for a concert, a play, a burlesque show at the Old Howard, or for dates with girls from the Emerson or Leland Powers Schools of Elocution who in those days were more popular with Harvard men than the "Cliffies." Somehow I discovered a Russian-Ukrainian colony near the Boston and Maine Railroad Station where Russian style parties were held. These always began with music and recitations, followed by dancing and the inevitable *letuchaya pochta* (flying post), a game offering a splendid opportunity to become acquainted with a member of the opposite sex by addressing a letter to him or her to be delivered by the appointed postman. I took my Harvard dining companions to some of these parties and it amused them to write letters to pretty Russian or Ukrainian girls, to dance and flirt with them, even though the girls knew little English.

But I worked hard and spent most of my time in the library under the guidance of Professor Wiener. I read virtually everything I could find in the collection on the two empire-shaking peasant rebellions in Russia, one in 1669–70 led by the illiterate Cossack Stenka Razin, the other in 1773–75 by Yemelyan Pugachev, another illiterate Cossack, when Catherine the Great was on the throne. The rebellions were guerrilla-type wars, in the course of which landed noblemen were murdered, their mansions sacked, their properties looted, and their lands appropriated. Both uprisings were finally put down in blood and their leaders hacked to death. But the rebellions demonstrated how easy it was to rouse the peasants not against the Czar whom they worshiped, but against the landed nobility whom they despised and whom they held responsible for all their woes.

Russian fiction about the muzhik was not only absorbing but often shattering. This was particularly true of Gleb Uspensky's novel *Vlast Zemli* (Power of the Earth), Leo Tolstoy's play *Vlast Tmy* (The Power of Darkness), above all of Anton Chekhov's story *Muzhiki* (Peasants) and Ivan Bunin's *Derevnya* (The Village). Uspensky's work was published in 1882, Tolstoy's play in 1886, Chekhov's novel in 1897, and Bunin's in 1910, five years after I had left my village for America. It was heart-rending to read of the poverty, agony, degradation, and barbarism in which the muzhik wallowed as late as 1910. One could quote passage after passage from Bunin, one of the most felicitous stylists in Russian literature, in illustration of the harrowing life of the muzhik. One of his village characters cries out in disgust and pain, "And the songs? The same thing, always the same: the stepmother is 'wicked and greedy'; the father-in-law 'harsh and quarrelsome' sits on the top of the oven 'like a dog on a rope'; the mother-in-law no less wicked, also sits on the oven 'like a bitch on a chain'; the sisters-in-law are invariably 'young bitches and tricksters'; the brothers-in-law are 'malicious scoffers'; the husband is either a fool or a drunkard; the old father-in-law bids him thrash his wife soundly 'until her hide rolls down to her heels'; while the wife, after she scrubbed clean the household, and baked the cakes, turned to her husband with the words 'Get up, you foul wretch, wake up, here is a dish of water, wash yourself, here are your leg wrappers, wipe yourself, here is a piece of rope, hang yourself.' And our adages, Tikhon Ilych, could anything more vile and foul be invented? And our proverbs? A man who has been soundly whipped is worth two who haven't been. . . . Simplicity is worse than thieving."

In truth, Bunin only echoes the same savageries of village life that had tormented Chekhov. Consider, for example, this passage in *Peasants*: "Who keeps the tavern and encourages drunkenness? The peasant. Who embezzles and drinks up the funds collected for the community, the school, the church? The peasant. Who steals from his neighbors, puts a torch to his property, bears false witness in a court for a bottle of vodka? The peasant. Yes, to live with them was terrible; still, they were human

beings, they suffered and cried like human beings and there was
nothing in their lives for which they could not find justification.
Crushing toil that made the body ache at night, beastly
winters, scanty crops, overcrowding and no hand of help from
anybody, nowhere to look for succor. Those who were stronger
and more well-to-do could grant no assistance. They were themselves vulgar, dishonest, drunken and swore just as vilely. The
most petty clerk or official treated peasants as though they were
vagrants; spoke to village elders and church guardians as to in-
feriors. Actually, can any kind of help or salutary example be
offered by lazy, avaricious, debauched men who come to the village for no other purpose than to affront, mulct and terrorize?"

Chekhov's and Bunin's novels were my own, bought in Maisel's
big Russian bookshop in New York, so I felt free to pencil comments on the margins. Sometimes I would go to Professor
Wiener's study to show him such marked passages and my scribbled comments. I had to explain to Weiner, who had never lived
in a Russian village, that muzhik life was not all mud, drunkenness, and brutality. Though I remembered the beastly winters,
the execrable mud, the drunken orgies, the grinding poverty, the
epidemics that took so many children, still I could never forget
the happier moments—the lively, colorful weddings, the gay
festivals of Christmas, Easter, and Trinity that brought joy to
everyone. I recalled the muzhik's love of song and dance, his gift
for storytelling, his sociability, his respect for learning, though for
centuries it had been assiduously kept from him. I spoke of all
these to Professor Wiener and even grew sentimental as I recalled
them. Yet Uspensky, Chekhov, and Bunin had perceived no joy at
all in village life, nothing but gloom and savagery, as though they
had been so overwhelmed by its dark and barbarous aspects that
nothing else counted. To them the village was the dark side of
Russia, where no sunlight pierced nor any ray of hope, not even
through the social work of the *zemstvos*, the local provincial
assemblies introduced in 1864.

We often discussed a possible solution to the Russian peasant
problem, and the professor disagreed with me that it must begin
with an equitable distribution of the landed estates, private, public, church, and Czarist. After all, I argued, the peasant knew only
the land; during serfdom he had summarized his age-old hunger

for land in the well-known adage; *my washi a zemlia nasha*—we are yours but the land is ours. Young muzhiks from my village, I told the professor, were coming to America not to stay here (though some of them did), but to earn dollars to go back and buy strips of land. Land to the peasant was not only a sanctity but a prime necessity. Without it he could see no end to his poverty and misery.

One day in the library I stumbled on a remarkable essay on the peasant's attitude toward land. It included scriptural passages that Bible-reading Protestant peasants, notably the Stundists (Baptists), cited in justification of their belief that the land rightfully belonged only to the people who worked it with their own hands:

"So shall ye divide this land unto you according to the tribes of Israel.

"And it shall come to pass, that ye shall divide it by lot for an inheritance unto you, and to the strangers that sojourn among you, which shall beget children among you: and they shall be unto you as born in the country among the children of Israel; they shall have inheritance with you among the tribes of Israel.

"And it shall come to pass, that in what tribe the stranger sojourneth, there ye shall give him his inheritance, said the Lord God." Ezekiel 47: 21–23.

"The land shall not be sold for ever: for the land is mine; for you are strangers and sojourners with me." Leviticus 25: 23.

"Woe unto them that join house to house, that lay field to field, till there be no place, that they may be placed alone in the midst of the earth!" Isaiah 5: 8.

Then like a sudden burst of lightning came the news of the February (1917) Revolution in Russia. It seemed incredible that the Romanov dynasty, which had ruled the country with an iron fist for over three centuries, had tumbled into dust. Instead of a Czar, there was now a "Provisional Government" in Petrograd, headed by Prince Lvov, with Paul Milyukov, Professor Wiener's close friend, as Minister of Foreign Affairs. The professor was the most overjoyed soul at Harvard. All the greater was his rapture— and mine too—when we learned of the very first decree of the new government. With one stroke, the Czar's successors wiped out ages of repression and tyranny. They granted an amnesty to political prisoners, proclaimed freedom of speech and press, equal rights of all religions and all nationalities, and universal suffrage in elections. At last the civilized values for which Russia's most cultivated and most dedicated sons and daughters had for generations been battling, often at the sacrifice of their lives, had become a living reality in the old homeland. It was all heady wine, too heady, not only for a graduate student like myself but also for so seasoned a scholar as Leo Wiener. But not even he had envisioned in the newly formed Workers' and Soldiers' Soviet in Petrograd a political power of potential magnitude that would harass and finally wreck the Provisional Government.

The Russian-Ukrainian colony in Boston celebrated the fall of the Czar and the rise of what appeared at the time a new democratic government with a ball. Several of my Harvard dining companions and I attended. There were speeches which were tumultuously acclaimed. The "flying post" game was busier than I had ever known it to be and the girls that paired up with men who had written them romantic notes were as ready to kiss as to be kissed. In fact, the ball turned into a hilarious affair in which my Harvard companions joined with as much spirit as did the Russians and Ukrainians.

Harvard and Boston greeted the February Revolution with dignified and hearty enthusiasm. A group of Bostonians arranged a mass meeting at Faneuil Hall to celebrate the historic event. The hall was jammed and overflow throngs milled around outside the old Boston shrine. Among the many speakers was Governor Samuel McCall of Massachusetts. I too was invited to address the meeting and though I was allowed only five minutes, it was long enough for a paean to the new day that had come to "dark" Russia. There was nothing else I could say, because I knew so little about what was really happening there.

My appearance in Faneuil Hall was reported in the Boston press and immediately I found myself in demand for addresses by one organization after another including a Harvard faculty club. A girls' finishing school invited me to deliver two lectures, and I fell in love with one of the students, a pretty, dark-haired, blue-eyed, seventeen-year-old girl, daughter of an old Boston family. Despite the girl's encouragement, nothing came of the romance for reasons that need not be stated here.

In all my speeches I stressed the urgency of a land reform in the new Russia. Professor Wiener shared my view, but insisted that so sweeping a reform as the distribution of land would require a long period of preparation before it could be carried out and should be done not by the Provisional Government, but by the Constituent Assembly which the government was pledged to see elected on the basis of a universal vote. Obviously, the professor was a constitutionalist. But he and I could only speculate, as we did day after day, on what was happening and what might happen in the new Russia. To enlighten myself more fully on events there, I subscribed to *Izvestia,* spokesman of the Workers' and Soldiers' Soviet, and to *Rech,* the daily newspaper that Milyukov was editing for the Constitutional Democrats, the leading non-Socialist political party in the country.

Looking back to that time, one can only marvel at the tranquillity that prevailed in Russia, even in the villages, in the early weeks of the Revolution—so, at least, it appeared to those of us observing the scene from our stalls in the Harvard library. Nor were we in error as far as the village was concerned. Years later in his monumental *History of the Russian Revolution,* Trotsky was to write, "In the first weeks after the February Revolution, the village remained almost inert. . . . The village was silent, and therefore the city was silent about the village."

But even before Lenin arrived in Petrograd April 1917, determined to smash the existing government and to impose on Russia his own type of proletarian dictatorship, disintegration had begun to set in, especially in the army, as we began to learn when the Russian newspapers started coming to Cambridge. The famous "Order Number 1" which the Soviet had issued without the approval of the new Cabinet called for the formation of soldiers' committees in each military unit that were to obey not their superior officers but the Soviet in all political decisions. The rank and file, made up overwhelmingly of peasants, welcomed the new order much to the consternation and anger of its officers, from sergeants to generals. The High Command was helpless to stem the corrosion of the fighting spirit of the soldiery, who more and more began to think of going home to claim an allotment of

land now that landlords, churches, and monasteries and the de-
throned Czarist family, no longer had the support of the old police
and the old gendarmerie.

Again and again I showed Professor Wiener the copies of the
Izvestia and *Rech* that I was receiving, which published stories
of the rot that was setting in in the armed forces at the front and
in the rear. The professor was beginning to be disturbed, and after Lenin arrived on the scene and set about forging a new force
for the enactment of his program, and even more, after Milyukov
resigned as Foreign Minister because he had committed himself
to the continuation of the war and to the fulfillment of Russia's
secret treaties with the Allies, the professor became apprehensive
and angry. He saw only ruin ahead for the country he had always loved, and from his standpoint he was of course right.
Democratic Russia, the dream of his life, was collapsing. New
forces were emerging that despised the social, moral, political
values that the intellectual Russian milieu out of which he had
come had always venerated. His speech grew increasingly shrill
as he heaped scorn and invective on Lenin and Trotsky and the
rising Bolsheviks. He was ready to believe all the tales that were
disseminated about the two leaders of the Bolshevik party, including the charge that they had sold out to the Kaiser.

Lenin and Trotsky were new names to me, too, and so was
the term "Bolshevik." I had read the *Communist Manifesto* years
earlier in Carl Baum's tailor shop and it had amused more
than enlightened me with its absurd prophecies of the doom that
awaited the individualist farmer in the Western world. I knew
nothing of Marxism. I was viewing the turbulent Russian scene,
as reflected in the newspapers I was receiving from Petrograd
and the daily stories in the American press, as a purely Russian
event, the outcome of the tragic history of Russia. That was why
I kept on saying to the distressed Professor Wiener that the most
urgent problem before the new government in Russia was an
immediate and nationwide land reform. I knew peasants well
enough to expect them to take the law into their own hands if
the reform was delayed much longer, whatever the practical or
political circumstances that might cause the delay. Professor
Wiener, who venerated Milyukov not only as a scholar-historian
but as a politician and a friend, wouldn't hear of it—only a Con-

stituent Assembly, he held, as did Milyukov, had the legal right to enact a land reform.

This is not the place to discuss the disastrous offensive against the Central Powers launched by the Kerensky government under the prodding of the hard-pressed Allies. However, in June 1917, when the nationwide Congress of the Soviets opened in Petrograd, the Social Revolutionary party, the party of the peasants, was the strongest of all the Socialist parties that made up the Soviets. They drew 285 deputies against 248 by the Mensheviks, who opposed an immediate Socialist revolution, and only 105 by the Bolsheviks who clamored for such a revolution. I have always thought that with so much political power in their hands the Social Revolutionaries, if they had had the audacity to push through a land reform, regardless of possible opposition from their more conservative political opponents, would have had an excellent opportunity to win the support of the peasantry, including the peasant soldiers, and thereby paralyze the advance of the Bolsheviks, their implacable foes. But Victor Chernov, leader of the Social Revolutionary party, lacked the boldness and the fighting spirit of Lenin and in the end he and his party were crushed.

However, despite Professor Wiener's growing wrath against the Bolsheviks, he never forgot that first and foremost he was a teacher, and when I told him that I was ready to begin writing my book on the peasantry, a difficult but necessary book, he not only approved of it but also helped me to work out an outline. And whenever I failed to find the necessary material, he would search through the stacks until he came up with a pertinent document or essay. An amazing researcher, he knew as if by instinct where to turn for the material I needed.

Once I spent hours in a futile effort to find statistical information on wage labor in the Russian countryside. I went to the professor's study and told him that I didn't think Harvard had any material at all on the subject. He immediately arose, went with me to the stacks, and quickly discovered a printed copy in German of a Ph.D. thesis by a certain Dr. Simon Blank on wage labor in the Russian countryside, province by province, though only in European Russia. Proud of his quick find, he chided me gently for assuming that the Harvard library would be lacking any material I might need. For those times the Russian section was indeed an extraordinary collection.

My year as a graduate student at Harvard was a high point in my life and the year was coming to an end. America had entered the war and students, graduates and undergraduates, rushed to enlist. In those days students would no more think of burning draft cards or fleeing to Canada or Sweden than of putting a bullet into their heads.

I was disqualified for active service because the doctor who examined me said I had a heart murmur. But I was kept busy speaking at rallies and training camps, especially where there was difficulty with Russian and Ukrainian immigrants who, against their will, were drafted into the army though they had never even declared their intention of becoming American citizens.

By the time the armistice was signed in November 1918, I was in New York continuing my studies and my writing in the excellent Slavic Department of the Forty-second Street library.

Chapter 20

An Author Finds His Subject

◀▶

After nearly three years of research and writing, I finished *The Russian Peasant and the Revolution.* Glenn Frank was already assistant editor of the *Century Magazine,* so I took the manuscript to him, asked him to read and to advise me which publisher, if any, might be interested in bringing it out. Frank read the manuscript and told me that my approach to the Bolshevik Revolution was completely new to him but was too "heavy" for the Century publishing company. He advised me to submit it to Henry Holt, then one of the most prestigious publishing houses in New York. I followed his advice, and some three weeks later I received a letter signed by Lincoln MacVeagh, a Holt editor, informing me that they would publish the book.

It came out in the spring of 1920 and got excellent reviews. But the sale was poor, as Frank had predicted, and I waited for an opportunity to write something lively enough to merit acceptance by the *Century Magazine.*

The opportunity presented itself in the summer of 1922 when I was lecturing on a Chautauqua circuit in Western Canada. At Nelson, British Columbia, I heard of a colony of Russian farmers in Brilliant, close to Nelson. These Russians, I was informed, called themselves Doukhobors. Did I know anything about them?

The mere word "Doukhobors," which literally means spirit-wrestlers, roused in me a flow of nostalgic sentiment. Of course I had heard about them, during my school years in Russia. To all of us boys in the school, they were a heroic people. However cruel the punishment they suffered under the Czars, they would not compromise with their consciences or abandon their simple and noble faith. They were all peasants, barely literate; and about ten thousand of them, so we had learned, had been exiled to the Caucasus wilderness and exposed to the perils of wild beasts and warring Tatars. Yet one day they rose up, not with guns but with hymns, against the Czarist government. Chanting hymns, they burned all their arms and vowed to be Christians in thought and deed: to kill no living thing, to refuse to use violence against violence. They vowed to avoid all excesses and dissipations—to refrain from meat, tobacco, liquor—and they pledged themselves to abandon individual pursuits and to build a commune where all would toil and enjoy and suffer together.

Thus they turned their backs on modern civilization. They rejected military service and forswore their oath of allegiance to the Czar. They were lashed, tortured, jailed, but they did not yield. Intellectual Russia applauded and idealized them and Leo Tolstoy became their foremost and most eloquent champion. With the help of the English Quakers, he made it possible for them to migrate to Western Canada in 1897.

I could hardly wait for the Chautauqua circuit to end so I could go to Brilliant and live in this extraordinary community.

It was a Sunday morning about five when I finally came to Brilliant, the largest Doukhobor colony in Canada, with a population of some 2500. The community lay in a beautiful spot in the Rockies, in a valley skirted on one side by the roaring Kootenay River and on the other by the swift-flowing Columbia and sheltered by a circle of high mountains. The Doukhobors had come here some fifteen years earlier, when the place had been a heavily wooded wilderness. Now as I swept my eyes over it from a high hill, I saw superbly cultivated orchards and gardens, clusters of houses set in green lawns bright with flower beds. Opposite the railway station towered mammoth grain elevators, a massive jam factory, and not far away on the rocky bank of the Kootenay sprawled a huge modern sawmill.

Yet the moment I entered the meetinghouse—Doukhobors gather early for services—I found myself in a world that was in strange contrast to the modern progressive community I had observed from the hilltop. In the middle of the room, which was a community kitchen and dining room—Doukhobors have no churches—stood a red-painted table, long and bare, and on it lay a big round loaf of dark bread; nearby stood a glass of water, a white pitcher, a dish of salt. The worshipers were standing, as

in a Russian church, the women at the right of the table, pictur-
esque in their bright shawls and richly colored blouses and skirts,
and the men facing them at the left, patriarchal in their homespun
white smocks and full unironed trousers.

The services were impressively simple and informal. There
were no books, no ceremonial, no symbols other than the bread,
water, and salt, no priests, and no leaders. Stepping up to the
table and facing the bread and water, they alternately took turns
at reciting a verse of Psalms, after which they bowed low, touching the floor with their heads, rose, sang a hymn, a special Doukhobor composition in long-drawn-out wailing tones typical of
peasant singing. Then followed an intermission. The men and
women relaxed, chatted sociably for a while, and then sang again.
They were tireless singers, and their hymns seemed interminable.

At the close of the services a group of men gathered about me.
Shut in among the mountains, keeping entirely to themselves,
strangers to the printed word—few of them ever read books or
newspapers—seldom visited by outsiders, they seemed ignorant
of the world beyond their valley. Was it true, they queried, that
there would be a new dynasty of Czars in Russia, with Lenin as
the first Czar? Was it true that in America working folk had decided to starve to death all capitalists? Did people in New York
go shooting and did they drink liquor? How much had I paid for
my suit, my tie, my collar? How did I earn the money to pay for
them? Was everybody in New York going bareheaded, as I was?
Possessed of boundless curiosity intensified by their seclusion,
they did not scruple to ask personal questions. Did I ever go
shooting? Did I eat meat? Did I smoke? Did I consume liquor?
No? Then my wife must be a happy woman. No wife? Ah, ah!

We squatted down on the spacious meetinghouse porch and
continued our conversation. Very eagerly they expounded to me
their beliefs and practices. They regarded it as a waste of money
to build churches. Usually, they gathered for services in their
houses or on a lawn or in an orchard. They worshiped in the
communal house in Brilliant as a matter of convenience; it ac-
commodated a larger crowd than any other place they had. They
did not believe in a clergy because clergymen "exploit the people.
When a man is born, the priest collects a tax on him; when he
marries, the priest collects a tax on him; and when he dies,

the priest collects a tax on him." Festivities of any nature were taboo. They had even discarded holidays. They did not observe New Year's Day, Christmas or Easter.

"Holidays make a man lazy, offer his mind a chance to drift into bad thoughts, and tempt him into evil acts. What did people in Russia do on holidays? Drink, quarrel, fight. Yes, and in this country are they any better?" In their disapproval of worldly pleasures they surpassed the most blue-nosed puritan. Aside from their songs, they had no music. Their weddings were simple affairs. The bridegroom announced publicly that he had selected such and such a girl for his wife and that she had accepted him and would "the brethren and sisters bless them?" No rollicking ceremonies such as rock a Russian village at an ordinary peasant wedding.

Quite remarkable was their explanation of their attitude toward the Bible. Such rationalism was as un-Russian as it was un-peasantlike.

"The Old Testament," they explained, "is an interesting book; we read it sometimes. But there are a lot of foolish things in it. It speaks of war and punishment and revenge and of God helping one army against another. That's all pure nonsense, so we think. The New Testament we read more often than the Old, but we do not regard it as an inspired book. We do not believe in inspired books. Men write them, and they make errors. The stories of the virgin birth, of the ascension of Christ to heaven in the flesh, of his bodily resurrection, are for children. They are contrary to the laws of nature. And when the New Testament speaks of submission to authority we do not know what it means. Christ says do good for evil, and supposing your ruler tells you to cast your brother into dungeon or to take up a gun and go to war? How can you do good for evil then? You see a man has to figure all these things out for himself with his own understanding and not accept everything as it is written down. That's why we do not go much by books, any books. We have no religious books of any kind. We do not print any of our psalms or hymns. We teach them to our children by word of mouth. In winter, when there is not much work on the land, every mother and father instructs the children in the things that a Doukhobor ought to know."

"What other education do your children receive?"

"The father or sometimes a neighbor will teach them to read and write Russian and arithmetic."

"And history and geography too?"

"No; that is not necessary. We don't believe in education. It is not a good thing for a man. It weans him from honest labor, makes him want to live by his wits, by deception. Is not that so?"

"But education," I argued, "enriches and beautifies life—"

An old man interrupted me with a laugh.

"*Nu*, brother," he began, "we have heard such words before. But, you see, we are simple people. We are happy as we are. To us education means being a good Doukhobor. That is, to love all living things and to do no evil, not to shoot, not to eat meat, not to smoke, not to drink liquor. We teach all these things to our children. And more, too. The mothers teach their daughters to bake and to cook, to spin and to weave and to embroider, and the fathers teach their boys to be handy with an ax, a carving knife, a plow, a team of horses. Such things are useful and are good, and the other things that you educated people speak of, *nu*, you can have them. We do not need them. Of what good are pictures, musical instruments, theaters, 'moova peachers'? They only excite your bad appetites, so to speak. You see? To us education means doing useful things."

"Supposing so," I contended, "if it was not that men have studied in universities and laboratories, you never would have had the engines and the boilers and the furnaces that you have installed in your jam factory; you never would have had the tractors, the reapers, the threshing machines that you use."

The old man only shook his head.

"And do you suppose machinery is a good thing?" he answered. "In the Caucasus we had small farms, no machinery. We did all our work by hand, and did not we enjoy life there? Did we not have enough to eat? Aye, better food than we have here. And we did not work so hard and did not have so much worry."

"Correct, correct," the other men muttered. From the expressions of their faces it was evident that they felt they had the better of the argument. I was on the point of mustering a new array of reasons in support of modern education, when a man who had all the time been silently leaning against the doorpost turned toward me and said:

"*Nu,* you look at your cities. I don't know much about them, but once in a while I read a newspaper, and I read of murders there, and robberies, and arrests and police and jails. And look at us. We have no education, and yet there are twenty-five hundred of us living in this community, and we have no police and no courts and no jails and no guns. And now, friend, look at the rulers of the world. They are educated, yes? They have been in universities, yes? And, *nu,* see what they have been doing. Have they been following Christ? They have been fighting wars instead. Merciful Lord, think! They have killed millions and millions of people, and all for what, can you tell me?"

He paused and gazed at me as though expecting a reply, and when I offered none, he continued:

"And yet, you know, they tell us, these educated people, that we ought to kill the wild beasts in the woods. *Nu,* have all the wild beasts since the beginning of time destroyed half as many lives as have the two-legged beasts in the last war?"

One of the men invited me to his house for breakfast. He lived in a colony, as they all did, on top of a hill across the railroad tracks. The colony consisted of a square row of frame houses in each of which lived several families. It was set off in an orchard of apple, plum, and peach trees loaded with ripe fruit. Hop vines in full bloom stretched in a network over the walls and porches. Flower gardens, free of weeds and with a varied assortment of flowers—dahlias, marigolds, roses—greeted the eye at every turn. The lawns were freshly cut and free of any refuse. The neatness of the Doukhobor in his surroundings, in house and person, was one of his outstanding virtues. As we entered the yard, a group of girls came out. They were barefooted, in bright shawls and long skirts; each carried on an arm the head of a sunflower plant from which she was picking the seeds with her fingers and eating them. "Glory be to God!" they greeted us, bowing. "Glory be to God!" my host responded, removing his hat and returning the bow. This was the customary manner of salutation among them. They had dispensed with the Russian "good day" and "good evening" and even with the general "*zdravstvuite.*"

Upon entering the house, what struck my attention most vividly was the hair style of the women. Some of them had their shawls off, exposing clipped heads—clipped close and all around

save for a straggling tuft in front. They reminded me unpleas-
antly of jail inmates. They explained that they began cutting their
hair about a dozen years ago. Why?

"Because," the cook, a ruddy, stout, affable young woman, replied, "it is too much bother to have heavy hair. It takes time to
care for it, and we are not like your women; we have no leisure,
we have to work in the field, help our men. And, then, heavy
hair is not healthy. It used to give me headaches, and sometimes
when a person works around the kitchen, hair falls into the
dough or the soup, and that is not clean. So we are now cutting
it."

"But hair makes a woman beautiful," I protested, thinking of
the numerous hair-tonic ads I had read extolling the glory of
woman's hair.

She waved her hand, shook her head, and smiled.

"We don't care for that kind of beauty."

Here my host, ever ready to philosophize, like all older Doukhobors, remarked:

"You see, *druzhok* [little friend], there is beauty of the spirit and
beauty of the flesh. What's beauty of the flesh? Today you have
it, tomorrow you lose it. Is not that so? Now, for example, you
have dark hair. Tomorrow it turns gray. Today it is heavy, tomorrow it falls out. Today you have a full face, tomorrow the
bones stick out. But beauty of the spirit, you understand, grows
with age. It is as lasting as God."

It was a charming bit of philosophy, but the cook probably
imagined it pictured the Doukhobor women as too unearthly, for
she hastened to add:

"We believe in bodily beauty; but to us such beauty means a
ruddy face, muscular arms, a strong body, flesh like blood and
milk."

I was riding up the mountain once with a white-haired Doukhobor. At one place we made a sharp turn in the road and
beheld a few rods ahead of us, and directly beneath a clump of
overhanging brush, several deer, wide-eyed and with uplifted
heads, staring at us. The Doukhobor halted the horses, gazed at
them, and shook his head in ecstasy.

"How handsome they are!" he said in a low voice, as though
fearing they might hear him and skulk away. "What a pity to kill

them! And yet in the fall the *Anghlicks* [Canadians] tramp all over these mountains and shoot them by the hundreds. But we never touch them, and they are wise beasts, oh, they are. They know we are their friends, and so they come down upon our land for shelter. They wander in our gardens and orchards like cows. And one night last fall a party of *Anghlicks* rowed across the river and shot fifteen of them upon our land. And that was the first time since we have been here that the blood of living things has been shed on our soil, and with God's help we hope it will be the last."

I asked him what they did to animals that foraged on their crops.

"We drive them off," he said; "we never kill them. Look at the squirrels this year. Lord! how they have been damaging our fruit! It seems there is a poor crop of nuts and berries in the mountains, and so they have been coming down to our farms for food. They have stripped bare our nut trees, and we had such an excellent crop! And now they have begun to attack our apple trees. And they are such unreasonable creatures! If they'd eat the apples, we shouldn't mind so much, but they nip off the stems, thinking they can carry the fruit to their holes as they do nuts, and they have not strength enough for that, and the apples fall to the ground. I have tried to drive them off, but it does no good. They come right back. The other day I caught one and I was so angry, may God forgive me, that I picked up a rod and spanked her. And when I let her go I said to her, 'You wicked thing, next time I catch you, even if I am a Doukhobor, I'll cut off your ears.' It would be best, I suppose, if we'd catch them, put them in bags, carry them way up the mountains, and let them out there. That's what I'll do if they keep coming again."

"And what do you do with bears? Do they ever bother you?" I had heard that there were a good many grizzlies roaming about in the neighborhood.

"They never touch us. Men only think that wild animals are dangerous. But we lived in the Caucasus, and there were Tatars and wolves and bears, and yet we burned our arms, and no one ever molested us. I'll tell you, *druzhok*, of an experience we had recently with a bear. A party of us went up the mountains to help put out a forest fire. We came to a place where a wind swept the flames all around us, and we had to flee for safety to a near-by big flat rock. We sat down and watched the flames, and all of a sudden a bear came out and sat down at the end of the rock opposite us, with his forepaws lifted in the air as though to show us his burns. There was an *Anghlick* among us. He picked up a rock and threw it at the bear. But the bear didn't stir. Think of it! Where could he go? He could not jump into the flames. The *Anghlick* picked up another rock. He wanted to kill the bear. But we grabbed him by the hand and said: 'Don't, brother! The bear is our comrade now. He has come here to save himself, even as we all have. Look at his feet. They are burned, and he is suffering.' The *Anghlick* sort of felt ashamed and dropped the rock. The bear sat beside us like a brother, and when the fire swept by, he rose and walked quietly away."

To a Doukhobor all governments were evil because they rested upon force. "The *Anghlicks*," they said, "want us to swear allegiance to their king. But how can we? Their king has armies and navies and fights wars. We owe allegiance to only one king—Christ."

They were as suspicious of the Canadian Government as a bride is of a domineering mother-in-law. For years they refused to register births, deaths, and marriages. They argued that such registration was merely a scheme of governments to collect additional taxes from the people and to keep count of the number of available soldiers. There were times when Canadian officials had to exhume their dead from the graves in order to ascertain the cause of death. In retaliation, the Doukhobors interred their dead in the fields and leveled off the ground to keep the police from locating the place of burial. They resorted to all manner of stratagems—to lies, most of all—to evade the Canadian school laws. They regarded these laws as inimical to their faith and their practices. They were afraid of modern civilization—afraid it would wrench children away from their fold and break up their society.

I broached the question of Canadianization to one of the oldest and most cultivated Doukhobors, and he summed up their attitude in words which it is neither easy to refute nor to forget.

"The *Anghlicks*," he said, "want us to give up our mode of living and our ideas. They want us to go to their schools and adopt their ways and be like them. What would we gain? A knowledge

of English? Good. More luxurious homes? Good. Better food?
Good. Finer clothes? Good. Automobiles of our own? Good.
Property, more and more? Good. And would we do more useful
work? Would we love our fellow men more? Yes, we'd become
worldly and educated. We'd want to go to the cities. We'd seek
a life of ease. We'd reach out for more and more of this world's
material goods. We'd scheme and cheat. We'd drink liquor and
smoke. We'd eat meat and carry guns. We'd go to war and take
human life. Our women would leave the garden and the orchards.
They'd want to be *baruini*—ladies. They'd be thinking of pretty
clothes and jewelry and paint and powder and dances and men.
Yea, they might even begin to smoke and drink and go to the bad.
Once a person starts to go down, there is no telling where he'll
stop. What would become of us then? Here, look at me. I am an
old man. I have not many more years of life. I have been in jail
in Russia and in Siberia, where I nearly froze to death because I
would not give up the Doukhobor faith. Merciful Lord! they
beat many of us to death in Russia because we were Doukhobors.
Nu, must we break up now because the Canadians want us to?
And, pray, who would profit from it? Each of us would be for
himself and against his brother. We'd lose our peace of mind and
our contentment and our simple ways and our love of Christ,
and then where and what would we be?"

I visited Kylemore, Saskatchewan, one of the largest grain-
growing colonies of the Doukhobors. Harvest was in full swing.
An army of reapers was hastily reducing the shoulder-high wheat
fields to huge sheaves. About thirty boys and girls were setting
up the bundles. The girls wore knickerbockers and caps and were
hilariously proud of their harvesting costume. Every hour or so
when the water boy drove round with barrels of freshly pumped
spring water, they came together, slaked their thirst, then sat
down to rest, to play, to sing. An older man was with them to
see that they did not make the rest period too long. Toward noon
he told them that he would release them from further work until
after lunch if they would lay aside "their childishness" and entertain with songs this "Russian man who has come from a far place
to see how we simple people Doukhobors are living."

With joyous exclamations they dashed after sheaves of wheat,
sat down upon them close together, with their backs toward the

observations of their surroundings and their manner of living. The material I had gathered begged to be digested and written up, which is what I did. I mailed the article to Glenn Frank who by this time was editor-in-chief of the *Century Magazine*. I remained in Kylemore, having the time of my life visiting Doukhobor homes, going off to the wheat fields, working with their young people and spending night after night in the barracks for the harvesters.

Then one day in my mail came a small letter-sized envelope from the *Century Magazine*. It was too small for a manuscript so I knew that Frank was not returning the story I had mailed him. Tremblingly I opened the envelope and a check for $250 fell to the floor. No money I had ever earned touched me so profoundly. There was also a letter from the editor congratulating me on the piece I had sent him and requesting another if I could gather the proper kind of material.

Chapter 21

Doukhobors and Dissenters

◆

From Canadians I heard sensational stories about certain Dou-khobors, men and women, who now and then descended on a town, disrobed in public and staged hymn-singing parties. But Doukhobors resolutely denied that they had ever indulged in nudism or that it had ever been a part of their faith. The nudists the Canadians spoke of, they said, had broken away from the Doukhobors and formed a sect of their own, called *Svobodniki*—Freedomites. No Doukhobor would deign even to exchange greetings with any of them and no Freedomite ever had a kind word to say about the Doukhobors. They regarded Doukhobors as traitors to the faith of their fathers, as men and women who had yielded to the sins of the flesh and had abandoned Christ.

The manager of the Doukhobor business office in Kylemore, a sandy-haired, blue-eyed, pale-faced man, whom I came to know well, told me that if I went to Thrums, British Columbia, I should find a colony of Freedomites, presided over by their most influential leaders; at once it occurred to me that a story about these sensationally wayward Russians, deep in the mountains of British Columbia, might make an acceptable story for the *Century Magazine*. But before leaving for Thrums I discussed the Freedomites with the Doukhobor manager, a highly intelligent man, who was himself interested in them and had made a searching study of their beliefs and practices.

Nudism, I learned, though the most sensational, was not the most significant aspect of their stern denial of civilization. God, they contended, didn't grow cooked foods, why then should man eat anything that was touched by fire? And they didn't. They subsisted exclusively on raw foods. Why cut hair and shave, they argued? If God didn't want flowing locks on man's head and a beard on his face, he wouldn't grow them. They wouldn't eat salt, sugar, pepper, vinegar, any spices or condiments. God, they maintained, created all living things to work out their own destiny in their own way. Therefore man had no right to subject any of them to his use. And the Freedomites didn't. Not only would they kill no living thing, they would not eat eggs, milk, or dairy foods, nor wear anything made of hides or furs. Several years earlier they turned all their livestock out on the prairies, to "free God's dumb creatures" from the slavery of man. They wouldn't even use a horse. Instead of plowing, they spaded up their land and did all their work by hand.

God, they held, wanted man to work and live in the open, in field and forest. Therefore man should abandon the city, the factory and the machine. They wouldn't live in the city or use any machinery whatever, which was one reason why they hated Doukhobors who saw no sin in the use of modern agricultural implements, the erection of a jam factory and the construction of a sawmill.

Once the Freedomites had heard of a strike of miners. To show their sympathy for the strikers and to protest against the employment of human beings in mines and factories, they called a mass meeting, delivered speeches, sang hymns, and concluded the meeting by burning an old reaper one of them had possessed. At another time a group of them assembled in a newly built village in Saskatchewan, stripped and built a bonfire of their clothes and, chanting Psalms, flung their money into the flames, one hundred and sixty dollars—all they had between them—as an example to the world of what to do with "the root of all evil." On still another occasion they had resolved to protect against the Doukhobors for their ever-growing worldliness and their compromises with civilization, as evidenced in their use of modern machinery, modern business methods, and their erection of a separate office building. They decided to burn the building in the hope the act would waken their erring brethren into a realization of their perverse ways and bring them to the fold of Christ. But before setting fire to the building, they pried open the windows, climbed inside, and with lighted candles in their hands marched from room to room, floor to floor, searching for birds, lest any perish in the flames.

The Doukhobor manager asked what I thought of all he told me about the Freedomites. I replied they would be fascinating people to talk to and write about. "Then go to Thrums," he said, "and if you write about them, please do not fail to tell your readers that they are *not* Doukhobors, and that the Doukhobors are heartily ashamed of them."

I found Thrums sprawling over a jagged valley that was a connecting link between two walls of mountains. A small community, it struck me as a slice of Russia grafted on Canadian soil. Russian speech floated in the air and Russian folk tunes with their long-drawn-out plaintiveness resounded over the mountainsides. Russian women and girls, barefooted with gay-colored kerchiefs over their heads worked in gardens and orchards. Nearly all the settlers there were Russian, principally Doukhobors who had become sick of community life and broken away from it. Now they were laborers in a near-by sawmill or independent farmers cultivating small but precious acreages on which they grew excellent fruits and vegetables.

From a group of ragged boys who gathered around me, I learned the location of various Freedomite farms. I came to one that nestled in the shadow of a wooded mountain, screened off from the road by a thick orchard. It was a small farmstead, not over ten acres, that rolled gently over a sloping hillside. On top of the hill slouched two small and outwardly neglected houses, built at right angles to one another. I walked over to one of the houses. The door was wide open and following peasant custom I entered without knocking. What a delightfully typical peasant home it was! The walls were freshly whitewashed, the girders unplaned and unpainted, long planks fastened to the walls taking the place of chairs and lounges. Here also was the eternal *polati* (wooden platform), stretching from one end of the room to the other that served as a sleeping place, precisely as in muzhik homes in my native village. But no ikons adorned the walls and no pigs and chickens strutted about the floor. This was a remarkably clean home, without a whiff of the smoke which darkens muzhik homes, without any of the smells that infest muzhik living rooms.

At an open window, with her back toward me, bent over a piece of sewing, sat a middle-aged woman, barefooted and bareheaded, with her thin gray hair slicked back straight and done into a braid with a white ribbon at the end, not at all in the manner of a person renouncing man-made aids of adornment. She did not hear me enter, and when I spoke to her, she turned round and eyed me with suspicion. Without waiting to be questioned, I explained who I was and what I had come for. Instantly she grew animated, leaped from her chair, and, excitedly muttering words of warm welcome, began to bustle about to entertain me.

"*Nu*, and I thought you were an *Anghlick*," she apologized, "come from the government with a complaint. Ah, a Russian from New York! *Nu synok* [little son], I'll set the table at once. How hungry you must be after such a long journey! And we have lots of food—lots." And suiting action to word, despite my vigorous protests that I had just partaken of a hearty meal, she rushed dish after dish upon the table. And what fare! Heads of lettuce, raw carrots, freshly pulled onions, raw peanuts, peaches, raisins, plums, and raw potatoes.

"Sit down, *synok*, sit down," she said and fairly shoved me into a seat at the head of the table. "Eat, eat, *synok;* don't say you are not hungry after such a long and arduous journey. You must be hungry; of course you must be, and our food is not like yours. It is unspoiled by cooking; it is just as God grows it, and as all of God's creatures save men eat it." Dish after dish rattled its way toward me.

"Maybe you'd like some of our bread? Ah, I've forgotten!" Off she dashed, soon returning not with a loaf, but with a glass jar filled with something that looked like corn meal sprinkled with pepper. She shoved a bowl toward me and emptied some of the substance into it. "That's our bread," she chattered on. "We make it ourselves, *synok*, from wheat, raw peanuts, raisins, sun-dried apples and plums, which we mix and grind. Delicious bread! *Nu*, just try it. Slice peaches and plums into it, as we do, and mix it. Wonderful food that is, *synok!* We eat barrels of it in winter. It's so strengthening!"

I plied her with questions, which she answered readily. Of course it took courage to be a *Svobodnik* in the face of the opposition of the whole world. It was hard at first to live on raw food. It made them sick; and every time the smell of *shctchui* (cabbage soup) reached their nostrils, they were overcome with a desire to taste cooking again. That was because their systems had been poisoned by their previous mode of living and craved unnatural things. But now, *ekh!* they wouldn't look at cooked dishes. Once one of their women fell sick. An *Anghlick* told her that if she ate hot soup she would get well. She followed the *Anghlick*'s advice, and of course they had to discharge her from the society. It was a great joy to be a *Svobodnik,* to live in tune with God and nature; only Canada was such a worldly country, even in the mountains, and offered so many temptations that seduced the young people. If they could only get back to Russia! Did I know Lenin? Couldn't I intercede for them and beg the new ruler of Russia to let them in and give them small parcels of land, enough only for fruits and vegetables for themselves? Did the Bolsheviks actually kill off people in Russia? It could not be that they were killing peasants? It must be landlords and the Czar's relatives they were putting to death. Why should any one want to kill muzhiks? Muzhiks had nothing, anyway. Ah, if they could only get back to the land of their birth!

Soon the man of the house entered. Ivan was his name. He was a leader of the sect, and what an arresting personality! Tall, gaunt, erect, with a massive head and heavy, dark hair that straggled in waves over his sun-baked neck and ears. His broad, bony face seemed sunk in a lustrous black beard, which, together with his hard, gleaming eyes overhung by heavy brows, lent him an air of medieval austerity that awed and yet fascinated. Greeting me cordially, he sat down beside me and, peasant fashion, pelted me, in between bites of onions, carrots, and radishes, with personal questions. At last he said:

"*Nu,* we are happy to entertain you. We are always glad to have strangers visit us, and quite a good many come, especially *Anghlicks.* You see, out in the world people think that we always go naked, that that is all we believe in. And do you know, brother, people come to look at us. Yes, and when they find us in our clothes, they are disappointed. Sometimes they will ask us to disrobe, go out in the sun, and pose for them, so they can take pictures. Why do you suppose they do it? Do they want to sell these pictures and make money? *Ekh,* what people will do for money! But we are simple-minded people, and we don't mind what others say or think of us. Christ says love thine enemy as thyself, and we believe in Christ. Our homes, our cellars, our orchards, our gardens, our hearts are open to all. That's the way Christ wants us to be."

"You see, *synok*," the woman interrupted, "we are not like the people in your world. Your people teach even children to be selfish and cruel. In your world, if a baby lolls around on the floor, and some living thing crawls near it, what do you do? You say to the baby, 'Kill it! kill it!' And sometimes you set the example yourselves and step on the innocent thing and crush it. Yes? And do you know what we do? We say to our baby, '*Va-va! va-va!* Don't touch! don't touch! It hurts, it hurts.'"

"But some creatures," I protested, "have to be destroyed."

"What ones?" Ivan flared back.

"Why," I replied, "flies and snakes and gophers. Think what—" But Ivan would not let me continue.

"Look, brother," he said pointing to the ceiling, the walls, the floor. "Do you see any flies in this house? Hardly any, yes? And it's the end of summer, too, with autumn smelling in the air, when flies rush inside houses for shelter. And do you know why we have no flies? Because we live a natural life. We don't do any cooking and don't use any sugar and other vile foods that attract them. And snakes? *Nu ladno* [very well]." He rose, took a few steps away from the table, and continued, acting out his words in the manner of a man taking the part of the gravedigger in *Hamlet*.

"Here am I, a man. *Da*, a man. I am walking along a road—a road. And here at this place I see a snake. And I, the man, step on the snake with my heel and crush it, and right here before me lies the snake, dead—dead! And now tell me who is the snake— the thing that's dead or I, the man?"

"So, so," said his wife and nodded with evident delight.

"And now you say kill gophers; they ruin crops. *Ekh*, brother, if every man would work as we do, there would be enough for gophers and for birds, more than enough. But do you know what it means to kill a gopher? I'll tell you what it means. You kill a gopher, you kill a mouse; you kill a mouse, you kill a rabbit; you kill a rabbit, you kill a squirrel; you kill a squirrel, you kill a cow; you kill a cow, you kill a horse; you kill a horse, you kill a man!"

We went out into the orchard and sat down on the ground in

the sun. Other *Svobodniki* joined us, long-bearded men and barefooted women, eager to talk themselves out.

"To the outside world we are a crazy people," Ivan explained. "Yes, crazy. We don't work horses, we don't use machines, we don't eat cooked foods, we don't kill snakes. Perhaps we are crazy. Who knows? We are not educated. We don't want to be. Why should we? Is God educated? You see, we believe in God, and do you know what belief in God means? Do you think it means going to church and dropping on your knees and crossing yourself incessantly and praying and sobbing yourself hoarse with repentance? What foolishness! We have no prayers; we don't pray. Once a Russian came to visit us. He was a poor man, and we offered him shelter. He stayed with us about half a year. He was Orthodox, and, ah, how pious! He'd rise in the middle of the night, get down on his knees in the dark, and pray, pray, pray, sobbing his heart out to God, and keeping us awake for hours. But we said nothing. We are *Svobodniki;* we believe in every one doing as he pleases. And one morning he was gone. He disappeared in the night. And then we discovered that the hundred dollars we had saved up had also disappeared. *Nu,* what good is prayer to such a man?"

He paused, brushed back the hair the wind had blown over his face, and continued:

"God, brother, means love, and do you know what love means? Love means freedom, absolute, everlasting freedom, to let everyone do, not as books and priests and man-made laws prescribe, but as his own inner spirit dictates. That's freedom. And, *nu,* how much freedom have you in your world? You have nations, governments, schools, property, and machines, the wickedest of all things, and all these kill freedom; and when you kill freedom, you kill love; and when you kill love, you kill faith in God. Smile, if you please; it's so, though. You are educated, yes? You live in a big city—New York. Is it as big as Chicago? I was in Chicago once, but I've never been in New York. And where you live, you've got to dress and eat and talk and pray just as other people tell you. *Nu,* how much freedom have you in New York? And then in New York you are all grasping after the cent; and when you get it, you clutch at it with all your might, as though the cent was all there is to life. No, brother, you have no freedom; you are all slaves in the outside world, slaves of the machine and of the cent. But we have freedom. We'd rather have freedom than food. Listen!

"It was about eleven years ago. A crowd of us marched into the village of Verigin, Saskatchewan. It was daytime, and we removed our clothes and threw them into a heap and set them afire, and then we took up all the money we had between us and flung that into the flames. You see, we had rid ourselves of our money, our clothes, of every bit of property we had; we had nothing left. We were as poor as on the day we came into the world; none could be poorer than we. And yet we were free. We felt so happy that we sang. When you have freedom, brother, you need no clothes, no money, nothing, to make you happy."

"So, so, so," said the other *Svobodniki*, nodding in elation.

Since he touched on the question of clothes, I asked for an explanation of the nude pilgrimages.

"It is simple enough, brother," Ivan began. "Now look! This is my shirt, made of linen which we ourselves have woven; and these are my trousers, likewise made of linen. We make these clothes ourselves, from spinning to sewing. And under these clothes is my body, and that's the work of God. Now the clothes are our own work, the work of man, and of them I am not ashamed; but the body is the work of God, and of that I am ashamed. *Nu*, is there reason in that? What is there about the body that man should be ashamed of? If God is not ashamed of it, if it is the very image of God, why should man be? Did Adam have clothes? Do beasts wear clothes? Do birds wear clothes? Supposing you threw a cloak over the back of a goat, how would it look? It's the same with man, brother. Only man's mind is poisoned; yes, poisoned by the things that rob him of freedom, and that's why he thinks that the body is a terrible thing and should be covered up. But we *Svobodniki* say, 'Freedom, freedom of the body from poison that gets in there from foods that are boiled and broiled and roasted, and freedom of the mind from false and poisonous ideas, from slavery and from the things that cruel, selfish people have invented who did not know what freedom meant.'"

As I was listening to these speeches I could not help thinking of Tolstoy. How that sublime primitivist would glow with joy at such fiery denunciation of Western civilization! In essence the *Svobodnik* view of life was boldly Tolstoyan. I was not sure but the ironic Christian nihilist would approve of the nude pilgrimages.

"I suppose you are followers of Tolstoy," I said. To my amazement, the name did not register animation.

"Tolstoy," one of them repeated. "Was he a general in the Czar's army?"

"No, he was a writer, one of the greatest that has ever lived."

"A writer?" Ivan repeated in a tone of indifference. "Then he was not of much account."

One evening we gathered in the home of a young *Svobodnik*. Ilya was his name, a blond, blue-eyed, wiry, handsome, boyish-looking youth, with a shrill musical voice such as good tenors have. He was married to Lusha, or, rather, lived with her, for *Svobodniki* did not recognize marriage. Like Tolstoy, they regarded celibacy as the ideal life; but when a man and woman did decide to live together, they were "brother and sister." Lusha was one of the prettiest Russian girls I had seen in Western Canada, slender, bobbed-haired, with deep-blue eyes, dark brows, full red lips, and a fine set of teeth. She was the daughter of a Doukhobor and no *Svobodnik*. In the morning, while Ilya would get his breakfast in the garden and orchard, she would bake potato pancakes for herself and fry potatoes and make tea. When I came to the house she was busy amid baskets of tomatoes and peaches that she was canning for winter use. When Ilya introduced her to me as "my sister," she indignantly protested, insisting she was his wife.

"I believe in absolute freedom," he explained, "and when a man has a wife, he has a possession, and there are no possessions in the kingdom of heaven. If Lusha ever falls in love with any one else—"

"But I won't," Lusha interrupted, almost with a scream.

"I only wanted to say that if you should—"

"I won't, though," she persisted. "You know I love only you."

Being a man, he yielded and did not refer to the subject again. Lusha served supper. At one end of the table sat the *Svobodniki*, and before them she set down plates of cucumbers, tomatoes, radishes, watermelons, onions; at the other end were a Doukhobor friend, she, and I, and before us she placed hot soup, cakes, bread and jam. It was one of the most memorable meals I've ever had. In the pale light of the lamp, in that whitewashed hut in the Canadian Rockies, the long-haired *Svobodniki*, in their white-linen garments, crunching away with relish at raw fruits and vegetables, made a touching scene of patriarchal simplicity. Ivan asked Lusha if she had any oatmeal in the house. She went to the cellar, soon returning with a big box of oatmeal, which she handed to Ivan. He poured some into a bowl, sprinkled raisins over it, poured in water, stirred the mixture, and began to eat it, praising highly its gustatory and nutritive qualities. He ate it with such relish that I had not the heart to inform him that the commercial oatmeal was no uncooked food.

There was an old *Svobodnik* woman at the table. She was over eighty, bent and toothless, and with a face that seemed like a lump of withered flesh without bones. She was one of the most talkative persons there, and in the course of the evening she narrated an experience she had that illuminated the *Svobodnik* attitude toward suffering.

"A group of us," she began, "had gone to a certain village on a pilgrimage. We stopped at the railroad station and began to sing. A crowd had gathered, and one of our men who could talk a little of the *Anghlick* language explained to the people there what it meant to be a *Svobodnik*. He told them that we believed in absolute freedom, and that even the clothes we wore were a sign of slavery. Then in protest against the slavery in the world, we disrobed. We were arrested and sent to an insane asylum. There they took us into a ward and told us we must go to work; but we refused. Then two persons threw me to the floor. Of course I did not resist. We *Svobodniki* believe if people want to beat us or cut us up, let them do it. Our spirit will make us insensible to the pain. Then these two persons jammed a brush into my hand and shouted, 'Now will you work?' And I shook my head and said: 'No. Let me out of here. I have done no one harm.' Then they grabbed my hands and beat them against the floor until I lost all sense of feeling, and after that they stood me up against the wall, seized my arms, twisted them back, forced my mouth open with an iron thing, which they rolled around inside until they wrenched two of my teeth out and tore off a strip of flesh inside of my right cheek, and the blood gushed forth and soaked my clothes. Then they flung me to the floor, dragged me around, kicked me into a corner, and left me there. And when I came to I clambered to my feet and stepped over to the window. I looked outside at the sky and the sun, and of a sudden I felt Christ in my heart, and light came to my soul, and I felt free and happy and began to sing."

That night I lay awake for a long time, meditating. How childish these *Svobodniki* seemed! How futile their outlook on life, and their impossible anarchic conceptions of freedom! To an Anglo-Saxon, with his orderly ways, his utilitarian aspirations, his search for a comfortable berth in the world, the efforts of these unread, unlettered muzhiks to attain a certain peculiar standard of spiritual perfection must appear absurd and irrational. But then, judged by Anglo-Saxon standards, are Raskolnikov, Prince Myshkin, Ivan Karamazov or his brother Alyosha, the saint, persons of normal mind? And what of Tolstoy himself, renouncing in his old age fame and fortune and fleeing in the dark of night from a comfortable home and a loving family to a distant wilderness in the hope of finding peace of soul?

As I lay there meditating, I was suddenly interrupted by a familiar voice.

"Are you asleep?" It was Ivan, the leader of the sect, standing at the doorway of my room.

"No," I replied. "Come in."

I lighted the lamp and he sat down on a box beside my bed.

"Don't think unkindly of me for coming again," he said apologetically. "I don't mean to disturb you, but there was something else about the *Svobodniki* that may interest you and the paper for which you are going to write about us, and as you expect to leave in the morning, I thought I'd come back and tell you about it. You see, we don't bury our dead."

I could hardly believe his words.

"No, we don't; we just throw them out on the grass."

"But—"

"I know what you are going to say, but this is the way we think. When a man is dead, his soul is gone, and his flesh is of no use for anything except a feast for the wild beasts. People think that's terrible. They think the body is something sacred,

But it is not. Leave it somewhere, and it rots and becomes filthy. Of course, the dead person's relatives cry and mourn, and they want to dress him up and put him into a casket with flowers and other ornaments, but he'll rot, anyway. When a man dies, his friends and relatives should rejoice and sing, for he has gone into the kingdom of eternal bliss. That's the way we think."

"But don't they arrest you for doing that?"

"I'll tell you what happened to us once several years ago. We went on a long pilgrimage, and we came to Fort William. One of our party died. It was winter. We got a sled, put the corpse on it naked, and covered it with a black cloth. We wanted to take it to the cemetery of the *Anghlicks* and throw it out there on the ground. But we didn't know where the cemetery was, and so, as we passed through the town, we stopped and asked. A policeman became suspicious, and he came over and asked us what we had on the sled.

"'A corpse,' we told him.

"'Where are you going with it?'

"'To the cemetery.'

"'Have you got a grave dug?'

"'He does not need a grave.'

"'How are you going to bury him?'

"'We won't. We'll just throw him on the ground.'

"'Have you a coffin?'

"'Of what use,' said we, 'is a coffin to him? He'll feel just as comfortable without one.'

"'Have you a permit?'

"'A permit?' said we. 'He's already got his permit from Jesus Christ.'

"'Well,' he said, 'you can't go.'

"Of course we wouldn't fight with him, and when we realized he wouldn't let us go to the cemetery, we lifted the corpse off the sled, threw it at the policeman, marched around several times singing 'Farewell, comrade' and departed."

Ivan rose to go.

"*Nu*, I won't disturb you any longer, brother," he said on leaving. "I only hope you won't remember us in evil. We are simple people. We have not got the nice ways and the nice things that educated people have. We don't want them. But we have given you the best we had, and if you come again, whether you write well or ill of us, we shall welcome you just the same. And if you tell your friends about us, and if they say that we are crazy, just tell them that perhaps we are, but that we are honest folk, we earn our living with our own hands and our great joy in life is to fulfill the will of Christ."

Fanatic though he was, Ivan's parting words sounded so earnest, so honest, so innocent of mischief that it never would have occurred to me that the sect of which he was the most eloquent spokesman would in the course of the years forge itself into the most monstrous terrorist organization Canada had known. The arsonist torch, the wrist-watch bomb, the Molotov cocktail were the weapons they wielded pitilessly on members of their sect who tired of its fanaticism and against Doukhobors who yielded however slightly to the assimilationist power of Canadian civilization. The Canadian Government could only respond with police power which finally brought to an end the depredations the *Svobodniki* had for some five years been perpetrating in the name of Christ.

However, I went back to Brilliant where I had excellent accommodations. I had brought with me a pack of notebooks on conversations with the *Svobodniki* and on their surroundings and their manner of living. I quickly typed out my story on my portable Corona and sent it off to the *Century*. It's title was "As in the Days of Adam."

But I lingered on in Brilliant, held there by the friendliness and hospitality of my new friends, until I received an enthuiastic letter of acceptance from Glenn Frank. He liked my story, he said, and had further plans for me, a proposition that I might be interested in—in fact, a matter of some urgency. Would I please see him as soon as I returned to New York? So I boarded the next east-bound train for the long trip back, wondering every mile of the way what the editor of the *Century* had in mind for me.

Chapter 22

My America

◄►

During my year at Harvard I had become better acquainted with Glenn Frank, who lived in Boston and was political secretary and intellectual mentor of Edward A. Filene, head of the department store that still bears his name. A small-town Missourian, Frank was a handsome man with a warm smile and a brilliant mind. He had attracted the attention of Morgan Shuster, president of the Century Company in New York. In 1919 Shuster invited him to become associate editor of the *Century Magazine*, and in two years, at the age of thirty-four, he was editor-in-chief.

As I have said, it was he who read the manuscript of my *Russian Peasant and the Revolution* and steered me to the right publisher. Then as editor-in-chief of the monthly, he had urged me to write for him. His aim as editor was to search out promising unknowns and he thought I had the making of a *Century* writer. He had already persuaded Albert E. Wiggam, an old-time Chautauqua and lyceum lecturer, to become a contributor.

Wiggam, a Hoosier, was over fifty years old and would no doubt have ended his days wandering over lecture circuits summer and winter had not Frank perceived in him the making of a quality writer. A dedicated eugenist, Wiggam had year after year been lecturing on the problems of heredity; then with Frank's encouragement and assistance, he wrote a piece which was the opening feature of the *Century* for March 1922. It was called "The New Decalogue of Science" and presented as "an open letter from the biologist to the statesman." The piece created a sensation and the Bobbs-Merrill publishing company signed a contract with Wiggam to expand the article into a book, which became a national best seller. Other books followed which also became best sellers and Frank was naturally proud of what he had helped Wiggam to accomplish. He was ready to help me too in any way he could.

But at the time I had nothing to offer in which I myself had confidence. While still in Dean Briggs's class, I realized that I had not the gift of language to become a literary figure. Style would win me no laurels. I could only write with more or less felicity about events or experiences that excited me. And so it was not until accident brought me into association with the Doukhobors and Freedomites that I stumbled on a subject which stirred me so profoundly that I felt compelled to write the stories which Frank accepted for publication.

Back in New York, as I sat opposite him at his desk, he told me that what had particularly impressed both him and Carl Van Doren, his literary editor, about my stories from Canada was my deep understanding of peasants and my ear for peasant speech. He therefore advised me to go to Russia and write about peasants there. As the author of *The Russian Peasant and the Revolution*, I was the logical man to report on the human aspects of the lot of the peasants under Bolshevism, of which hardly anything was known in America.

Unfortunately, Frank continued, the magazine was in no position to finance the trip, but he was certain that he could publish a sufficient number of my stories to cover at least the major part of my expenses; and I could sell articles to other magazines and perhaps bring out a book. Of one thing he had no doubt—a trip to Russia and publication in quality magazines would automatically raise my lecture fees and also make me more in demand. Like Dr. Gunsaulus, Frank held no exalted opinion of lecturing as a profession. Privately, he spoke of it as "intellectual masturbation." But it was an ideal means of supplementing a writer's income.

Nobody could have offered me friendlier or sounder counsel. I had in fact toyed with the idea of going to Russia ever since Lenin had proclaimed Nep—New Economic Policy—in March 1921. Among other things the new policy had done away with the requisitioning of grain that had so infuriated the peasantry. It had also legalized free trade in small-scale private enterprise, a measure the peasantry could only welcome. I viewed Nep as a smashing victory for the peasantry over Lenin and his strait-laced ideology. But the difficulty of getting to Russia had appeared insurmountable. I didn't have the money to finance the trip, nor was I certain I would obtain a visa, and even if I did, I had no assurance that with the peasants in a surly mood, the Bolsheviks would permit me to travel in villages, above all to visit the village of my birth where I could be certain of hearing muzhiks speak without fear and without reservations.

Now Frank's proposal helped me to overcome the principal difficulties. A request for a visa from the editor of the well-known *Century* would not be lightly disregarded by Moscow's Foreign Office. Nor were finances any longer a serious problem. As for other difficulties, particularly travel in the Russian countryside, I would take my chances. After all, Russia was a muzhik country and I could hardly escape meeting muzhiks wherever I might travel.

Yet autumn was no time to go there. I remembered the ugly autumn weather in the Russian countryside, the floods and the deep mud that had so often cut off my village from the outside world. So I told Frank I would wait until spring before leaving for Berlin, where there was a Soviet Embassy at which I could apply for a visa.

Meanwhile, to enlarge my understanding of events in Bolshevik Russia, I proceeded to make a study of the Russian publications that were arriving in some profusion in the United States. The fresh material confirmed my conclusion in *The Russian Peasant and the Revolution* that in the last analysis the peasantry would be the decisive force in the Bolshevik battle for power. The Revolution was of course city-made, with Petrograd the center of the plotting and the fighting. But it was clearer than ever now that had the soldiery, overwhelmingly peasant, turned their guns on the rebellious workers as they had done in 1905, they would have drowned the Revolution in blood as they had the earlier one. Nor was it any longer disputable that the principal reason the peasant soldiers hadn't shot down the workers, was that the Bolsheviks had dangled before them immediate land reform and immediate peace which would enable them to take prompt advantage of the reform. Tactically the Bolsheviks had outsmarted all other political parties, including the Social Revolutionaries.

The freshly arrived Russian publications confirmed the view

of those observers of the scene (including myself) who held that despite all Bolshevik pretensions and protestations to the contrary, this Revolution could on no account be regarded as the beginning of an age of "proletarian internationalism" but was a purely national event, as Russian as the ancient Kremlin in which Lenin now lived and worked. The proof of this was to be found in accounts reaching this side of the Atlantic of the Bolshevik-German peace negotiations begun in Brest-Litovsk on December 5, 1917.

It is well to survey briefly the story of the German-Bolshevik encounter at Brest-Litovsk, a shattering episode in the Revolution and a dramatic revelation of the frenzied self-deception of the men who had come to power.

In his farewell letter of April 8, 1917, to the Swiss workers on the eve of his departure for Russia, Lenin had written, "The Russian proletariat single-handed cannot successfully complete the socialist revolution." He can only *start the revolution* [the italics are Lenin's]. . . . render more favorable the conditions under which its *most important* and trustworthy and most reliable coadjutor, the European and American *socialist* proletariat, will undertake the decisive battles."

Of one thing Lenin, who was determined to overthrow the government that had succeeded the Czar, had not the least doubt: *"The German proletariat is the most trustworthy and most reliable ally of the Russian proletariat."*

These assertions, which history has refuted, demonstrate how ill-informed the Bolshevik leader was not only of the mind of the American worker, but also of the German proletarian. Though Lenin had lived in Western Europe, principally in Switzerland, for some fourteen years and was conversant with Europe's three major languages—English, French, and German—he might as well never have left the straggling town of Simbirsk, high on the west bank of the Volga, where he was born, for all that he had learned about the American and European working class. The same was true of Trotsky, Bukharin, and other leaders, who in the pre-revolutionary years had lived as exiles in the West. To the end they remained Russian, unable to think beyond the abuses and barbarisms of their own history. Full of hatred for these ancient wrongs and burning with fiery passion to destroy Russia's capitalist system, such as it was, they called for a "dictatorship of the proletariat." With the proletariat in power, the leaders imagined that the class consciousness of workers of all nationalities would transcend their national and other interests and emotions: "Workers have no Fatherland," "Workers of the world, unite!" exhorted the *Communist Manifesto*.

Lenin and his associates were convinced that if German and Russian soldiers fraternized across the trenches, the German would as gladly lay down his arms as the Russian; and then, once peace negotiations had unmasked the imperialist aims of the Kaiser's Germany, the German proletarian, Russia's "most trustworthy and most reliable ally," would realize how brutally deceived he had been. He too would rise in revolt.

At Brest-Litovsk, Trotsky had indeed brilliantly unmasked the aims of the Kaiser's government, but when his debating and oratorical skills failed to move the German representatives into acceptance of peace "without indemnities and annexations," he withdrew from the negotiations and proclaimed the slogan "No peace, no war." This was Trotsky's last desperate effort to waken "the revolutionary consciousness" of the German worker and the German soldier. But Trotsky only demonstrated that he was as naïve as Lenin in his judgment of the temper and mentality of both. At the command of their generals, the German soldiers forgot "fraternization" and continued to fight and the German worker forgot his "class-consciousness" and failed to paralyze industry and transportation with strikes, while the German army continued to advance deeper and deeper into Russian territory. In consequence, on March 3, 1918, the Bolsheviks were obliged to sign the disgraceful treaty imposed on them at Brest-Litovsk.

Lenin had gambled on the militant support of at least the German worker and soldier and the gamble had proved a disaster, the greatest Russia had known since the Tatar invasion in the thirteenth century.

In his *Literature and Revolution* Trotsky would have us believe that "even in Brest-Litovsk when first we refused the Hohenzollern his peace, and later signed it without reading it, the revolutionary party did *not* [my italics] feel itself vanquished, but rather the master of to-morrow." Trotsky is unabashedly romancing. Utterly helpless, their dream of a German uprising, shattered by the German high command, the leaders of the Kremlin, contrary to Trotsky's boasts, were actually "shivering in their boots," as I learned over and over again, even on my first visit to Russia.

The truth is that had it not been for the victory of the Western powers over the German army, the Kaiser's government would have smothered Bolshevism and dismembered Russia, reducing it to a second- or third-rate power. But the armistice of November 11, 1918, obliged Germany to renounce the Brest-Litovsk treaty, and two days later, with the menace of German military might swept off the scene, the Soviet Government annulled the treaty, though without any mention of the debt it owed to the Allied forces. Since then no Soviet historian, politician, or general has ever admitted that it was not "proletarian internationalism," but Allied guns that had rescued Bolshevik Russia from defeat and collapse. Fanatical faith in Marxist dogma or Marxist prediction and fatal misreading of the mentality of the Western and more notably the German worker backfired with a vengeance on the Kremlin leaders and the provincial Russian people. Any comfort these leaders may have derived from the few isolated uprisings that briefly installed Soviet or Communist dictatorships in Finland, in other Baltic states, in Germany and Hungary was short-lived. Everywhere attempts at Kremlin-style dictatorships were savagely put down.

This is of course past history, but it is still alive with historical meaning. It dramatizes, as no other events of the time, the one unshakable truth about even the best-educated Bolshevik leaders, regardless of their knowledge of foreign languages and the length of time they had lived in Western countries: they could no more divest themselves of their Russian heritage than of their hot Russian tempers and their gift for invective. The hatreds and desperations they had brought with them from Russia clung to them as tightly as the skins to their bodies. In their self-delusion, they imputed to the Western worker their own violent moods or the violent moods of the far more disadvantaged and primitive Russian worker.

Nowadays it requires no great hindsight to perceive in the collapse at Brest-Litovsk of "proletarian internationalism," as envisioned by Lenin and Trotsky, the beginning of the downfall of Trotsky and the beginning of the rise of Stalin with his purely nationalist doctrine of "socialism in one country," which in time he transmuted into Russian chauvinism and finally into rank imperialism. Whether Stalin would have had the cunning and the strength to disgrace and annihilate Lenin as he had done Trotsky, nobody of course knows. Lenin died before a test of strength between him and the Georgian autocrat could possibly have occurred.

But once installed in the seat of power, Stalin centered all his attention on the problems of the internal struggle. Though it was now a country freed of capitalism and private enterprise, it yet remained, to my mind, the same Russia that Peter the Great had ruled. His ruthless imposition of Western sciences, industrial methods and even dress and manners had no whit altered their basic Russian character.

Never, even in those faraway years when I was preparing for my first trip back to Russia, did I cherish any illusions as to the international nature of the Bolshevik Revolution. I viewed it as an explosion of a people bottled up within its diminished borders, forced to solve, one way or another, its own purely Russian problems, political, economic, and social. Of course, the Kremlin leaders did not completely abandon the crusade for world revolution. In 1919 they set up the "Comintern" (Communist International) for the purpose of promoting Marxist uprisings wherever possible. Kremlin ideologists continued to advocate their brand of Marxism and to assert the inevitability of a world-wide proletarian revolution. I soon tired of the tortuous ideological dissertations, which twisted and falsified facts to suit a particular theoretical tenet or a particular Bolshevik prediction. I became convinced that ideology alone, by whomever expounded—Lenin, Trotsky, Bukharin, or some other Kremlin personage—was no reliable or comprehensible guide to the nature of the Bolshevik Revolution or to events in Russia. One would have to be in the country, wander around, observe and listen, ask questions and digest answers to obtain some comprehension of the sweep and meaning of these events. Fortunately for me I knew the language, I was widely read in Russian history and literature, and I had had first-hand experience in a muzhik village and on an American farm.

That spring, with a third-class ticket in my hand, I stepped aboard the S.S. *Olympic,* one of the finest and fastest liners of its time. Eighteen years before I had made the voyage to America with my mother, brother, and two sisters as a passenger in steerage, quartered in a huge, crowded, barracks-like hole more foul than any muzhik hut or barn, where we spent endless days in our hard bunks, groaning with seasickness. Steerage quarters were a thing of the past now, and my third-class cabin was clean and airy, with courteous stewards—to be tipped, of course—always on call.

In a way it seemed only yesterday that I had driven out of the mud-drenched village on a straw-padded springless cart. Then again it all seemed very long ago, like something in another life. Now that I was on my way back to the Old Country, perhaps to spend a whole year there if the Bolsheviks gave me permission, I realized that I was curiously lacking in any emotional feeling about my return. My village, not Russia, had been my country. My interest in Russia was coolly professional; it was a country to observe and report, but never to live in again.

It was only when I thought of the old village that I felt a stir of emotion. That, not the realm of the Czars, had been my attachment. Mine, I realized, was a peasant's attitude—a deep love of one's birthplace and indifference to the land that lay beyond the familiar meadows and forests. My nostalgia was all for one particular spot, the fields where we picked berries and mushrooms, the woods where we gathered oak leaves for our mothers to wrap around the fresh-baked loaves or searched for fallen branches for firewood, where we had raided gardens and orchards, climbed tall trees to tear down crows' nests.

I wondered whether the majestic white storks still nested in our trees and on the thatched roofs of the muzhiks' huts. One-eyed Sergey was part of the scene too, that most important man with his inexhaustible store of folk songs and tales about house goblins, *rusalkas,* ghosts of the departed and forest spirits, which I had so often drawn on to write a school or college theme. If he was still on earth I would seek him out and tell him how I had carried his stories to the New World. He would be very proud of that, I felt sure.

The third class was crowded with Americanized immigrants

and their families, principally Germans and Scandinavians who were returning to visit their homelands. The American-born boys and girls, some of them of high school and college age, always spoke in English. I learned that with some exceptions they had at best acquired a smattering of their parents' language, and to me it seemed regrettable that they should have relinquished so rich a part of their heritage. But then—that was America; its powers of assimilation were so enormous that even the foreign-born parents spoke mostly in English, however incorrectly, and with however pronounced an accent.

I mingled freely with these immigrant groups, and while they spoke proudly of their native lands, they even more proudly proclaimed that now they were Americans. They were visiting the Old Country as Americans, and they would return to their homes, principally in Minnesota and Wisconsin, as Americans. Some were farmers and we often discussed farming methods in the Old Country and in America. It was illuminating to hear these men, who had done well in their new homes, point out how much the European farmer with his comparatively small holdings could learn from the American farmer with his larger acreage. It was obvious that experience with American farming had been a transforming influence in their lives as it had been in mine or in the lives of the Bohemian settlers I had come to know and admire in Iowa and Nebraska.

Even in the premotorized age when I first worked on a farm in upstate New York, I had been impressed by American farm machinery. For efficiency and ingenuity the muzhik knew nothing like it. Another aspect of my American education was my changed attitude toward animals. I could no longer imagine myself gleefully demolishing crows' nests. As a farm laborer I had learned to appreciate the usefulness of crows to the farmer. Nor would I hunt wild creatures any more, not even woodchucks, though I would never stop dogs from settling accounts with these despoilers of clover fields and meadowlands. I had learned the meaning of kindness to horses, cows, pigs, cats, and dogs, a kindness I was never taught in the old village, where even now, after some fifty-two years of revolution and of earnest government efforts to inculcate a more humane attitude to animals, Soviet children in city and country are still often as cruel as were the muzhik children in my old village.

I often receive letters from college students asking how best to prepare themselves for the study of Soviet life and Soviet civilization. Invariably I advise them that before they contemplate going to Russia, they should spend a summer on a well-operated mixed farm, where field crops are as important as livestock. I always tell them that it is necessary to be able to distinguish a well-cultivated field from one that is poorly tended, a good stand of grain, in stalk as well as in ear and kernels, from a poor one, and that to learn to appraise the quality of a cow, a pig, a chicken by merely looking at it is of inestimable aid to anyone who seeks to discover the reasons for the perpetual crises, in spite of occasional advances, in Soviet animal husbandry.

Then there is the discipline and the habits of work that one inevitably acquires on a well-tended American farm, which would enable a farm-trained American observer to judge the quality of the performance of Soviet agricultural workers.

And even more important, a first-hand knowledge of farming is the surest way of establishing cordiality and trust between the American visitor and the personnel of a Soviet farm, whether ordinary workers, executives, or Party secretaries. The ability to discuss crops and livestock or soil and agricultural implements disarms the most hardheaded Soviet executives or functionaries of any suspicions they may harbor against the foreign visitor. They are as eager to learn from him as he is to learn from them. But I also warn prospective young American sovietologists not to inject ideological or political topics into their conversation with Soviet farm people. If they do, they are certain to rouse suspicions and emotions that spoil good fellowship and ruin the possibility of a frank exchange of opinion and experience.

The time of my voyage on the *Olympic* was the age of jazz and the flapper. Scott Fitzgerald's *Flappers and Philosophers* was published in 1920 and his *Tales of the Jazz Age* in 1922. Yet for all I could see, the daughters of the immigrants in third class were uninfluenced by the cult of the flapper, either in dress or manners. They were more like the farm girls around North Brookfield; they dressed simply, they never used green eye-shadow or smoked cigarettes in long holders. They liked to chatter, to banter, to dance, to flirt, but in all of this there was nothing brash or sophisticated. They came from a world I knew and I could easily make friends with them. As for the flappers, they seemed, from what I had heard and read about their doings, as remote and strange as creatures from another planet. I thought that were I ever to meet one I would prove tongue-tied and awkward with her. The America I had known had inculcated in me nothing of the cynicism, the restlessness, or the spirit of rebellion that I associated with the flapper's world and the jazz age.

I happen to belong to the college generation of Vincent Sheean, Malcolm Cowley, and Scott Fitzgerald with whom I was to have a memorable encounter years later.

In an interview with a reporter of the New York *Times* (March 14, 1969), Sheean said, "There is no place that I can call home. . . . I've always been rootless." In his *Exile's Return*, Cowley makes a similar statement: "Our whole training was involuntarily directed toward destroying whatever roots we had in the soil." Sheean and Cowley are of course native-born Americans, as I am not. Yet to this day I am baffled by the intellectuals of my college generation who speak of themselves as rootless, without a home, without a feeling for home. I had been uprooted once, when I left Russia, and had I remained in the slums of New York, I too would probably have remained rootless and might have become as fiercely rebellious as the rest, some of them journalists who went on assignments to Russia about the time I did. But the America in which I lived after my flight from New York—an America of hills and valleys, of woods and swamps, of fields and streams, and of people who lived on the land—had been so congenial to my taste and temperament that I could not help striking roots into it, roots that were growing deeper and stronger. Though over sixty years have passed since I first went to the small farming village of North Brookfield, I have come to regard it as home. The fact that I do not live there is of no consequence. I only know that socially and emotionally it is as indispensable to me as the bed in which I sleep and that whenever I go back there I feel refreshed and exhilarated. I can conceive of no greater misfortune than to find myself cut off from the farming community in which I spent some of the happiest and most fruitful years of my youth.

I too was influenced, though not profoundly, by what Cowley calls "the revolution in morals," which he holds "began as a middle-class children's revolt." Though I was not a drinking man, I too detested prohibition and its by-products. Among other evils, it invested law breaking with a false aura of daring and adventure. Nor was I a puritan: one can hardly have survived boyhood in a Russian village and come out with any strait-laced notions about sex. Sex there was out in the open, at flax-spinning parties, at dances, at any home gatherings during the long winter evenings where young people openly kissed and embraced without disapproval or censure. So the "breakdown in morals" that came to America after the First World War meant little to me.

I had read *This Side of Paradise,* which was supposed to have fostered that breakdown or at least to have proclaimed the end of the more rigid aspects of Victorianism. But the novel, however widely acclaimed by youth as its declaration of independence, left me untouched. The egocentric, pleasure-seeking young Princetonian and the glamorous, money-minded girls he moves among were alien creatures in the America I had come to know and love. In the world of the young Fitzgerald's characters I would be the complete outsider.

But H. L. Mencken of *Smart Set* proved an exciting discovery. Though he wittily damned the Protestant ministry, knowing nothing of their very real contributions to rural culture, his fulminations against ignorance, complacency, and bigotry were both amusing and disturbing. I enjoyed his sharp assault on Irving Babbitt's brand of humanism to which I had been so antipathetic during my brief stay in his class. Mencken's racy and incisive prose was a joy to read. From him I learned certain new approaches to literature which readily fused with my own tastes. But his philosophy of life rarely touched me. Though in his writings he could sound like an ogre, in private life, I later discovered when Dr. Horsley Gantt, a Johns Hopkins psychiatrist, once invited me to join him for a beer at Mencken's house, he was a charming and congenial host.

Yet neither Mencken nor Fitzgerald nor any other iconoclastic writer of the time had made a cynic or rebel out of me, as they had done to others of my age, and I never qualified for membership in the so-called "lost generation." To me it was enough to be living in a society that knew no feudalism and nothing of the prerogatives that go with it that divide humanity into the privileged and the lowly. America had given me confidence in myself and a sense of inner security that I never lost.

Of course, I was to know moments of self-doubt and frustration. But unlike some intellectuals of my college generation I didn't seek escape in the circles of New York's Greenwich Village, which Cowley tells us was "not only a place, but a mood, a way of life . . . a system of ideas" strongly flavored with Bohemianism. The discipline I had acquired, a very strong discipline, during my farm years, cut me off from the irresponsible life I associated with Bohemianism.

Nor did I succumb to the Freudian fashion of the "couch confessional." I abhorred the confessional as I understood it, with its morbid emphasis on sex as the root of all ills. Rightly or wrongly, I thought of psychoanalysis as a form of self-indulgence for both patient and practitioner. The resulting introspection and self-concern among young people I knew, especially in matters of sex, in women more than in men, at times amused me and at times bored me to distraction. The one thing these young women did achieve was to freeze any desire a man may have felt for them.

Whenever I was seized with a mood of desperation or hopelessness I rushed upstate, hired out for a month or so to a dairy farmer, or spent time with a former schoolmate in North Brookfield who had become an independent farmer, helping him in milking and field work. It was astonishing how a spell of sweating labor on a farm restored my composure and self-confidence.

I was especially intimate with a former schoolmate whose name was Bert Ramsdell, son of Johnny and Eve Ramsdell, who since my arrival in North Brookfield had been among my closest friends. A chunky, freckle-faced youth, Bert in all ways met the local tests of character. He was not only an excellent farmer, but he also had a passion for the history of Central and Northern New York since pioneering times. Walking with him along an abandoned country path or driving over a country road was almost like reliving the past, so fresh and vivid were his accounts of movements both civilian and military along these once important arteries of travel and traffic on foot, on horseback, in horse and cart. Now and then we might stop at an old, out-of-the-way cemetery, and reading the headstones with Bert as a guide, was like looking into another age. Bert was an impassioned gun collector and every gun he managed to buy represented an epoch or an episode in the history of the country he loved. Spending a few days with him, helping him with chores and field work, examining his gun collection, or roaming the back country with its overgrown footpaths and trails and listening to his endless accounts of events of the faraway past, including the trials and triumphs of his pioneering ancestors, was invariably an edifying and heartening experience. Bert's irrepressible vitality and optimism dissipated whatever frustration or disappointment I might have brought with me.

Actually, close association with land and people who lived on the land, this alone fortified me against any idea that American life was empty, stupid, and ugly, which led so many intellectuals and pseudo-intellectuals of my college generation to seek "salvation in exile," as Cowley puts it. There were even those who fled to Russia to live in a Socialist society that would be free from the sordidness and exploitation of American capitalism. I had no desire to "help build Socialism," especially after my name began to appear in the *Century Magazine*. That the way to fulfillment had opened before me only deepened my awareness and appreciation of the benefits that had already come to me from America.

Thanks to my awareness of the positive aspects of American civilization, I never for a moment shared the notion that the Moscow-ruled Comintern possessed the power, through whatever American agencies it could muster, to bring about a revolution or a "dictatorship of the proletariat" in the United States. I vigorously opposed outside military intervention in the Red-White civil war in Russia. My sympathies were with the Red armies, because the White armies whom fourteen foreign nations, including Great Britain, France, and America, were supporting symbolized to me a restoration of autocracy and landed feudalism, both of which would bring back the old injustices and the old barbarisms, including repression of national minorities and pogroms of Jews. After the Bolsheviks won the civil war, I could and did view with abundant sympathy their plans and efforts to reconstruct and modernize slovenly and primitive Russia, without however subscribing to the doctrine of the inevitability of Marxist Russian-style Bolshevik world revolution. Out of the context of Russian history and Russian conditions, Bolshevik doctrine made no sense to me, least of all its so-called "messianism," with its commitment to the destruction of world capitalism.

So when Dr. Horsley Gantt telephoned me long distance to come to his home in Baltimore on the evening of February 14, 1933, to meet Scott Fitzgerald and his wife Zelda, I imagined that I was being invited to one of those delightful and stimulating parties for which he was famous among Baltimore intellectuals. Over the telephone Dr. Gantt gave no intimation whatever that my views on Bolshevik messianism or the Bolshevik concept of world revolution were in any way related to a fear that was haunting the celebrated author of *The Great Gatsby*, to me one of the most stirring novels in American literature.

When I arrived at Gantt's house, the Fitzgeralds were already there. I was introduced and when I saw them close up I was painfully shocked. I had thought of them as one of the most glamorous couples on the American scene; now they looked anything but glamorous, especially Zelda, supposedly the original American flapper—a term, I was given to understand, derived from Zelda's capricious practice of wearing her galoshes unbuckled so that they flapped as she walked. The Webster's International Dictionary on my desk, published in 1943, defines the slang word "flapper" as "a girl or young woman whose behavior and costume are characterized by daring freedom and boldness" and does not relate the word to Fitzgerald's wife.

Zelda sat in a corner in a big armchair, all huddled up as though from cold or timidity, her broad-brimmed dark hat casting a shadow over her angular ashen face. I had read that her eyes were beautiful and deep blue, but now they were black and staring, without the least flicker of her famous vivacity. I wondered how a Southern blue-blood came to be called "Zelda," a common name among Jews in Eastern Europe. But her staring eyes, her tight-lipped mouth, her air of aloofness discouraged conversation and I didn't put the question to her. All evening long she sat speechless and unmoving in the armchair, a ghost of her once beautiful and exciting self. It was only after she and Scott left that Dr. Gantt told me that she was under treatment by Dr. Adolf Meyer, head of the Phipps Psychiatric Clinic at the Johns Hopkins Hospital.

Fitzgerald too appeared a ghost of the handsome, triumphant, fiery youth, the *enfant terrible* of American letters. Of course, at thirty-seven he was not young any more. Still, it was impossible to think of him as no longer young, as withering into middle age. His face was pale and flabby, his hair was thinning, and he had acquired a visible bulge in the midriff. The long-fingered hand trembled as I shook it. But his blue eyes, his warm smile, his finely cadenced voice lent him a charm that made one think of the Fitzgerald of earlier and happier years. He was a model of humility, with no hint of the arrogance and exhibitionism that were part of his legend. He was an easy talker and an intent listener. I told him that *The Great Gatsby* was one of the most moving novels I had read; its comparative brevity and direct dialogue made me think of Turgenev's *Fathers and Sons*. He appeared pleased at that and spoke of Turgenev as of one of his favorite novelists.

We talked on about books and writers, when suddenly Dr. Gantt intruded with a question that surprised me: "D'you think there is any danger of Communist revolution in America?"

I had first met Gantt in 1923 in Helsinki, where we were both waiting for Soviet visas, he to go to Leningrad to study conditioned reflex with the Nobel prize-winning physiologist I. P. Pavlov, I to write for the *Century Magazine*. During his five years with Pavlov I frequently saw him in Leningrad. He learned to speak Russian fluently, and together we called on our Russian friends, who in those times were not officially discouraged from inviting foreigners to their homes. We had discussed Bolshevism countless times during his years in Leningrad and we both agreed that the Bolshevik Revolution could only be understood as a purely Russian phenomenon, directed against a social structure that had never existed in the United States.

In reply to his question I reminded Gantt that of all my friends none knew better than he did what I thought of the possibility of a Communist revolution in the United States.

"I wish," he said, "you'd explain to Scottie why you don't think a Communist revolution is possible here."

I knew that he must have some reason for asking this, though what it was I couldn't imagine. So I proceeded to explain myself to Fitzgerald, centering my attention as I had done in my writings on the sharp historic contrasts between the Russian muzhik and the American farmer and between the American Homestead Act and the processes of acquiring land in Russia, even after 1861 when the muzhik was liberated from serfdom. Fitzgerald asked question after question and I answered to the best of my ability. Whether I convinced him that his fear of a bloody Communist revolution was unfounded, I didn't know.

Some time later I learned from John Dos Passos, one of Fitzgerald's closest friends, that Fitzgerald was given to passing obsessions of one kind or another, and apprehension over the possibility of a revolution in America was, for a while one of them. Yet as long as it lasted, it must have been intense, else Gantt, a psychiatrist, would not have called upon me to show Fitzgerald the groundlessness of his fear.

Not very long ago Gantt showed me a page in his guest book signed by Fitzgerald about a year after our conversation. Instead of scrawling his name as usual across the page, he wrote in a large round clear hand:

> *Greetings to Horsley Gantt*
> *from*
> *Lenin*
> *Trotsky*
> *Fitzgerald*

I hope that his facetiousness was the measure of his peace of mind in at least one respect.

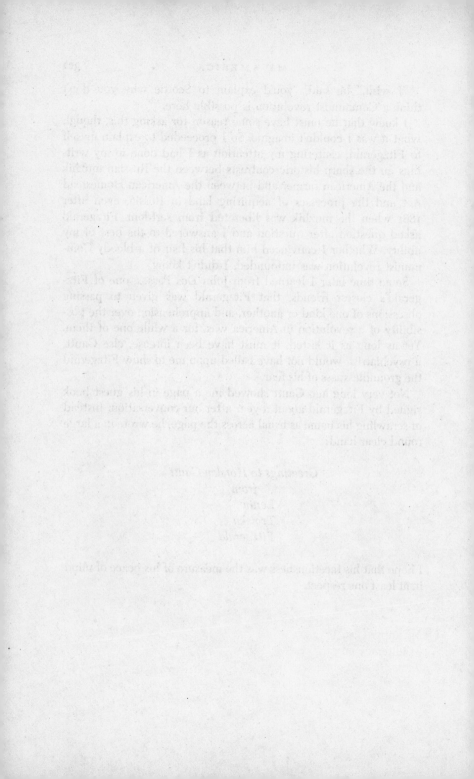

Chapter 23

America and Russia:
Reflections on Two Worlds

◆

"Aren't you afraid to go to Russia?"

The question was flung at me countless times by fellow passengers aboard the *Olympic*. My answer—that if I were afraid, I wouldn't be going there—usually released an envenomed rehearsal of the outrages committed by the "bloody Bolsheviks" who were ruling and ruining the country.

Like the rest of the American public, my fellow passengers carried in their minds a lurid image of the new Russia as a vast slaughterhouse where a barbarous dictatorship was energetically engaged in the butchery of its best educated, most cultured, and most useful citizens.

I was only too keenly aware of the blood and terror of the Revolution. But now, with the end of the civil wars, with the collapse of foreign military intervention and the disastrous rout of the Polish offensive, with constitutional government superseding army rule, the Revolution had taken a sharp turn away from the rigidities imposed in the name of Lenin's Marxism, a relaxation exemplified by the New Economic Policy.

At long last, stifled creative energies were being released for the transformation of a backward nation. Though I had only read about the reforms instituted by the new government, there was much evidence to show that they were being carried out. I could only applaud such a measure as the nation-wide crusade to stamp out illiteracy and to open the schools and universities to all racial and national minorities on a basis of complete equality, as well as to workers and peasants who hitherto had been unable to attend institutions of higher learning. The liberation of women from their ancient disabilities had been long overdue. I had known girls in my native village to be forced into loveless marriages by their fathers; and I recalled Anna, a neighbor's daughter, one of our village beauties, who had been deeply in love with Lohvin, a poor peasant with no great prospects. But Anna's father, against her pleading, had bestowed her on a sickly hunchback from another village who stood to inherit a large farm, well-equipped with the best implements and plentifully stocked with cows, pigs, and horses.

Nothing of the sort, I was convinced, could happen now under the new dispensation. Now a girl could defy parental tyranny and be upheld by the local authorities; she was no longer chattel. Nor would a young wife whose husband was away serving in the army or at work in the city be forced into sexual relations with her father-in-law—an old story in peasant life. The new village officials would protect her.

This granting of equal rights to women, a measure dreamed of by Russian intellectuals long before Lenin was born, ushered in an era of liberation from the ancient patriarchal tyrannies for millions of women in the rural world, which was most of Russia. That this freedom would in time degenerate into the enlistment of women to toil side by side with men in the mines, in heavy industry and on construction projects, on highways and railroads I could not foresee.

I had also read with great interest of the new health service, dedicated to the eradication of the frequent epidemics that for centuries had ravaged the countryside. With memories of my old village where there had been no defense against disease but prayer and old wives' wisdom, I could only rejoice that at last medicine and sanitation were being brought to the peasantry.

My older sister Minnie had come to the pier to see me off on the *Olympic*. She, like my mother, had strongly disapproved of this trip, even though it was being made for professional reasons. Least of all did she favor my visiting our native village, of which she had only grim memories of filth, vermin, and poverty, where muzhiks had fed the pigs in their own sleeping quarters, had spat uninhibitedly on the floor, and had blown their noses without benefit of handkerchief. The memory of the old squalor revolted her: here in America a person could keep clean. So why would anyone want to go back to that Godforsaken mudhole? She remembered how mother had given birth to her eleven children in the straw on the floor, with no doctor, no *feldsher*, no midwife in attendance—only an old muzhik woman from across the way. "That was the way I was born," she finished ruefully, "and that was the way you were born." But I was beyond persuasion. I cherished a warmth of feeling for the old life which she couldn't share.

But the most important reform of all to me was the deathblow the Revolution had dealt landed feudalism, of all Czarist institutions the most obstructive to social progress. But I did not need Marxism to teach me that no country could take its place in the modern world with most of its acres in the possession of a few great landholders.

I was no great student of Marxism, and the Marxist ideology promulgated by the Bolshevik press only exasperated me with its rigid formulas, its glib analyses and pat solutions to all problems, and seemed frequently at odds with the intentions of the prerevolutionary Marxist writers I had read. So even before my return to Russia I was judging the progress of the Revolution not in terms of Kremlin doctrine but in terms of human effort by Russians to solve the problems of Russian human beings. These were problems my acquaintances on the *Olympic* had hardly heard of and found difficult to understand. I thoroughly agreed with them that the new Russia was far from being a democracy and that it was ruled by an inexorable dictatorship. But nevertheless that dictatorship, I pointed out, was committed to improving the human condition of a primitive, exploited, and war-ruined nation of many millions of souls, most of them ignorant peasants. So I was on my way there to see with my own eyes what was happening to a people in the process of being transformed from the backward peasantry I had known in my boyhood into members of a modern industrialized nation. It was one of the biggest upheavals in history and I wanted to write about it.

Nor was I like many returning immigrants, a few romantic young idealists and certain headlong journalists—most of whom eventually suffered bitter disillusionment—fleeing from a brutal capitalist society to a socialist utopia. I had studied too much Russian history and experienced too many of the hard realities of

Russian life to be able to delude myself into believing that an ideal Socialist state with economic security, political and intellectual freedom for all could suddenly be conjured into existence by some fiat of Marxist magic in the Russia I had known.

Not that the abuses of American capitalism were any less familiar to me than to the seekers of a classless utopia. That saintly atheist Clarence Darrow, a doughty fighter against the machinations of moneyed power and privilege, had been my mentor and had taught me much about the arrogance and iniquities of the great corporations. But never for a moment had I forgotten that it was America, with all its shortcomings, that had made it possible for me, poor as I was and lacking in influential connections, to obtain as good an education as any son of the native rich could aspire to. And this had been the experience of thousands, tens of thousands, like me. I knew of nothing like it anywhere in the world.

In America I had been subject to no social or class discriminations, to no political oppression. I thought of the newly arrived peasant boys from Eastern Europe that I had known on the farms around North Brookfield. Being illiterate they would often come to me on a Sunday to get me to write letters home for them, and invariably they had made a point of telling their families how they sat at the same table with the "landlord" and ate the same food he did. And they would boast too of having a room of their own and a bed to themselves.

Even with the new restrictions on immigration, such as the literacy test imposed in 1917 and the quota system of 1921, the poor and the landless, mostly from Southern and Eastern Europe, still clamored at the gates of America, ready to pay in hard work for the dignity of becoming citizens of a democracy.

And so in that spring of 1923, as the *Olympic* plowed eastward toward the Old World, I carried no hostilities with me for the country I was leaving behind. On the contrary, I was taking with me a store of experiences and ideas gained in America that I believed would serve me well in understanding the human drama I was about to witness and record.